THE DUAL DEVELOPMENTAL STATE

To Benedict Stavis
Mentor and Friend

The Dual Developmental State

Development strategy and institutional arrangements
for China's transition

MING XIA
The City Univeristy of New York
The College of Staten Island

LONDON AND NEW YORK

First published 2000 by Ashgate Publishing

Reissued 2018 by Routledge
2 Park Square, Milton Park, Abingdon, Oxon OX14 4RN
711 Third Avenue, New York, NY 10017, USA

Routledge is an imprint of the Taylor & Francis Group, an informa business

Copyright © Ming Xia 2000

All rights reserved. No part of this book may be reprinted or reproduced or utilised in any form or by any electronic, mechanical, or other means, now known or hereafter invented, including photocopying and recording, or in any information storage or retrieval system, without permission in writing from the publishers.

Notice:
Product or corporate names may be trademarks or registered trademarks, and are used only for identification and explanation without intent to infringe.

Publisher's Note
The publisher has gone to great lengths to ensure the quality of this reprint but points out that some imperfections in the original copies may be apparent.

Disclaimer
The publisher has made every effort to trace copyright holders and welcomes correspondence from those they have been unable to contact.

A Library of Congress record exists under LC control number: 99076154

ISBN 13: 978-1-138-70830-3 (hbk)
ISBN 13: 978-1-138-70826-6 (pbk)
ISBN 13: 978-1-315-20119-1 (ebk)

Contents

Acknowledgments	*vi*
List of Abbreviations	*viii*

1	Introduction	1
2	The Developmental State and the Hybrid Mode of Governance	14
3	The Adoption of the Developmental State Model	40
4	The Pillars of the Chinese Developmental State	67
5	The National People's Congress and China's Transition	100
6	Developmentalism and the Provincial People's Congresses	136
7	The Shenzhen Revolution and Central-Local Synergism	178
8	The Logic of the Dual Developmental State	208

Bibliography	*228*
Author Index	*254*
Subject Index	*256*

Acknowledgments

Thanks go to three American families: Alvin and Sally Magid, Henry and JoAnn Rosement, Benedict Stavis and Marjatta Lyyra, for helping me to pursue my Ph.D. degree in the United States and to have finished it at Temple University of Philadelphia.

Temple University political science faculty gave me incredible help during my six-year stay there. Joseph Schwartz, Lynn Miller, Harry Bailey, Jr., Lloyd Jensen, Aryeh Botwinick, Elliott White, Frederick Herzon, and Gary Mucciaroni were caring and inspiring. Since the major ideas of this book were first developed in my dissertation, my dissertation committee (Benedict Stavis, Robert Osborn, Richard Deeg, and Cathy Walker) helped me think through my thesis. The dissertation fellowship from Temple Graduate School provided crucial financial help for my research. The Bernard Watson Best Dissertation Award from Temple University in the 1997 graduating year encouraged me to complete my work. Helpful were several travel funds from Temple University Center for East Asian Studies, University of Chicago Center for East Asian Studies, and the APSA Foreign Graduate Travel Fund. Robert Kidder and Gale Johnson, both directors for the Centers for East Asian Studies at Temple and Chicago, provided gracious help to me in getting travel funds.

Thanks go to my classmates at Temple: Philip Avila, Angela Bailey, Patrick Cannon, Brigid Callahan, Mark Cohen, Sharon Gramby-Sobukwe, James Heasley, Chieke Ihejirika, Carol Jenkens, Sharon Leacock, Sam Miller, Donald Rieck, Theresa Singleton, Sonja Moore-Siler, and Gyonwoo Yun. They enriched my intellectual, cultural, and spiritual life. I will always retain a warm memory of these wonderful years.

My colleagues at the City University of New York, the College of Staten Island have provided me sustaining support. Daniel Kramer read the entire manuscript, provided comments and saved me from many embarrassments. Nathan Greenspan, Larry Nachman and Michaela Richter helped me juggle heavy teaching and extensive writing during my first two years of teaching at CUNY. The PSC-CUNY Research Fund provided financial support to me to do further research and collect more data in China during the summers of 1998 and 1999. The Presidential Release

Time Award from the College of Staten Island gave me time to focus on my writing.

Several chapters were respectively presented to the annual conferences of American Political Science Association, Northeastern Political Science Association, Association for Chinese Political Studies, and the Workshop of Parliamentary Scholars and Parliamentarians. Kevin J. O'Brien (Ohio State university), Jean-Marc Blanchard (University of Pennsylvania), Feiling Wang (Georgia Institute of Technology), Don-Yun Chen (University of Rochester), Guoli Liu (College of Charleston), Philip Norton (University of Hull), made valuable comments. In writing chapter 7, I got generous help from Sheying Chen, Principle Investigator of "Public Policy and Development Strategy: An International Comparative Study" Project, for introducing his contacts to me. During my visit to China to collect data in 1998 and 1999, many Chinese scholars and officials provided tremendous help. Here I cannot thank them by name in order to protect their anonymity that I promised.

Two chapters have drawn materials from my two articles published in the *Journal of Legislative Studies*: "Information Efficiency, Organization Development, and the Institutional Linkages of the Provincial People's Congresses in China," vol. 3, no. 3 (Fall 1997), "China's National People's Congress: Institutional Transformation in the Process of Regime Transition," vol. 4, no. 4 (Winter 1998). I thank the publisher, Frank Cass & Co Ltd. for allowing me to incorporate part of these two articles into the book.

My friend, Alan Ponikvar and his father, Adolph, took great pains to proofread the entire manuscript and made it presentable.

I take sole responsibility for any errors that escaped my scrutiny.

M.X.
Staten Island, New York

List of Abbreviations

CDS   Capitalist Developmental State
CPC   Communist Party of China
CPPCC   Chinese People's Political Consultative Conference
MITI   Ministry of International Trade and Industry
NIE   Newly Industrialized Economy
NPC   National People's Congress
NPCSC   National People's Congress Standing Committee
PBC   People's Bank of China
PC   People's Congress
PD   Renmin Ribao Haiwai Ban [People's Daily, Overseas Edition]
PPC   Provincial People's Congress
PPCSC   Provincial People's Congress Standing Committee
PRC   People's Republic of China
RMRB   Renmin Ribao Guonei Ban [People's Daily, National Edition]
SC   Standing Committee
SDPC   State Development Planning Commission
SEZ   Special Economic Zone
TVE   township and village enterprise
WTO   World Trade Organization

1 Introduction

The Puzzles to be Explored

The developmental state model originated in Japan and later spread to other East Asian countries. Over the past decade it has ascended to the status of the leading paradigm for the study of the East Asian political economies (Johnson 1982, 1995; Deyo 1987; White and Wade 1988; Amsden 1989; Haggard 1990; Wade 1990; Fallows 1994; Evans 1995; Simone and Feraru 1995; Chan, et al, 1998; Woo-Cumings, 1999). After the summer of 1997, a financial crisis swept over this region and severely challenged the developmental state model (Krugman 1994; Lingle 1997; Sanger 1997; Kim 1998). Despite this fact, it is very unlikely that scholars will abandon this paradigm for explaining the miraculous economic take-off in this region over the past four decades. Moreover, many of the well-known Asian specialists have suggested that this model has been emulated in China. Thus, the largest Asian country has become part of the "flying-geese" pattern of development led by Japan, followed by the "Four Little Dragons" and the other East Asian countries (Perkins 1986; White and Wade 1988; White 1991; Overholt 1993; Simone and Feraru 1995; Cheng 1998; Gilley 1998). The words of the Chinese leaders, those specially of Deng Xiaoping, as well as the policies recently implemented have further confirmed this view. Given this development, it is disappointing that no case study on China has been conducted within the context of the developmental state theory. Meanwhile, the institutional arrangements for development in other East Asian countries have been examined in relative detail. This study is designed to fill this academic lacuna.

With regard to the East Asian developmental state, China has shared several important similarities with Japan and other East Asian Newly Industrialized Economies (NIEs include South Korea, Taiwan, Singapore and Hong Kong and are often referred as "Four Little Dragons"). For example, China has a Confucian culture, a very high savings' rate, and a miraculous economic growth rate driven largely by exports. Like these

2   The Dual Developmental State

countries in their early stages of modernization, China has followed the same one-party authoritarian system to guide its economic development. But these similarities do not conceal two qualities that distinguish China from the other East Asian NIEs. First, China's territory is more than eighteen times larger, and its population is almost six times greater than the "Four Little Dragons" and Japan combined. Understandably, the Chinese are pursuing the goal of modernization under much stressful conditions due to their environment. Second, its economic and political transitions are being carried out under the leadership of the Communist Party of China (CPC) and thus are proceeding within the context of a different set of ideological background conditions. The socialist political and economic legacies (e.g., egalitarianism, Stalinist bureaucracy, and a centrally-planned economy) have imposed tremendous constraints upon this transitional process.

The logic of the situation raises the following questions: Considering its vastness and its Communist economic and political background, how has it been possible for China to emulate the developmental state model which is capitalist in nature and has originated primarily in relatively small countries? If, as most scholars believe, China is following the developmental state model, I suspect the adoption of this model must have been assisted by major institutional adaptations within the Chinese state and economy. What then, if any, are these adaptations? How have these newly adapted institutions been constructed to support the developmental state model in China? Within what kind of environment and following what kind of strategy has such institution building become possible? Once established, what has been the impact of these institutions upon the Chinese political economy?

According to the classic developmental state model, what is crucial to a developmental state is state capacity, which is defined as the ability of a government in getting its job done and includes its capacity to mobilize society, to extract resources, to steer development and to legitimate the regime (Wang and Hu 1993, 235). From the political perspective, the secret of the model's success for maintaining state capacity relies mainly on two important institutional arrangements: the suppression of local autonomy and the negligible role of legislatures. These institutional arrangements set the stage for administrative guidance from a competent bureaucracy of the central government. However, in China, Deng Xiaoping started his reforms with decentralization and legislative development. In the twenty-year course of reform, the local governments were given regional property and autonomy, and the legislatures both at central and local levels were encouraged to expand their institutions and powers. Obviously, at the level of institutional arrangements, China has deviated in two important respects from the other East Asian developmental states. The issue is then: to what extent do these two institutional deviations disqualify China as an emulator of the developmental state model? Is there any connection between the different ecological conditions and unique political legacy of China and these two institutional deviations? In other words, when China adopted the developmental state model did it not have to adapt it to its unique heritage?

To provide explanations for the discrepancy between the Chinese practice and the original model, I will propose in this book a "dual developmental state model." By "dual developmental state," I mean that the Chinese developmental state is defined and sustained by both the legislative and local political institutions. There is a dual structure from the central to local levels, between the governments and the People's Congresses (PCs). The system of PCs has developed to become an indispensable part of the Chinese ruling machine by legitimating the government, integrating the nation, and by making a huge number of laws for governing and for market creation, as well as for the supervision of the government and judicial branch. Furthermore, this "dual developmental state" also has a two-tiered structure in which the developmental role of the central state is nested within the context of the central/local synergism. Reform-minded central leaders, for a long time led by Deng Xiaoping, have encouraged local leaders to explore new policies and experiment with ideas in order to generate experiences and learn lessons. But since local leaders have come to need a mandate from the center, the central state and local states have formed an interdependent relationship. The mutual needs of both levels of the governments have helped to establish and maintain an equilibrium over the past two decades, despite the oscillating nature of the central and local power relationship. As a result, the dynamics of China's developmentalism cannot be solely attributed either to the central or the local governments. It has arisen out of their interaction, which in turn has mutually strengthened their developmental orientation.

If the Chinese developmental strategy is included in the family of developmental states, then the existing theoretical model needs to be stretched to accommodate the Chinese deviations. This creates several

4   The Dual Developmental State

problems. First, has the integrity of the classic developmental state model been destroyed? Second, is it too far-fetched to apply the developmental state model to China, given the institutional deviations that exist in the Chinese developmental state? Third, if the Chinese developmental state has been characterized by a power-sharing mechanism among the central state, local states, and various legislatures, how can it maintain its coherence and efficiency?

To solve these problems, I have tried to restructure the classic developmental state model by introducing a new concept: the mode of governance. According to Oliver Williamson (1975, 1996), economic and social transactions (or exchanges, interactions) are basically organized into three types of institutional matrices, or three modes of governance: market, hierarchy, and hybrid. Most scholars agree that the developmental state approach is neither a market, nor a hierarchy, but is, instead, a hybrid. To be exact, this hybrid mode of governance in the East Asian countries is a network.

Several scholars have pointed out that one important limitation of the developmental state model, namely the assumption of an insulated and autonomous state, lies in its failure to incorporate the network analysis into its theorization. By following this line of reasoning, they have "introduced a network approach as an extended modification of the developmental state paradigm" (Chan, et al, 1997, 10). Peter Evans (1995) introduces the concept of "embedded autonomy" to help us understand the linkages, connectedness, and ties between the states and societies, political elites and industrialist elites, and the connection between the capital and bureaucracy through a hegemonic ruling party in the East Asian developmental states. Manuel Castells (1996), one of the most important thinkers within the developmental state paradigm, obviously sees that the developmental states in East Asia have been evolved in the context of the connection culture, business networks and network society there. He also has confidence in that the combination of cultural and traditional values with modern information technology in Asia helps it enjoy a comparative advantage over other regions in the new information age (Castells 1996, 173).

The network approach enables me to transcend the existing construct of the developmental state and move to a higher level of abstraction and generalization to assess it. Thus, in light of the network approach, all East Asian countries have shared one common institutional feature. This is networks and networking. In their political, economic, and social life, complex networks among individuals (e.g., connections), families, businesses (e.g., *keiretsu, chaebol,* crony capitalism, and business groups), and politicians (e.g., the patron-client relationship) are easy to identify. Based on the institutional nature of networks, the Chinese institutional arrangements that promote its development do have an affinity with and share the homogeneity of the East Asian developmental states. Moreover, how the Chinese state has maintained its institutional coherence and state capacity for steering the economic transition can be explained. Specifically, the National People's Congress (NPC), the Provincial People's Congresses (PPCs), and local governments have asserted and institutionalized their power by means of a network strategy, which places more emphasis on embeddedness [that is, institutions are more embedded into instead of insulated from each other], connectedness and reciprocity rather than on insulation, open conflict and autonomy. The central state and local states also have been bound together by means of sophisticated institutional linkages.

That China is a new species within the parameters of the developmental state theory explains how the Chinese system has changed itself even while maintaining the state capacity. Therefore, decentralization and legislative activism, which usually are twin challenges to the state capacity in other countries, have not posed an immediate threat to the maintenance of the state capacity nor to the integration of China as a nation.

To support my central thesis of a dual developmental state, I will utilize the institutional economic approach to interpret China's emulation of the East Asian experiences, as well as to interpret its industrial policies and major innovations within the state. By focusing on the NPC, the PPCs and the Municipality of Shenzhen (the first and most influential Special Economic Zone or SEZ), I will try to highlight the legislative and local perspectives of a multifaceted developmental state as it manifests itself in China.

My central thesis is that in the process of creating a market-oriented economy, China has intentionally emulated the practices of Japan and the East Asian "Four Little Dragons" and successfully adopted the developmental state model. To accommodate and support this model, the Chinese state--owing to its territorial and demographic size and its Communist background--has also transformed itself and adapted to the

6 The Dual Developmental State

new choice-set imposed by this model. The two most important institutional arrangements have been decentralization and legislative empowerment that have led to the reduction of transaction costs and to the creation of markets (marketization). Actually marketization has provided the dynamics for the institutionalization of some important structures (such as the PPCs and the center-periphery relationship) within the Chinese state. But the developmental state model has provided a context, shaping and structuring the styles and characteristics of these processes of institutionalization. In other words, the concern of the state capacity has imposed constraints upon the way in which these institutions have developed and restructured their relationship with other existing institutions. In summary, the institutionalization of legislatures and decentralization have followed the network strategy, and because of this strategy, the Chinese political system has been characterized by a matrix of power and institutional linkages. Furthermore, its pattern of interaction has been one marked by reciprocity and consultation. Coupled with the culture-rooted informational ties and connections, these linkages have greatly helped the powerful actors to exchange information, coordinate policy, reduce misunderstandings, and manage conflicts. As a result, the newly established institutions have been market-facilitating because they often have successfully granted autonomy to the institutions which needed it. At the same time, these institutions being connected with each other have avoided generating unmanageable conflicts.

When a developmental central state coexists with local developmental states, a developmental executive coexists with a developmental legislative system in China, a dual developmental state is formed. This new institutional construct provides an organizing principle for the Chinese leadership to conduct its regime's transition as well as a fundamental guideline by which we are able to understand the current Chinese political economy.

A Note on Methodology

My research relies heavily on the analytical concepts developed by comparative transaction costs analysis (Coase 1937, 1960; Williamson 1975, 1985, 1996; Williamson and Winter 1993; North 1981, 1990; Drobak and Nye 1997). As Thrainn Eggertsson (1990, 14) has summarized, "Transaction costs are the costs that arise when individuals exchange ownership rights to economic assets and enforce their exclusive rights." Its fundamental idea is that transaction costs include the cost of arranging a contract ex ante and monitoring and enforcing it ex post. Or as Oliver Williamson (1996, 379) puts it simply, "the costs of running the economic system." These costs could be money, time, or merely inconvenience.

Comparative transaction costs economics is a theory of the firm. According to this theory, the firm has chosen different strategies for organizing economic transactions: (1) either within the hierarchy (the firm, or any other organization), transactions are "placed under unified ownership" and "subject to administrative controls," for example, through vertical integration, or (2) through the market, "the arena in which autonomous parties engage in exchange," or (3) a third way: hybrid, for example, by establishing "long-term contractual relations that preserve autonomy but provide added transaction-specific safeguards" (Williamson 1996, 377-9). The trade-offs among these three modes of governance (the market, the hierarchy, and hybrid) vary, depending on the needs of the transactions. As Williamson (1996, 151) argues:

> The main market and hierarchy trade-offs involve comparative assessments of adaptability, incentive intensity, and bureaucracy. Markets are superior in autonomous adaptability respects, employ high-powered incentives, and are less subject to bureaucratic distortions. Hierarchies enjoy the advantage in bilateral and multilateral adaptability respects, work out of low-powered incentives, and are beset by intertemporal bureaucratic distortions. Hybrids are located in between.

The hierarchical governance (the firm, bureau, bureaucracy, and organization) can help human beings minimize the boundedness of rationality [i.e., the limitations upon human cognitive competence], reduce opportunism, and therefore, reduce the transaction costs. However, the hierarchy has its own limitations. For example, it cannot replicate some advantages of the market, and it also incurs some other transaction costs (i.e., organization costs). It cannot be extended without limit and must be used in a discriminating way. All forms of feasible governance are flawed. There is no frictionless, costless market, just as there is no benevolent, omniscient government. For this reason, in choosing the mode of governance, both market failure and organization failure (or state failure, or government failure) have to be considered. Therefore, to minimize

8　The Dual Developmental State

transaction costs, a comparison of the different modes and their efficiency for economizing transaction costs is needed in order to determine which specific mode shall be applied. The most important point is to compare different modes of governance with respect to their ability to economize on transaction costs (or organization costs) and then consider the issue of trade-offs. As Charles Wolf (1988, 6) argues:

> Moreover, the choice cannot be dichotomized, as Galbraith and Friedman sometimes imply, as choice between relatively perfect governments and imperfect or inadequate markets (the Galbraith view), or between relatively perfect markets and imperfect or inadequate governments (the Friedman view). The choice in actuality is among imperfect markets and imperfect or inadequate governments, and various combinations of the two. The cardinal economic choice concerns the degree to which markets or governments--each with their respective flaws--should determine the allocation, use, and distribution of resources in the economy.

Some scholars have argued that the network mode of governance, as a hybrid between the market and the hierarchy, is a third form of governance, which offers a "a middle ground" or "a third way" for organizing transactions (Powell and Smith-Doerr 1994, 368-402; Ouchi 1984; Knoke 1990; Granovetter, 1994; Nohria and Eccles 1992; Wasserman and Faust 1994). Despite the fact that the comparative transaction costs theory has not covered the network mode of governance, its hybrid mode leaves the door open to it. Williamson (1996, 231) himself also agrees that his hybrid mode of governance can be complemented by the network strategy. As an approach and as a means of governance, Walter Powell and Laurel Smith-Doerr (1994, 383) define a network as follows:

> [A] network is composed of a set of relations, or ties, among actors (either individuals or organizations). A tie between actors has both content (the type of relation) and form (the strength of relation). The content of ties can include information or resource flows, advice or friendship, shared personnel or members of a board of directors; indeed any type of social relation can be mapped as a tie. Thus, organizations typically are embedded in multiple, often overlapping networks-resource exchange networks, information networks, and so on.

Because networks provide connectedness and embeddedness among organizations, they encourage organizations to learn from each other. They also facilitate coordination and emulation among organizations, increase responsiveness of organizations to each other, and also reduce transaction costs for organizations. For example, they can avoid the disconnection and barriers among actors found in the horizontal relationship, and also reduce the dependency upon a rigid vertical structure. Coordination and monitoring become easier. Diffusion of information becomes more efficient. Moreover, a network strategy encourages reciprocity so as to guide the patterns of interaction among individuals and organizations. Self-restraint instead of a confrontational style becomes more common in their relationships. These merits have encouraged the development of networks in political and economic governance.

Although transaction costs analysis is a theory of the firm, it has utilities for our understanding of politics, international affairs, sociology, and law. For institutionalists, to some extent the legislature, the bureaucracy, and interest groups are "political firms" (Moe 1995). Transaction costs theory has a variety of relevant ways to enhance the study of reforms and development in the former Soviet Union, Eastern Europe, and China (Williamson 1993, Introduction; 1995, 14; 1996, chapt 13). Indeed, by following this line of thought, studies of the US Congress and Constitution, public bureaucracies, public policy, and even China's central/local relations have been attempted (Wu 1994; Montinola, et al 1995; Weingast and Mashall 1988; Moe, 1989, 1995).

R. H. Coase (1988, 117) himself believes, "The government is, in a sense, a super-firm (but of a very special kind) since it is able to influence the use of factors of productions by administrative decision." According to Coase, to be qualified as a firm, this organization must have the ability of a firm to perceive its interest, to calculate the costs and benefits consistently, and then to make a choice in accordance with its best interests. He argues that the state has more freedom and autonomy than a firm because the state has more "authoritarian methods" and "the government is able, if it wishes, to avoid the market altogether." Clearly, in Coase's case, when he discusses the state in general terms, the state to which he refers is a strong state. But not all non-economic organizations have such an ability. In fact, some states have a weaker capacity to make effective choices than do firms, even as some have a stronger capacity. If a state is too strong and moves to a Stalinist model that drives out the market altogether and essentially relies on administrative control, it is less like a firm. In such a case, a theory of the

10   *The Dual Developmental State*

firm will have more difficulty in explaining the state. Therefore, this theory of the firm is more applicable to a state that stands in the middle between a pluralist democracy (which tends to be too weak) [1] and a Stalinist model. These strong states that use both administrative decisions and market mechanisms can act more like a firm. Japan, the East Asian developing countries, some authoritarian and semi-democratic states in Latin America, and Africa are examples. Even after it started its marketization in 1979 China has remained as a strong state, and thus, is precisely a state which has the ability to act like a firm. A theory of the firm should have a strong explanatory power when applied to China.

Several more reasons justify the argument that China has many of the characteristics of a firm and is more appropriately to be treated as "China, Inc.," just as there are "Japan, Inc.," "South Korea, Inc.," and "Taiwan, Inc." First, both the corporate structure and the Chinese state are basically characterized by a hierarchical and authoritarian governance. The Chinese political elites (the Communist ruling apparatus) act as the owners of the state. The ordinary Chinese are their employees and have no rights that would enable them to select the leadership or to participate in decision-making process. As Eggertsson (1990, 37, 49) argues, "under a dictatorship, state ownership can approach the system of private property with the economy resembling a huge corporation." Second, the ruling Communist party has dominated Chinese politics for half a century. The state in China has a strong capacity to control social and economic life and to decide whether to choose one governance or another in organizing the political economy. Third, the ruling status of the CPC is not based upon competitive elections. Instead, its political legitimacy is based upon "economic performances." Economic gains and political gains overlap. The state works more like a business. Terms such as "developmental state," "economic state" (Chen 1996) and corporatism (Unger and Chan 1995; Oi 1995) make this evident. Fourth, the central state as the primary owner of property-rights coexists with many other forms of property owners in competition: local state, collective enterprises, private firms, and joint ventures. As property rights have diversified, the central government has had to deal with other actors (for example, local governments, and autonomous firms) more through an exchange of interests and benefits. Thus, China has become an even more diversified business-like network. Fifth, the state is the most important institution for providing and distributing services and values in Chinese society. The Chinese state is like a political firm. The political elite is the board of trustees, while the top leader of the state is an executive

Introduction 11

officer. Thus, a comparative institutional approach to all modes of governance is clearly relevant to China. Many Chinese political scientists and economists have taken heed of this approach and noted its analytical power within the Chinese context.[2]

Plan of the Book

In Chapter 2, "The Developmental State and the Hybrid Mode of Governance," I review the major works pertaining to the developmental state theory for the purpose of showing how this theory relates to the practices of development in China. I also point out the limitations of the theory in the context of China. Instead of the neo-liberal approach, the new institutional economic approach is applied to the economic and political analysis of the East Asian countries. Based on important concepts and the research methods of institutional economics, especially comparative transaction costs economics and network analysis, I try to construct a new framework in an attempt to give a satisfactory explanation to the institutional arrangements for economic development in China. My research questions are also developed here. In Chapter 3, "The Adoption of the Developmental State Model," I focus on the basic characteristics of the developmental state model and its adoption by China. I demonstrate how China has intentionally emulated the successful practices of Japan and the East Asian NIEs, and has come to adopt the East Asian developmental state strategy. By following the theory of the developmental state school in analyzing the interactive relations between China's economic and political institutions, I expect to identify the developmental state as a choice-set or context in which Chinese political institutions are evolving. A coherent explanation of the changing Chinese political economy is constructed based on this choice-set. In Chapter 4, "The Pillars of the Chinese Developmental State," I discuss the major institutional arrangements at the central government level that support the existence and functioning of a developmental state in China. On the one hand, I discuss how the Chinese government has followed in the steps of other East Asian countries by transforming and restructuring its governmental institutions and policy in order to strengthen its capacity to steer the modernization process and macro-manage its national economy. On the other hand, I indicate that many potential problems with the Chinese

12 *The Dual Developmental State*

developmental state have to be addressed within a larger context; namely, within the context of legislative and local politics. In Chapter 5, "The National People's Congress and China's Transition," by focusing on the NPC, I try to explain why the NPC was introduced by the Chinese leadership almost simultaneously with the start of Chinese economic reforms. I also show that because the NPC has a peculiar institutional arrangement and follows a network strategy for institutionalization, it has expanded its role, but not at the direct expense of the state capacity. In Chapter 6, "Developmentalism and the Provincial People's Congresses," the PPCs are used as a further example to demonstrate that legislative activism and local decentralization have helped the central state address the transition problems. Particularly, this chapter discusses the institutional linkages as the most efficient way for institution building, and the politics of consultation and smoothness, the interaction pattern of cooperation through competition as an often-used strategy for exerting power by the PPCs. It demonstrates how the network politics has been conducted in the Chinese legislative development and even in the larger context of political and economic transitions. In Chapter 7, "The Shenzhen Revolution and Central-Local Synergism," I use the municipality of Shenzhen as a case study to illuminate Deng Xiaoping's strategy for China's transition, and to further highlight the indispensable role of local developmentalism in the national strategy and the symbiotic relationship between the center and the localities. My conclusion, Chapter 8, "The Logic of the Dual Developmental State," serves two purposes: here I explicate the logic and spirit of a dual developmental state and summarize my findings and their implications for many other research topics in Chinese studies. Finally, I anticipate the future changes of the Chinese system and some possible policy consequences.

Notes

[1] In Terry Moe's study (1995, 127), the state in America is a weak state; American bureaucracy has less authority and capacity than a firm: "In the economic system, organizations are generally designed by participants who want them to succeed. In the political system, public bureaucracies are designed in no small measure by participants who explicitly want them to fail." This insight can also be applied to the US constitutional system. Another mainstream liberal theorist, Robert Dahl (1985) argues that the American state is different from corporate America: the former is a pluralist democracy, but the latter is an authoritarian hierarchy. In American corporate capitalism, the economic structure of the firm

is the least democratic one among major institutions in American democracy. The firm is still governed by a hierarchical system, the employees have no democratic rights to participate in decision-making process. In other words, US firms are more an "authoritarian" structure relative to their employees than the American government is relative to its citizens.

2   Many economists have used institutionalism and transaction costs analysis in their studies on the Chinese political economy. For example, He Qinglian (1998) applies the concepts of "rent seeking," "transaction costs" and "path-dependence." Other examples are: Liu Xin, "Property Right and Transaction Cost in Actual Market Economy," *Nankai Economic Studies* No. 1 (Feb. 1995), pp. 3-9; Wang Dingding, "From 'Transaction Costs' to the Equilibrium of Game," The Economic Studies (Beijing) No. 9 (1995), pp. 72-80; many articles in Zhang Wenmin, et al, (1996, 1997, 1998).

2 The Developmental State and the Hybrid Mode of Governance

Like all Communist and post communist countries, China has been on the path of a triple transition: to marketize its economy, to democratize its polity, and to build a civil society. The rapidly changing nature of China's political economy has caused anxiety among her neighbors and major Western nations. This worry comes from two opposing concerns: One is the possible ascendancy of a new "Middle Kingdom" with enormous economic and political clout, while the other is the possible break-up of China and the emergence of a "Muddle Kingdom" suffering from political, ethnic and regional conflicts (*Foreign Affairs* 1998). These two scenarios for the future China seem totally different. However, if we examine them carefully, they are actually twins begotten by a common observation: China has done well in the economic but not in the political realm. Such an unpredictable "China threat" (no matter which scenario is considered) has intensified the urgency for both decision-makers and academics to grasp accurately the logic underlying the Chinese system in order to interpret her behavior and gauge her future policy projection. But her rapidly changing economy and persistently opaque politics have increased the difficulties of placing her in a broader comparative and interdisciplinary perspective, and thus, of interpreting the dynamics and directions of her political and economic development (Shambaugh 1993).

Despite the accelerating progress by China specialists and comparativists to reach out to each other for a fruitful dialogue over the past decade, the accommodation of the China case to general theoretical studies is still inadequate. This inadequacy is reflected in the fact that none of the most fashionable paradigms in comparative studies has satisfactorily solved any of the important issues posed by China. The field of Chinese studies is still in a warring state. This failure has compounded the problem of perceiving China as a volatile and eccentric factor in world affairs. Thus, the failure to provide a sound explanation for the developmental pattern and its underlying logic in China has further strengthened the uncertainties surrounding this country. Uncertainties produce anxieties and misperceptions. A vicious cycle acquires its own momentum.

In this chapter, I will review three major perspectives used to explain China's transition and the two fundamental ideologies supporting them. Basically, I will discuss the inadequacy of the neo-liberal approach within the context of China's experiences. I will also discuss the weaknesses of the developmental state theory that jeopardize its validity and applicability. To repair the developmental state model, I will go to its theoretical foundation, namely, institutionalism, to search for conceptual tools. Institutionalism will provide the major inspirations and ideas for my re-conceptualization of the developmental state theory. The keystone for this re-conceptualization is the network as both an institution and an approach. Based on institutional economics, the developmental states commonly found in East Asia can be interpreted as instituting a hybrid form of governance to organize economic, political and social transactions. More exactly, these East Asian societies are characterized by the networks that have features and a logic different from both the market and bureaucratic modes of organization.

Three Paradigms, Two Philosophies

Major comparative approaches to Chinese studies have placed China within three contexts, or three theories of "convergence": China's convergence with the West, with Eastern Europe (including the former Soviet states), or with East Asia (McCormick and Unger 1996). These discussions have been going on at both the normative and empirical levels. The former asks whether it is desirable to have one kind of convergence; the latter asks whether China has been converging with one of these areas. Few scholars think that the experiences of Eastern Europe provide a distinctive model that can serve as an ideal type for China to emulate. However, some scholars believe that a sudden death of Communism leading to a birth of Western-oriented development could be a good strategy for China. The convergence with Eastern Europe might serve merely as a transitional stage leading China to the Western-style development. Thus the polemic at the normative level narrows down to the difference between East Asian "Confucian democracy" (Huntington 1991, 307) and Western liberal democracy. Thus, there is a divergence between two different strategies and the philosophies meant to

16   *The Dual Developmental State*

bring these strategies into being (Pye 1985; Berger and Hsiao 1988; Keyfitz 1988).

In 1989, Francis Fukuyama (1989) already apocalyptically claimed that the fall of the Communist regimes in Eastern Europe and the Soviet Union indicated the disappearance of Communism as an ideological challenge to liberalism. The end of the Cold War closed the ideological conflict between the East and West. The final and permanent triumph of liberal democracy with a market economy all over the world announced the "end of history." But history seems to have moved in another direction. Samuel Huntington's provocative thesis about "the clash of civilizations" reminds us that the value-laden debate arising from basic differences between cultures will go on (Huntington 1993). The two different patterns of regime transition in East Asia and Eastern Europe essentially reflect two different economic ideologies. The developmental state model is based upon German economist Friedrich List's ideas for a "national economy and deliberate development," while the foundation of Anglo-American economic thinking was laid down by Adam Smith with his idea of the "invisible hand" and automatic growth theory (Fallows 1994, chapter 4; Thurow 1992). Since a discussion of whether China should follow the Western or East Asian experiences involves so many fundamental issues of culture and philosophy (Rosen 1990-91; Rosemont 1991; Nathan 1985, 1990; Liu 1990; Yan 1992a, 1992b; Ogden 1995; Friedman 1995), my discussion focuses on both a philosophical divergence and an empirical question: In recent years, has China been following the steps of the West, Eastern Europe, or East Asia?

(1) The West as an Analogical Framework

During the last two centuries, the Enlightenment model of the rational, autonomous individual (the Lockean ideas in political theory, and Smith's philosophy of the free market in economics) has triumphed over the challenges from Marxism and achieved the status of an established theory (Rosement 1991, chapter 3). First, for most Westerners it has provided a basic framework, a lens to perceive the world, an ideology to guide their economic and political operations, a moral standard to analyze and evaluate their own and other societies. Second, the isomorphism between political and economic liberalism has been regarded as orthodoxy.

According to classic liberalism, the economy is viewed as being in a state of equilibrium, operating in a zero transaction cost framework. Rational actors as individuals are engaged in instantaneous exchanges of identical commodities in a concentrated market in a single arena that is perfectly competitive, and for which the enforcement of contracts is automatic. Each producer and consumer is so small in comparison to a "thick market" that not one of them can affect the price alone. "It is scarcity that calls economic activism into being. Where exchange is free, consensual, and reasoned, laws of supply and demand direct the flow of economic activity. This fact alone diminishes anarchy. Quite general laws discipline all, and bind all together under significant constraints" (Novak 1991, 105). The market, for Adam Smith, is "the invisible hand" of God that guides the economy. For Hayek (1945, 528), it is a marvel, a "spontaneous order" resulting from the co-actions of private choices and evolving naturally without being designed by any individual or central power. Once established, the market is self-sufficient and self-regulating. As Hayek argues (1945, 527-8), the market is a kind of spontaneous governance "which we can perform without thinking about it." "The price system is just one of those formulations which man has learned to use...after he stumbled on it without understanding it." These beliefs are reflected in two famous liberal canons: "the free market" and "the self-regulating market." Although some orthodox economists agree with the idea of market creation, it is the idea that "manufacturers form the market" instead of the state (Shiraishi and Tsuru 1989, 16).

In addition, neo-liberal theories also assume an inefficient state in matters pertaining to the economy. The state is either regarded as a "necessary evil" or a predatory, rent-seeking bureaucracy. Although the neo-liberal economists recognize market failure and the necessity for compensation from the state, the market as a marvel is believed to be more efficient than the state, as state involvement is unavoidably related to rent-seeking behaviors. Thus, the neo-liberal view is also dubbed as "state minimalism" and "pricism" (Streeten 1992, 15-16). Consequently, the neo-liberal theory has constructed a linear development in which the state will be replaced eventually by a more efficient market in the organizing of the economy. A free market will produce a free polity. Only a liberal democracy then is to be the natural match for a market economy. This linear development can be expressed by the two following pairs of polar extremes:

Pole 1: Perverted or Deviant	Pole 2: Right or Natural
State-controlled Economy	Free Market Economy
Autocratic Political Regime	Liberal Democracy

A movement from Pole 1 to Pole 2 is a process towards development and civilization. It is also imperative that just as an apple always falls to earth, the free market goes with liberal democracy, marketization with

18   *The Dual Developmental State*

decentralization, and consumers' free choice with the voters' right to choose their leaders. The desire for both a market economy and liberal democracy lies in each individual's impulse to control his (or her) own life and fate. "The law of supply and demand is as immutable as the law of gravity: as a country moves up the economic ladder, political freedoms almost always follow" (Johnson 1995, 287). Consequently, as Chalmers Johnson (1995, 55) ridicules, under the Anglo-American orthodoxy, mostly built up around the American model, its doctrine has become "monotheistic:" "There was only one capitalist god and He lived in the United States."

From this Western pluralist democratic perspective, some people have argued that China has been on a dual track of liberalization and democratization meant to converge with Western liberal democracy and the market economy. It might take time, and the Chinese leadership might resist; but the convergence between Chinese and Western norms and practices is inevitable in the long run, if the market economy is allowed to continue.

During the early 1980s, because reforms in China coincided with the liberal philosophy, China was turned into an incarnation of the Western liberal doctrine. Westerners were excited to see the biggest country in the world changing herself in the image of the West, especially, the United States (Nathan 1990, chap. 4, 71-81). For this reason, its leader, Deng Xiaoping was chosen the person of the year by some US major news magazines and was widely acclaimed in the US (He got an honorary doctorate of law from Temple University). Some Chinese at home, Fang Lizhi being the most famous one, were also optimistic about the necessity and possibility for a "wholesale Westernization." As Charles Horner argued, this sentiment "was especially pronounced in 1989, at the height of China's democracy movement. The interest among China's best and brightest in Western parliamentarism and human rights had reached unprecedented heights, and the recovery of China for Western-derived political values and institutions seemed at hand" (Horner 1994).

But as Deng repeatedly delayed some reforms of the political system instead of fulfilling the liberal expectations for a simultaneous development of marketization and democratization, many Westerners became increasingly uneasy with the course of China's reforms. When the military was mobilized to crack down on the pro-democracy movement (or "Westernization impulse") in 1989, Deng was immediately condemned as a butcher. The Chinese economic reforms were believed dead, and the political regime doomed. The way for China to escape the current crises was believed to lie in the return to the aborted course, namely, the continuing economic liberalization and political democratization (Schell 1989, 1994; Lichtenstein 1991; Ruan 1994; Yan 1992; Liu 1990; Nathan 1990).

As China's image has changed from a romanticized pioneer for liberalization in the 1980s to an evil empire in the post-cold war era in certain Western circles (especially the US policy makers and mass media), the convergence argument turned from descriptive ("China is becoming more like the West") to prescriptive ("China should move to the Western democracy"). As Christopher Clark, a US State Department specialist, argued in 1991, "China does not seem likely in the foreseeable future to adopt a Western-style multi-party system of competition for power; it lacks most of the historical, cultural, and socio-economic conditions normally associated with such a transition" (Joint Economic Committee, US Congress 1992, 2). Thus, the Westernization argument (both normative and empirical) lost ground in China studies.

However, after China's reforms in favor of a market economy got back on track in 1992, a new wave of China fever (or "Sinomania") surged throughout the world. The hope for China's return to the liberal developmental strategy was rekindled. Stephen Robert (1994), a New York financier, explicitly voiced this optimism:

China's move from a wholly state-controlled to a largely free-market economy has already changed that country socially and politically....[E]conomic freedom is also a powerful social force. Once you let people make financial choices, you've unleashed their desire for other liberties--and these liberties are already taking shape in China...The vast middle class now forming in China almost assures the triumph of democracy and its freedoms.... Capitalism is nothing more than democracy of the marketplace--the right of people to make their own decisions about economic matters. Once a free market system is established, it is but a short step to political democracy.

Not only we have heard enough talk about China's next inevitable step toward democracy, some serious Western scholars even have claimed that the democratic developments have occurred in China but have been neglected by the outside world. China is reportedly moving towards a Western-style democracy by stealth. By focusing on the representative institutions at the village and local levels, several scholars have identified the "early sprouts of democracy," especially in the dark soil of countryside (Ogden 1993; T. White 1992; Lawrence 1994; Manion 1996). For example, Suzanne Ogden has found that as China's reforms proceed, the old democratic facade (for example, PCs), has been given real meaning and

20   The Dual Developmental State

importance. Melanie Manion also found that since the village committees were established and their elections conducted in the late 1980s to meet the fundamental economic changes in rural China, an electoral connection between village leaders and villagers has taken shape, holding the former more responsible to the later. She argues,

> Nonetheless, the electoral connection in the Chinese countryside is also a revolution of sorts. In theory, it reverses the Leninist relationship between leaders and masses; in practice, it is transforming the relationship between leaders and ordinary citizens at the rural grassroots....[T]he democracy that is slowly growing in Chinese villages is likely to have implications as profound as the changes in economic organization that created the demand of it....The "mundane revolution" of voter choice appears to be catching on in the countryside of one of the world's few remaining communist powers. (Manion 1996, 745)

As with Manion, when Tyrene White (1992) casts her eyes on the Chinese countryside, she sees the beam of a democratic future for China. She even thinks that the locomotive for Chinese democratization maybe be the Chinese peasants, another "countryside surrounding the urban centers." She argues, "Peasants, unlike their urban counterparts, have become property holders and taxpayers with a vested interest in how village affairs are conducted. In time, they may teach the urban populace a thing or two about the development of democratic institutions." This view distinguishes her from many other authors (for example, the authors of *River Elegy*) who think of the Chinese peasantry as "the most important stabilizing factor" for the current regime (Joint Economic Committee, US Congress 1992, 66) and expect the emerging urban middle class (especially intellectuals and entrepreneurs) to drive the democratization process.

In contrast, within the same liberal orthodox framework, there is another group of people who sticking to an either/or demarcation between democracy coexisting with economic growth and autocracy with economic stagnation, are skeptical that the current situation in China has anything to do with democracy. Since democracy and economic development foster each other, if China is resisting democratization and her Communist leadership has resorted to military crackdowns on the democracy movement, then this indicates that the Chinese political structure is an ossified Communist authoritarian system. Therefore, either the ossified political structure will stifle economic development, or economic development will burst its political structure and lead to the installation of a democracy. The introduction of a market economy should cause institutional decay within the Chinese political structure. This conflict between economic development and the political structure will eventually explode the "bubble" of China's success (Hornik 1994; Segal 1994). Before this finally happens, China will be regarded as "schizophrenic," "a contradiction," "a split personality," a paradox and an "ambivalent dualism" in tension, a "fascist country led by a Communist Party," a "Market-Leninism" with "two faces," "the yin and yang of China" (Schell 1994, 414; Kristof and WuDunn 1994, 430; Baum 1994, vii).

(2) The East European Experience as a Frame of Reference

The argument that China is following in the steps of Eastern Europe gained recognition after 1990 when former Communist countries fell like dominos in Eastern Europe and the Soviet Union. Because economic development generally causes the political decay of an authoritarian regime, many scholars have argued that it is a "logical impossibility for a Leninist system to reform and to marketize" (Lichtenstein 1991, 127). Any attempt to do so will be like shaking down a Humpty-Dumpty, only leading to a grand failure, or a quicker disintegration of the Communist system as a whole (Huntington 1968; Brzezinski 1993; Rozman 1992; Dahl 1970, 121). Reforms for marketization have to be started under a new political framework, namely a parliamentary democracy. Marketization and democratization have to be pursued at the same time (Crawford 1995).

In contrast to China, the former Soviet Union and other East European countries have tried the neo-liberal strategy. Adam Przeworski (1991, 8) has noted that "the road the new elites and the people in Eastern Europe want to take is the one that leads to Europe. 'Democracy, market, Europe' is the banner....They will thus reenter Europe. They will become a part of the West." These strategies, "the big bang" and "shock therapy" are examples that advise the states to withdraw themselves from the economy. A price-mechanism and the market will immediately fill this vacuum. As Bernard Chavance (1994, 205) describes,

The economists, inspired by free market ideas in the East as well as the West, have been particularly optimistic about the transition. Their implicit point of departure was a simplified model of Western capitalism: a system characterized by market coordination based on private ownership. Thus they saw the transition as a shift from an artificial and irrational order based on planning and

22   *The Dual Developmental State*

state ownership, through universal deregulation, to a spontaneous, self-regulating, and rational order: the market economy.

Since democratization was regarded as an integral part of the transition, at the end of 1993 free elections both at the national and sub-national level have also happened in Eastern Europe where parliaments have predominated (Remington 1994, 13-14). Even in the former Soviet republics, where strong presidents have emerged, a strong president always has to face a critical, assertive parliament (Remington 1994, 20). The bloody conflict between Boris Yeltsin and the Russian parliament in 1993 was an example. In all former socialist countries in Eastern Europe, one-party authoritarian rule was ended and free elections held with multi-party competition allowed. Parliamentary democracy has been established and parliaments have increasingly played a large part in the political economy (Remington 1994; Hahn 1995; Olson and Norton 1996). At the same time, almost all these countries have decentralized more powers to sub-national units, and localism and regionalism have been increasingly on the rise (Kim and Zacek 1993; Whitefield 1993, 11).

Unfortunately, for the leaders and ordinary people in these countries it has proved an illusion that they could move into a Western-type democracy and market economy within a short period of time. They failed to fully realize that even though an old economic system can be dismantled quickly, the creation and stabilization of a new one takes a long time. Their unrealistic strategy for transformation failed to take into account that this kind of systemic change entails an evolutionary process and gradual learning (individual, organizational, social). So it is not surprising that the simultaneous pursuit of liberalization and marketization did not produce economic prosperity but chaos and disillusion.

Some Communism specialists tend to see China approaching a "grand failure." Despite fundamental economic changes in the past twenty years, the Chinese political structure is believed to be ossified and too rigid to adapt itself to economic changes. The out-dated Communist system with its anti-liberal policy constitutes the root problem and is seen as breeding a total crisis within the Chinese system. The economic development has been "threatening to rupture the entire Leninist political structure as well " (Schell 1994, 431-432). Quite conceivably, the yesterday of former Communist countries in Eastern Europe will be China's tomorrow. This eventual crisis possibly will endanger the very survival of China as a nation state (Schell

1994; Lichtenstein 1991; Shirk 1993; Ruan 1994; Jenner 1992; Goodman and Segal 1994).

By focusing on the PCs (their elections, institutional arrangements and operations), Barrett McCormick has identified a fundamental hypocrisy within a Leninist state: the divergence between public discourse and private experience. "[I]t is apparent that China's present electoral and parliamentary arrangements are fairly typical of post-Stalinist Leninist states." On the one hand, the communist leaders make extravagant claims regarding the PCs as the highest democracy and most representative organ; on the other hand, they keep tight control over the public sphere and make elections meaningless and PCs powerless. However, when the society gained a little autonomy and some limited meaningful choices were presented to the people the political myth evaporated overnight. The Leninist regime started to crack because once parliaments are opened and activated, no Leninist regime has survived long. This dilemma caused the sudden collapse of all Leninist systems in Eastern Europe. Based on the similarities of power structure between China and other former communist regimes, there are enough reason to believe that "China might also follow that path" (McCormick and Unger 1996, 29-53).

Many scholars think China's political structure is suffering from political decay defined as the "loss of public trust, organizational deterioration, internal corruption, and declining effectiveness." The Chinese system has lost cohesion and coordination (Pei 1994, 65-66). David Goodman and Gerald Segal (1997) have claimed, "As more power was decentralized, the rulers pretended to rule and the ruled pretended to be ruled." The rise of localism and legislative power in China were believed to pose major challenges, because in so many former Communist countries parliamentary democracy has also been accompanied by localism. Regionalism and nationalism aggravated decentralization and ethnic conflicts. The free local parliamentary election became a precursor for the collapse of the Communist system. Thus, it seems that parallels between China and the East European states exist when we look at legislative activism and issues pertaining to decentralization and localism.

(3) The East Asian Model as a Frame of Reference

The third group of ideas associated with the developmental state theory argues that China and her East Asian neighbors are converging. This argument was first developed in the mid-1980s, and revitalized after the

24   The Dual Developmental State

1989 crackdown and the restart of China's reforms in 1992. It has become the hegemonic paradigm in China-related studies. As the Chinese have gained more confidence in their culture, they have been "less inclined to try out Western-derived solutions to their problems," but have tried instead to seek an "alternative world view to American-style liberalism" (Horner 1994). Consequently, nationalism and anti-Americanism have swept over the nation. And as a result, the relevancy of Western liberal democracy to today's Chinese political development has been questioned (Horner 1994; Tyler 1996; Ling and Ma 1999).

The Chinese leadership has shown no intention of following the liberal democratic, or American model. This has been illustrated by its persistent political campaigns against "bourgeois liberalization." The official propaganda machine has repeatedly denounced the Westernization of China as undesirable, impossible, and despicable. As Deng Xiaoping put it, "We are not against the parliamentary elections in Western countries. But mainland China cannot follow. We shall not adopt the 'separation of three powers' and bicameralism." The reasons are that "the United States actually has three governments, they fight with each other and cause a lot of troubles and delays." China's system is advantageous for avoiding deadlocks and developing the economy. "If we follow the Western model, only chaos will come" (Deng 1987). At the same time, they have declared that the East Asian NIEs are models to emulate. Therefore, for many scholars, China is intentionally resisting the Anglo-American liberal approach and is instead emulating the East Asian developmental strategy.

Most East Asia specialists think China is following a "gradual transition" model like the "Four Little Dragons." The East Asian pattern, sometimes also called the "developmental state model" or "soft authoritarianism," has two pillars: a repressive government and a high-growth economy. Relating these institutional traits to the Chinese context, several noted scholars consider that the developmental state model characterizes China's situation and have followed this model when examining recent developments in China (White 1988, 1991; Perkins 1986; Overholt 1993). Richard Baum (1992-93) summarized this neo-authoritarian alternative in Chinese politics as follows:

> [A] highly centralized, non-dogmatic political system under a strong leader who would govern in consultation with bodies such as the Chinese People's Political Consultative Conference (CPPCC) under the nominal supervision of an indirectly elected National People's Congress....In the absence of

The Hybrid Mode of Governance 25

competitive political parties, directive legislative elections or constitutional separation of powers, neo-authoritarian leaders would solicit "consent of the governed" through periodic plebiscites, opinion polls and routinized articulation of group interests. There would be, however, little political participation in the selection of leaders or policies. Incipient political discontent or opposition would be discouraged through strict controls on permissible speech and behavior.

In the East Asian developmental state model, a one-party authoritarian system can change, transform itself, and institutionalize state power after achieving economic development (Huntington and Moore 1970), as South Korea and Taiwan (its ruling party, the Kuomintang, was a Leninist party) have shown. Judging by the successful experiences of all the East Asian NIEs, if China could successfully adopt this model, there would be a great possibility for a smooth, gradual transformation towards a more open, market-oriented economy followed by a more relaxed political system (Harding 1987, 300; Kristof and WuDunn 1994; Perkins 1986; Overholt 1993; H. Wang 1994).

The aforementioned three different arguments have diverged over the following empirical questions: Are the political institutions in China suffering from decay and, as a result, constraining the further development of the economy? Is the Chinese state flexible enough to change in response to economic challenges, or is it too rigid to reform? Is the tension between economics and politics so strong that it will lead to a final showdown that disrupts the whole structure of the political economy? If Chinese political institutions indeed have transformed, what is the impact of these institutional changes upon the marketization process? Have they facilitated or retarded it? Are these transformations going to assist the whole Chinese communist regime to finish a gradual transition to a more democratic system?

Many recent studies have identified substantial changes in the party-state relationship, cadre transformation, the relationship between the center and localities, governance at the grassroots level, and the public service (Hamrin and Zhao 1995; Lee 1991; Manion 1993; Jia and Lin 1994; O'Brien 1990; T. White 1994; Ogden 1994). These changes had not eroded the political rule of the CPC, but rather had assisted the party to adapt to the changing environment. More important, some scholars have found that some newly developed political mechanisms were helpful to the economic development. For example, Gabriella Montinola, et al (1995, 50-81), have argued that "Federalism, Chinese style" is "market-preserving federalism."

26   *The Dual Developmental State*

Yasheng Huang (1996) has argued that the effective administrative capabilities of the central government to control local governments helped to stabilize the Chinese macro-economy and contributed greatly to Chinese economic development.

If substantial changes did exist within the Chinese political system, and these changes also were facilitating the economic growth, not dampening it, we then have to explore another possible conjecture: As the political structure in China has been in constant change, the positive effects of these changes may have alleviated the tension between the economy and the political structure and, therefore, may keep the tension at a manageable level. In other words, China's economic success may have political foundations (Shirk 1993; Montinola, et al, 1995; Goldstein 1995). If I can identify systematic data to support this conjecture, it will cast doubt on the doom-sayers' view of a possible start of warlordism and the end of China that would follow from the political decay and disintegration. If some mechanisms are functioning within the Chinese political structure, alleviating the tension between the economy and this political structure, then we have to consider two possible implications: Are these changes the first steps toward democratization, as Ogden, T. White, and Manion have suggested? Or alternatively, do these symptoms lead to some other mode of political and economic development?

In recent years, regime transitions have been studied in Latin America, Southern Europe, the East Asian NIEs, and the former socialist countries (the former Soviet Union, the East European countries, and East Asian socialist regimes) (O'Donnell, et al, 1986; Diamond, et al, 1989; Di Palma 1990; Huntington, 1991; Przeworski 1991; Wekkin, et al, 1993; Haggard and Kaufman 1995). Janos Kornai (1995, x) has argued that all these transitions are on only one road, namely capitalism. But on this road to capitalism, if one looks closer, one sees that "it consists of numerous greater or lesser main roads and side roads, zigzagging paths, ascents and precipitous slopes." At least two strategies or two prototypes of capitalism exist. One is the Anglo-American liberal strategy leading to the American model, or the liberal democratic/free market model. The other is the Bismarckian-Meiji strategy leading to the Japanese model, or the capitalist developmental state. These two paths are based upon two different historical patterns. They follow two different strategies and have two different institutional arrangements. We have discussed the neo-liberal approach and its ideological foundation. We now need to turn to another viable approach to the political economy, namely, the developmental state theory.

Prototype of the East Asian Developmental State Model

The "developmental state school" has different names used by different scholars, such as the "East Asian development model," the "strategic capacity" model, "bureaucratic authoritarian industrializing regimes" ("BAIRs") and "authoritarian capitalism." However, scholars within this framework have basically argued that Japan, South Korea, Taiwan, Singapore, and Hong Kong did not take the Western-style pluralist democracy as a model for their developments. Japan as the Asian pioneer has developed a new approach to the political economy, a new development strategy, and created a new Asian political and economic system, possibly a systemic new theory for capitalism and democracy (Fallows 1994; Thurow 1992; McCord 1991).

What is the "developmental state model"? According to Chalmers Johnson (1995, 28), a capitalist developmental state (CDS) has two characteristics: "the state-guided capitalist developmental system, or to put it in different terms, a plan-rational economy with market-rational political institutions." Manuel Castells (1998, 270-271) offers this definition for his "CDS":

A state is developmental when it establishes as its principle of legitimacy its ability to promote and sustain development, understanding by development the combination of steady high rates of economic growth and structural change in the productive system, both domestically and in relationship to the international economy.

For Gordon White (1984, 97), a developmental state is a "crucial stimulant and organizer of socio-economic progress," and "a major agent of social transformation." In the "guided market economies" of East Asian developmental states, the state plays a substantial role as "the executor of a national economic interest but encourages a vibrant micro-economy operating in a competitive market context" (White and Wade 1988, 25). A developmental state usually has four important characteristics:

(1) There is an active role for the state and a collaborative relationship between the state and the economy. To qualify as a developmental state, Johnson believes, "one of the things a state committed to development must do is develop a market system" (Deyo 1987, 141). The state must be "market-fostering," "market-facilitating," and committed to nurturing markets. In contrast to the passive role of an instrumental state perceived by

28   *The Dual Developmental State*

liberalism, the states in East Asia are "active states" or "strong states." Their roles are far beyond providing a framework for the economy. They act as agents or transformers in the economy and the society (Coporaso and Levine 1992, 181-196).

(2) The government provides an industrial policy. An industrial policy is the "development, guidance, and supervision of industry" by the government (Johnson 1995, 64). According to many studies, the secret of success in East Asian developmental states is the implementation of "deepening industrial policies;" that is, the ability and flexibility of the state to "move in and move out of sectors, to promote this or that industry" (Cumings 1987, 74, 81). One study found, "South Korea, Taiwan, and Singapore all have dirigiste bureaucracies capable of extracting and channeling resources to targeted industries and selectively altering and sequencing the system of industrial incentives, including those for foreign investors" (Deyo 1987, 102).

For the purpose of making and coordinating industrial policies, in all these East Asian countries there exists a famous economic "general staff" which is one powerful bureaucracy or includes many ministries. For example, there is the MITI (Ministry of International Trade and Industry) in Japan, the Council for Economic Planning and Development, the Industrial Development Bureau, and the Council for Agricultural Planning and Development in Taiwan (Wade 1990, 196), and the Economic Planning Board in South Korea.

(3) A dictatorship of development exists. A dictator (Park Chung Hee in Korea, Lee Kuan Yew in Singapore, Chiang Ching-kuo in Taiwan) or a group of ruling elites (in Japan) are in control. Fearing that a full democracy might lead these East Asian countries "to spin out of control," the ruling establishment purposefully delays the process of democratization (Johnson 1995, 48). One scholar rhetorically wonders: "How does a backward country like Korea make an economic miracle? The one-word answer is authoritarianism" (Fallows 1994, 366).

The political arrangements follow a "four-part model." First, an elite group dominates the ruling establishment. Second, interest groups are limited and weak. Mass movements, especially the labor movement, are weak. Third, the importance of political decisions based on the market mechanism as a means of intervening into the economy is emphasized. And fourth, national pride and nationalism are nurtured, but are not a constitutional development (Johnson 1995, 47). Because of these institutional characteristics, the state is insulated from social forces. It is

The Hybrid Mode of Governance 29

autonomous, and thus, is always strong and effective. But to distinguish it from the old authoritarianism, this authoritarianism is often referred to as a "semi-authoritarianism," "neo-authoritarianism," "soft authoritarianism" or a "paternalistic authoritarian system" (Johnson 1987; Berger and Hsiao 1988, 83). For, it is development-oriented, based on meritocracy, and enthusiastically for social equity in the process of development. The legitimacy of such a system is not based on democratic procedures but on its economic accomplishments and performances.

(4) The executive's dominance over the legislative institutions, or its administrative guidance is a typical institutional characteristic under a developmental state. The developmental state theory emphasizes the role of the executive and the administrative institutions at the national level (a competent bureaucracy in particular), in making and implementing strategic economic policies (Johnson 1987; Woo-Cumings 1994; Simone and Feraru 1995, 163-164; Ziya 1991: 109-126). The "administrative guidance" pushes the economy forward. Basically there is no place for the legislature and local governments. The state is always identified with the "executive authority," "bureaucracy," or some important political-economic organizations at the national level. The role of the legislature is negligible in a developmental state model. As Johnson (1995, 13) argues:

> Who governs is Japan's elite state bureaucracy....The bureaucracy drafts virtually all laws, ordinances, orders, regulations, and licenses that govern the society. It also has extensive extra-legal powers of 'administrative guidance' and is comparatively unrestrained in any way, both in theory and in practice, by the judicial system.....Article 41 (of the Japanese constitution) says that "The Diet shall be the highest organ of state power, and shall be the sole law-making organ of the state"; but this stipulation is not only untrue, it also conflicts with the Japanese political culture inherited from Japan's century of defensive modernization.

Robert Wade (1990, 327, 195) shares this view of the role of the legislature in Japan. The legislature from the beginning until the present has had less influence in the major decisions that affect the national welfare than in any other industrial democracy, while meritocatically selected technocrats have had more. Wade believes this description also applies to Taiwan and South Korea. In Taiwan, he argues, "Still today economic policy making is intensively centripetal, it is carried out entirely in Taipei and almost entirely within the executive branch, with some input from the top of the party. The process is dominated by little more than a dozen individuals."

30 *The Dual Developmental State*

Not only the legislature but also the local governments have almost no role to play in economic development. In the classical developmental state model, the relationship between the center and localities is often neglected. For example, in South Korea and Taiwan, decentralization and local democratization happened recently after these countries experienced a successful economic take-off (Kim and Zacek 1993, 195-214; Tan, et al, 1996). As for Hong Kong, one observer commented in the early 1980s, that it was "about as democratic as the Soviet Union" (Deyo 1988, 108). The tiny size of the most successful developmental states makes it unnecessary to discuss the relationship between the center and localities in the developmental state theory.

The above summary of institutional characteristics is based on five well-recognized developmental states or areas (Japan, South Korea, Taiwan, Singapore, and Hong Kong). One central interest for academics is whether this model can be applicable to other countries, especially those that are huge in size and diverse in background, such as China.

Institutionalism as a New Angle

Based upon the "laissez faire" doctrine, a strong state intervention would retard an economic take-off. Thus, an autocratic regime should not be able to develop a market economy. But if, nevertheless, such an economic take-off occurs, then it is only an abnormal phenomenon and cannot last, for the liberalizing effect of a market economy will eventually erode the political basis of autocratic rule. Starting with this dogma, the neo-liberals have demonized the experiences of Japan, South Korea, Singapore and other East Asian countries. Especially after the East Asian financial crises broke out in 1997, this demonization has run very high. However, the "Asian miracles" were not a mirage without theoretical justification. In fact, institutional economics can make important contributions to our understanding of the economic, social and political life of these countries.

"Institutionalism" is not a new word in either political science or economics. But the "to bring the institutions in" movement called for a "paradigmatic shift" and aroused a new interest by scholars in institutional studies during the 1980s (Evans, et al, ed., 1985; North 1981, 1990; March and Olsen 1984, 1989). For institutionalists, "institution" basically can be divided into two categories: an institution as an organization, and an institution as rule. Institutions are designed to structure and regularize

The Hybrid Mode of Governance 31

interactions between actors, and to provide regularity and predictability. As Herbert Simon once argued, individuals are "intendedly rational, but only limitedly so." Therefore, the rationality of individuals is bounded (Simon 1961, xxiv; March and Simon 1958, 11). For minimizing the bounded rationality, organizations are created. For, "organizational systems could compensate for the cognitive limitations of individuals" (Williamson 1995, 38). According to this line of thought, rational individuals under liberalism are not as rational as expected. And organizations are not as irrational as predicted. According to Douglass North, the role of institutions, their constraints upon economic actors and their impact upon economic policy and performance, should be emphasized. It is just as important to understand commodity transactions (goods and services) as it is institutional transactions (definition and delimitation of a choice-set), production costs, transaction costs, and the role of technology within institutions. The transactions do not happen in a frictionless or transaction-free market. There are significant costs in negotiating contracts, acquiring information, enforcing contracts, etc. The transaction costs actually account for a large part of the total costs of economic activities. Just as technology is important for production costs, institutions are important both for production and transaction costs (North 1981, 1990). The institutions, structures, and rules provide "the choice sets" that "define the arena of choices for individual utility maximizing agents" (Bromley 1989, 6).

Based on institutionalism, the market is not merely a mechanism, or the putting to use of some macro-economic policies. The market should be treated as an institution. "Therefore, the market overall is a mixed bag of institutions" (North 1990, 69). Daniel Bromley (1989, 50) argues, "In a market economy these institutional arrangements would consist of a different constellation of constraints and opportunities--the tax laws, wage rates, contractual obligations for workers, product liability for commodities, health insurance premiums and coverage, and the like. This is a bundle of norms, conventions, habits, practices, customs, laws, and administrative rules that define a choice domain (a choice set)." Geofry M. Hodgson (1988, 174) gives an institutionalist definition of the market:

> We shall here define the market as a set of social institutions in which a large number of commodity exchanges of a specific type regularly take place, and to some extent are facilitated and structured by those institutions. Exchange...involves contractual agreement and the exchange of property rights, and the market consists in part of mechanisms to structure, organize, and

32 *The Dual Developmental State*

legitimate these activities. Markets, in short, are organized and institutionalized exchange. Stress is placed on those market institution which help to both regulate and establish a consensus over prices and, more generally, to communicate information regarding products, prices, quantities, potential buyers and potential sellers.

When the market is defined as an institution, our understanding of the market and its social ramifications has to be deepened and complicated. For example, it is difficult to judge the social consequences of the market from only one perspective. The market is neither a marvel as Hayek claimed, nor a chaotic order as Marx critiqued. It is a complicity of institutions and has multi-dimensional characteristics and is open to the shaping forces from the social, cultural and legal contexts. The performances and external influences upon the market are not necessarily homogeneous and coherent. Instead, they are a much more complex and puzzling phenomenon. As North argues, some institutions within the market are efficient, but some enduring institutions could be wasteful.

For most nations, the reason to embrace the market is its ability to provide an abundance of goods and services to meet the people's needs. The market is the biggest mechanism of provision and a big provider. It is believed to be equivalent to the Western way of life, and is the basis of economic prosperity and affluence. Actually, the market is not merely a mechanism of provision. The market is also a mechanism of denial and exclusion. The market always serves someone with endowments, against those lacking endowments, and often produces the "Matthew effect": making the rich richer, and the poor poorer. Its inefficiency in regard to social justice is a notorious "market failure." Its foundation (for example, the protection of the property rights) works for some people as it guarantees their power over some goods and their right and privilege to consume these goods. For this reason, it also must prevent other people from impinging upon this right and privilege to establish a social order in which private property is inviolable. At this time, the market is a "mechanism of denial and exclusion instead of provision" (Shiraishi and Tsuru 1989, 54). If we argue that the market as a mechanism of provision is fostering democracy, then the market as a mechanism of denial is more likely to strengthen the coercive aspects of the state and thus is related to political autocracy. Because the market has this double-edged effect, it is wrong to argue for the absolute correlation and logical connection between the market and democracy.

The Hybrid Mode of Governance 33

These ideas shed fresh light on our understanding of the state-market relationship and the role of the state in the process of marketization. On the key issue of the political economy, namely, on the interactive relations between the state and the market, there is a spectrum of ideas. On one extreme there are classical liberals, neo-liberals, institutionalists, statists (state-centered school), and market socialists. On the other extreme, there are Stalinists and central planners. Few scholars would treat the state and the market as an alternating "either/or" choice. As one economist claims, "The 'mystique' of the market--the supposition that the market does no wrong, that markets do not malfunction (only governments do)--is more the work of propagandists than economic scientists of any era" (Phelps 1985, 379). Actually, as the command economy in the Soviet Empire and other Communist countries stagnated and eventually collapsed, the East Asian "economic miracle" expanded, both socialism and minimalism have been under the same fierce attack. Today, while scholars near the classical liberalism pole have realized the "market failure" and scholars near the Stalinist pole the "state failure," the complimentarity or synergism of the "invisible hand" (marketplace) and the "visible hand" (state intervention) is gaining recognition (Putterman and Rueschmeyer 1992).

Gabriel Almond (1991) once summarized four pairings of the relationship between capitalism and democracy: capitalism supports or subverts democracy, and democracy supports or subverts capitalism. In this relationship, both the state as a democracy and economic system as a free market economy can promote and hinder development. Under some conditions, the state can compliment the market. But under other conditions, the state can damage the market, and vice versa (Dutt, et al, 1994; Putterman and Rueschemeyer 1992, 20). Charles Lindblom (1977) has a vivid metaphor for the state-market relationship. In his *Market and Politics*, the market and the state are the two basic instruments for social control, mobilization, and organization. The state is more like "strong thumbs," in contrast to the market that is like flexible "fingers." This metaphor makes more sense when considering the differing effectiveness of the state and the market in economic development. Usually, at the initiation stage of industrialization, the state is more efficient in mobilizing resources and achieving social equity. When the economy becomes mature and complex, the market is more efficient in organizing production and allocating products. Therefore, in the combination of the state and the market, which ingredient shall play a greater or lesser role to a large extent depends on the stage of economic development in which a specific nation stands.

34   *The Dual Developmental State*

Institutionalism provides conceptual tools to look inside the institutional arrangements of both the state and the market and to desegregate them into a complex system of institutions and structures. Their interactive relationship has also been complicated as a result of interaction of all these institutions. Because there are too many variables, the linkage between the state and the market is more uncertain. It is difficult to believe the assumption that has the creation of the market mechanism occurring suddenly and simultaneously. "Market making" must be seen as a process of evolution and institution building. "Today's markets did not simply appear *de novo* but rather represent the product of decades of institutional change" (Bromley 1989, 68).

Market creation is not equivalent to the withdrawal of the state from economic activities. Therefore, the neo-liberal prescription for a radical disconnection from the old command economy and the sudden jump into a market economy becomes precarious. The nature of market creation, its maintenance as a public good, and the protection of property rights give a large role to the state. It was the state that took on the responsibility to help the market to develop and nurture other supporting institutions indispensable for the survival of the market. Institutionally, the state has to do two things: to create prerequisites for the existence of the market and to maintain the market. As some economists have argued, "the invisible hand" is not the "hand of some god, some natural agency independent from human effort;" it is "the hand of the lawgiver," "the hand of government acting in the role of rule-maker and umpire" (Samuels 1989, 3). Karl Polanyi (1975, 139, 140) even argued that during the golden years of laissez faire capitalism in England the market was never totally free. Its survival was dependent on assistance from the state. He observed, "There was nothing natural about laissez-faire; free markets could never have come into being merely by allowing things to take their course....laissez-faire itself was enforced by the state." He continued, "The road to the free market was opened and kept open by an enormous increase in continuous, centrally organized and controlled interventionism. To make Adam Smith's 'simple and natural liberty' compatible with the needs of a human society was a most complicated affair." In Polanyi's words, "the market is instituted" (Polanyi, et al, 1957, 243-70).

Under today's circumstances, the state should not be expected to play a lesser role than the states of advanced capitalism several hundred years ago in establishing a market order. According to Gerschenkron (1962), if the backwardness is deeper, then a stronger role from the state is needed. World system theorists also correctly point out that today's different international environment requires the state to intervene in the economy to protect its own national industry or expand its markets overseas. Therefore, for a "late late-comer" state such as China (Levy 1966, 16) the role of the state looms large in the process of development.

Alec Nove once pointed out a fundamental error in Marxism: "The belief that the task of replacing the market by the deliberate decisions of the 'associated producers' would be 'simple and transparent.'" Conversely, it is also a fundamental error to think that replacing the command economy by the market would be "simple and transparent" (Putterman and Rueschemeyer 1992, 39). De-Communization is more challenging than mere marketization. For most transitional societies, not only must a traditional economy be dismantled, at the same time a centrally-planned command economy must also be dissolved to restore the market economy. This dual processes complicates the marketization. A joke may be illustrative here: It is easier to turn an aquarium into fish soup than the other way around (Islam and Mandelbaum 1993, 2).

Limitations of the Developmental State Model

Based upon the policies, institutional designs, and the interactions between the state and the economy in China, which I will discuss extensively in the coming chapters, this author endorses the developmental state model and examines the development in China within this theoretical context. However, my endorsement is not without reservation, because, there are several serious flaws with the current developmental state theory:

The developmental state theory is a state-centered approach. Its "state" often exclusively means the "central state," particularly in terms of its executive and administrative aspect. For example, Skocpal (1979, 29) defines the state as "a set of administrative, policing, and military organizations headed, and more or less well coordinated by, an executive authority." "Moreover, coercive and administrative organizations are only parts of overall political systems. Nevertheless, the administrative and coercive organizations are the basis of state power as such." This definition of the state gives an impression that state is a singular and monolithic actor, and unavoidably neglects other actors. The developmental state theory was generalized on empirical studies of small countries in East Asia. The small geographic and demographic setting has caused the theory to fail to

36   *The Dual Developmental State*

accommodate local aspects of developmentalism and the local efforts for development from the local states. As a result, the interactive patterns between the central state and local state are missing.

Graph 2-1: Two Different Models of Economy and Economic Development

The Anglo-Saxon Model	The Japanese Model
-Individual capitalism	-Communitarian capitalism
-Consumer economics	-Producer economics
-Economic philosophy: Adam Smith	-Economic philosophy: David Ricardo
-Rational utility-maximizing individual	-Empire-builders: strategic conquest
-Individualistic: more leisure and consumption	-High saving and high investment society; Team-building and business groups
-Profit-maximization	-Market-share marketization
-Shareholders first, customers and employees a distant second and third.	-Employees first, customers second, and shareholders third.
-Labor as rented factors of production can be disposed	-Labor as a strategic asset to be nurtured
-Success flows from individual Brilliance	-Success flows from a skilled team.
-Risks of economic change are carried by the individual.	-Risks of economic change are carried by the group.
-More a laissez faire state.	-Strategic policies from the state.

Source: This graph is made based on the arguments by Lester Thurow, *Head to Head: The Coming Economic Battle Among Japan, Europe, and America* (New York: William Morrow & Company, Inc., 1992).

Most studies clustering around the developmental state theory have stayed at the level of institutional arrangements and policy. Their conclusions on the developmental states, particularly those in East Asia, tend to exaggerate the East Asian exceptionalism. For, most of its advocates have failed to answer this question: Do the developmental states in East Asia constitute a new terminal category independent and different from the American-style capitalism and democracy, or are they only transitional stages that eventually will converge with the American-style political economy? Some scholars seem to argue that the developmental states in East Asia are unique and have formed a new type of political economy different from the patterns we have seen in the United States. But even if we believe that the East Asian developmental states have developed their own logic and

The Hybrid Mode of Governance   37

created their own institutions, many scholars are still not convinced that we can juxtapose the developmental states with American capitalism and democracy because the concept of the developmental state smacks of an authoritarian political rule and lacks the legitimacy that the American model enjoys. There is a need to eliminate value judgments and to base the political and economic practices in East Asia on a solid theoretical foundation. The developmental state theory has to ascend to a higher level of abstraction in order to tease out the deeper nature of the developmental state. This higher level of theoretical abstraction and generalization reveals that the developmental states in Asia follow the network approach mentioned in institutional economic sociology. We then are able to integrate it into the general theoretical discussion on different modes for organizing political, economic and social transactions.

Developmental states can be treated as a mechanism of governance of the political economy that is characterized as a series of networks. In the light of the three modes of governance for a political economy (namely, the hierarchy, the market, and the network), the East Asian developmental states have all pursued a strategy of networking and have been moving towards network societies (Redding 1990; van Wolferen 1990; Hamilton 1991; Orru, Biggart and Hamilton 1991; Gerlach 1992; Castells 1996; Weidenbaum and Huges 1996; Hsing 1998; Wank 1999). In his comparison of the three most powerful economic units, Lester Thurow points out the fundamental differences between the "Anglo-Saxon model" and the "Japanese model." One difference is that in the latter groups, networks, and communitarian interests take precedence over individuals, free markets, and individualism. In his famous *Megatrends Asia*, futurologist John Naisbitt (1996) concludes that the East Asian economies follow the pattern of "the networking model," which is more conspicuous in the Overseas Chinese network. Based on thousands of clan networks, the overseas Chinese entrepreneurs have penetrated into their local communities, expanded to mainland China, joined the global network, and sent their children to the best schools, in each case for the purpose of engaging in networking. This "truly global, tribal network" will become a powerful player in the emerging global market. Its strength lies in this network. Since the network mode of governance has been developed within the social and cultural contexts of these countries in Asia, social and cultural norms, rules, and customs tend to resist easy change. Therefore, it is safe to say that the market mode of governance in American political and economic life, and the network mode of governance we have seen in the East Asian developmental states will continue to follow

38   *The Dual Developmental State*

their own logic, and the gap between them will remain. To some extent, the East Asian developmental states are in transition to their final settlement of a network society.

The developmental state model has instigated little discussion on the prospect of change, especially the possibility of democratization, for the East Asian countries. Since many developmental states have fallen victim to the East Asian financial crises that began in 1997, some commentators have argued that the developmental state model was the root cause and that, as a result, this model is doomed. The only way out for the East Asian countries is to jettison this model and to embrace an American-style capitalism. However, if we examine the East Asian crises in the context of the network strategy, we still can find enough space for East Asian countries to explore and to innovate as they follow their distinctive logic. Democratization is also conceivable. Manuel Castells (1996, 173) even argues, "If the informational/global economy is better suited to the network form of business organization, then East Asian societies, and their organizational forms of economic activity, would have a distinctive comparative advantage in global competition, because such an organizational model is embedded in their culture and institutions." There is no reason to believe that Americanization is the only way for East Asian societies to change.

Even as a believer working within the basic concepts and approaches of the developmental state school, I think these serious problems cast doubt on its applicability. A further consideration of the developmental state is needed in order to expose its nature as a network and to fix these limitations. Based upon the network approach, a new explanation can be constructed to accommodate the practices in China that deviate in important respects from those of Japan and the "Four Little Dragons." From the perspective of the network society, all the variations between China and the classic developmental state model become insignificant. The Chinese case illustrates the true nature of developmental state, only if our analysis moves one level higher to see the developmental state approach as a kind of network strategy and as a way to maintain state capacity. These important institutional innovations have helped China to maintain the integrity of the developmental state model, namely, a strong state with a developmental orientation. Although China has adjusted the developmental state strategy and produced a new type of practice with its own peculiarities, it still is definitely within the general parameters of the developmental state model. Here I coin a special term, the dual developmental state, to account for the new patterns of power relationships between the center and sub-national units, and between the executive and legislature. As a result, the prerequisite for the standard developmental state model is relaxed, its content widened, and its applicability extended in my study.

3 The Adoption of the Developmental State Model

A dominant assessment of China's post-Mao reforms is that they have been an economic success but a political failure (Lichtenstein 1991; Shirk 1993; Shell 1994; H. Wang 1994; Pei 1994). For example, after praising the success of the strategy of growing a market economy, Barry Naughton (1995, 310) adds the following qualification:

> This achievement is both obscured and rendered fragile by China's failure to achieve political reform. China lacks not only democracy, but also minimum level of accountability and legitimacy. The political system is simply not adequate to cope with the challenges that confront it. The dysfunctional political system might prevent the Chinese people from quickly building the kind of future economic system they would prefer; it might even jeopardize the achievements of recent decades. However, the inadequacy of China's political system is chronic and long-standing.

According to some scholars, because the Chinese political system has failed to adapt itself to the country's economic development, the change of the latter has led to the decay of the former. A troubling sign of this syndrome of political decay is that the control of the central government over the country is slipping away. As economic growth soars, decentralization deepens, and changes in local/central relationships follow. The state capacity of the central government, both politically and economically, has declined drastically (Zheng 1995, 3; Jia and Lin 1994; Segal 1994). The reason why this regime has not collapsed can be attributed primarily to China's economic prosperity. When a government is able to continue providing more goods and services people are satisfied. To borrow Habermas (1973)'s terminology, the success in dealing with the efficiency crisis has helped the Chinese government alleviate its legitimation crisis. All in all, it has become a cliché that China's economic performance has not benefited from its political system. Even if it did not happen in a political vacuum, the political system only hampered the economy from achieving its

The Adoption of the Developmental State Model 41

full potential. According to this view, the political system now depends on robust economic growth for its survival.

The striking contrast between the political and economic aspects of China's reforms leads me to ask: How can a system that is full of innovation and pragmatism on economic issues have no imagination in politics? If a market economy has to be instituted and embedded in a sociological, legal, and political context, how could a "dysfunctional political system" have steered the development of the market economy and sustained its evolution for two decades? If Dwight Perkins (1986, 60) is right about East Asian development in that "sustained rapid growth depends most of all on a supportive political environment," and if the development of the market is context-dependent, then how could China be an exception that has maintained and sustained rapid growth without a supportive politics? Considering its huge size, this exception is even more puzzling. It may be true that a "democratic deficit" is conspicuous in China's reforms, especially when judged by Western standards (see Chapter 5 and 6). But, does this "democratic deficit" indicate that China's political system has been rigid and inadequate in the process of fostering the growth of the market economy?

Another group of scholars has argued that the economic miracles in East Asia could be explained by the adoption of an appropriate development strategy: the Bismarckian-Meji strategy. In contrast to a laissez faire Anglo-American pattern, this strategy is characterized by developmental authoritarianism, or developmental dictatorship. Therefore, it is also called the "developmental state model." Because most successful cases have been found in East Asia, it is also known as "the East Asian developmental state model." It is then argued that the recent economic take-off in China can be attributed to the emulation of this model.

A strategy for development does not focus only on one aspect or part of the development, but refers to the overall development of a nation's political and economic life (Griffin 1989, 25). In a broader sense, we can take this strategy as an institution, if institutions are defined as "the rules of the game in a society or, more formally, are the humanly devised constraints that shape human interaction" (North 1990, 3). If a development strategy is a system of rules and norms that come into being as a result of intentional political calculation and rational choice, why did the Communist Chinese system adopt the developmental state strategy? And, to what extend has China adapted the institutional arrangements of this model to fit China's situation?

42   *The Dual Developmental State*

In this chapter I begin by looking at how the Chinese leadership have assessed and been affected by the Hungarian model of rationalizing reforms of market socialism, and then by the East Asian model of a market economy. Later I discuss how the East Asian model was finally adopted and how it has had institutional ramifications for China's political system. In the light of the spirit of the East Asian developmental state model, I conclude that the Chinese political system has changed accordingly. The ingenuity and creativity of its political development are comparable to what has occurred in its economic development.

To Experiment with Strategies for Reforms

In chronological order since 1976, China has gone through three different development strategies: the classical Stalinist model, the Hungarian model of market socialism, and the developmental state model. After almost one decade of experiment, they finally settled on one that is comparatively most efficient in terms of reducing transaction costs and transition costs (the cost involved in moving to a new system). Because the government did not announce that it would follow one specific development strategy, and because it is impossible for China to follow another country's model in its entirety, a careful examination and comparison is required to identify the basic ways in which China is similar with other states. Only in this way does it become possible to explicate China's evolution.

In the aftermath of Mao Zedong's death, China was a deeply traumatized nation. As James Bryce (1959, vol. 1, 80) wrote, "Suffering, and nothing else, will implant that sense of responsibility which is the first step to reform." We can argue that this is the greatest merit of the Cultural Revolution for the Chinese people. This "Cultural Revolution syndrome" made the whole nation, from the very top to the grassroots, realize that the old system could not continue. For Hua Guofeng, the hand-picked successor to Mao, the most urgent task was to restore social, political and economic order, and, at the same time, to boost the morale of the nation and restore its political legitimacy. They believed that "the chaos of the Cultural Revolution was only a temporary interruption in the march. Only if we restore the order prior to the Cultural Revolution, return to the path chosen before the Cultural Revolution, speed up the pace, we still can recover the lost decade and catch up" (Zhang, et al, 1989, 685). For this reason, the strategy of the post-Mao

The Adoption of the Developmental State Model 43

leadership was "to set old policies, which have been thrown into disorder, right" (*boluan fanzhen*). The policies from 1977 to 1978 looked like a déjà vu of the good old days of the 1950s.

For Hua, returning to the golden Fifties meant first strengthening the Stalinist economic system. Underestimating the scope and depth of the structural crisis confronting China, he failed to realize that it was a systematic crisis of the whole Stalinist system. Consequently, under his "Great Leap Outward" policy, the central planning was strengthened, and the command economy was consolidated. These wrong-headed policies did not solve the problems embedded in the system, such as rigidity, bureaucratism, and a lack of incentives and innovation, but, instead, led China into a series of new crises.

Hua's failure highlighted even further the problems of a Stalinist command economy and finally forced the leaders to abandon it. An alternative program for China's political economy was advocated by a new political coalition built by Deng Xiaoping. For Deng, China needed comprehensive economic and political reforms, a "second revolution," instead of a continuation of the old good policies. The landmark Third Plenum of the 11th Party's Congress in December 22, 1978 symbolized the triumph of Deng's policy over Hua's and indicated a strategic shift away from the classic Stalinist system. But a "shift to where" was not quite clear. However, Deng (1983, 319) realized that "(t)o this end (modernization--added by the author) we must conduct conscientious investigations and studies, compare the experience of other countries and work out realistic plans and measures by drawing on collective wisdom."

For a late-developer, the modernization process has to be a mixture of innovation and emulation, adaptation and adoption (Black, et al, 1975; Westney 1987). Once Deng had led the nation to embark on a completely new path for development, he needed to learn from, so that China might emulate, the experiences of other countries. As the Stalinist strategy was finally discredited in the late 1970s, China was faced with three coherent developmental models that were in competition as possible models for emulation. First, there was the East Wind. This referred to the East European reforms in which there was a socialist system under a Communist party, and a planned economy augmented by a market mechanism. Second, there was the South Wind. This referred to Hong Kong and the East Asian NIEs (Newly Industrialized Economies) experience in which there is a capitalist system and market economy under a dominant party rule. And finally, there was the West Wind. This referred to the American or Western model in

44 The Dual Developmental State

which there are a liberal democracy and a market economy. To some extent, China's reforms became a decade-long process of comparing four development strategies (the classic Stalinist model, the Anglo-American liberal pattern, the East European market socialism, and the East Asian developmental state model). For historical and ideological reasons, China did not have an affinity for any one of them. No matter which new strategy was to be followed, it was to represent a discontinuity with the current policy. Therefore, to understand which route was finally chosen, we have to understand the choice-set of the Chinese leaders. That is, we have to understand their concerns and goals as well as the criteria that guided this emulation and selection process.

There is a key concept that can deepen our understanding of the evolution of the developmental state model in China: path dependence. In Douglass North (1990, 94)'s words, path dependence is "the consequence of small events and chance circumstances [that] can determine solutions that, once they prevail, lead one to a particular path." The formation of one strategy does not start with a *tabula rosa*. Instead, it is an accumulated result following from a long evolutionary path, and is shaped by many events and chance occurrences that take place within a specific social context. From this perspective, any strategy is created as a historic, dynamic, evolutionary, and accumulative process. Any rational decision-maker often tries to follow a model that economizes most of the transaction costs within the system. At the same time, the change from one pattern to another produces transition costs. If the path dependence effect is not considered, a radical break from the past increases this transition costs dramatically. It adds to transaction costs and makes the cost of establishing a new model too high, and therefore, undesirable.

For China, two important factors affected its move: (1) The "lock-in" or "choice set" formed by the existing institutions, which included China's traditional values, the Communist economic and political legacies, and the experience of a series of failures such as the Great Leap Forward and the Cultural Revolution, and (2) the feedback process by which human beings (leaders, people, etc.) perceive and respond to the choice set (North 1990, 7). North argues, "The agent of change is the entrepreneur, the decision-maker(s) in organizations. The subjective perceptions (mental models) of entrepreneurs determine the choices they make. The sources of change are the opportunities perceived by entrepreneurs. They stem from either external changes in the environment or the acquisition of learning and skills and their

The Adoption of the Developmental State Model 45

incorporation in the mental constructs of the actors" (North, in Sjostrand 1993, 37). The role of perceptions also plays a part in institutional change (North 1992, in Knight and Sened 1995).

In the last two decades, a series of important institutional changes were made possible by many significant changes both in China and abroad. In particular, there was the contrast between the energetic economies in the Special Economic Zones (SEZs) and the ailing state-owned enterprises inland. There was also the contrast between the collapse of the socialist economies in Eastern Europe and the take-off of the East Asian economies. These important institutional changes were also made possible by the change of the mental constructs that guided the thoughts of the Chinese leaders.

Deng Xiaoping, as was the case for most of his colleagues, was a victim of the Cultural Revolution. The Cultural Revolution shaped his diagnosis of the old system, as well as his new goals and strategies. For Deng, the lessons of the Cultural Revolution were two-sided. First, there was the problem at the top. Mao's personal dictatorship paralyzed the consultative decision-making mechanism and made wrong and irrational policies inevitable. It opened the door to political careerism and opportunism, irregular political struggles, and led to one decade of chaos. Second, there was the problem at the bottom. As a result of the mobilization and manipulation of the masses by one leader for his personal power, the masses turned into an irrational and destructive force. The subsequent popular explosion paralyzed normal political institutions and processes. The combination of these two irrationalities extracted a very high price from both the political elite and ordinary people. In the language of comparative transaction costs economics, the risk of bounded rationality and opportunism within the political system, the rampant bureaucratism, and the low incentives for ordinary people to work hard rendered the classic Stalinist system too costly to maintain. The organizational costs of the old system were too high.

In discussing regulatory politics in Western countries, we have been accustomed to starting with the concept of market failure. Market failures are always remedied by solutions from non-market institutions, such as the state, government, or other public, social and religious organizations (e.g., Churches). But in China as all other former Communist regimes, the market had been suppressed to a minimum and the states played an enormous role in the form of state ownership, economic planning, and state-controlled distribution. The state's failure had always preceded any market failure. The origin of socialism is closely related to Marx's critiques of market failure in terms of social equity and economic justice leading to

46 The Dual Developmental State

his call for the state to play a role in the economy. However, most former Communist states were failures, suffering from deep crises within the regime. These non-market failures are usually called "state failures," because the state or the government is the most important and largest source of non-market solutions (Wolf 1988, 38). The collapse of Communist regimes in the former Soviet Union and East European countries, and the start of economic reforms in China have resulted from the state failure, the impossibility of the state to replace the market in running a modern economy efficiently. Rigid central planning, the absolute dominance of state-ownership, and a centralized administrative control deprived other economic actors of their autonomy and of any incentive to innovate. This caused the economy to stagnate and culminated in a deep crisis that threatened disintegration. In the late 1970s, when Deng Xiaoping finally consolidated his power and launched his "second revolution" in Chinese Communist history, he faced the typical problem of state failure. Here was how Deng (1983, 310) himself viewed the problem in the Chinese political economy:

> Bureaucracy remains a major and widespread problem in the political life of our Party and the state. Its harmful manifestations include the following: standing high above the masses, abusing power, divorcing oneself from reality and the masses, spending a lot of time and effort to put up an impressive front, indulging in empty talk, sticking to a rigid way of thinking, being hidebound by convention, overstaffing administrative organs, being dilatory, inefficient and irresponsible, failing to keep one's word, circulating documents endlessly without solving problems, shifting responsibility to others, and even assuming the airs of a mandarin, reprimanding other people at every turn, vindictively attacking others, suppressing democracy, deceiving superiors and subordinates, being arbitrary and despotic, practicing favoritism, offering bribes, participating in corrupt practices in violation of the law, and so on. Such matters have reached intolerable dimensions both in our domestic affairs and in our contacts with other countries.

To solve these problems, Deng's solution was simple as well as inevitable: to introduce the market mechanism of competition. But by introducing the market to counter-balance the state's failure, China encountered problems arising from the market failure. For example, to resort to a market mechanism after thirty years of Communist rule, the immediate need is to create a market. However, a market system can take decades or even centuries to evolve by means of a "spontaneous order." As

The Adoption of the Developmental State Model 47

a result, the state is expected to play a facilitating and developmental role in assisting market creation. Besides, a market economy does not necessarily reduce corruption and the rent-seeking behavior of the officials. To the contrary, it may create more opportunities for corrupt officials to seek rents. Moreover, a market economy creates externalities, for example, pollution and environmental degradation. The market itself cannot solve these problems. Finally, a market economy always favors those with endowments of intelligence, wealth, and various other natural capacities that create a series of problems with respect to social justice. All these problems have to be addressed, and it is the state that is most likely to address them. However, if the state is a failure, it is difficult to expect it to play a developmental role in fostering the market and transforming the economy. Ultimately, by starting China's reforms, Deng situated China in a classic dilemma or "orthodox paradox": the solution (market mechanism) for the state failure has side-effects, and the problem (the state) is expected to be a solution for these side-effects (market failure).

To deal with the problem of high organizational costs, Deng attempted to minimize irrationalities in the decision-making process and to reduce bureaucratism in policy implementation. But he did not want these steps to weaken the state authority and capability. He wanted to energize the incentive of the people and enterprises at the grassroots, but not lift the lid and free the genie of mobocracy. Deng followed the same gradual strategy in political development as he did in economic development of "crossing the river by groping for the stone."

Although Deng also talked about democracy, his understanding of democracy was clearly anti-liberal. It seems that his personal experience in Western countries did not make him pro-Western. Deng spent a formative five years and two months (from Oct. 19, 1920 to Jan. 7, 1926) in France. However, "the evils of the capitalist society," the "sufferings and humiliations" in France had "a great influence" on him and turned him into a Communist revolutionary (Deng 1995, 58, 80-98). In his two important trips to the United States (1974, 1979), he might have been impressed by American material opulence. This probably reinforced his ideas for modernization in China (Evans 1994, 200, 246-247). But he might also have been annoyed by the hustle and bustle of American society. It is not difficult for him to imagine how that could be magnified out of proportion if imported into China. Therefore, he did not show much admiration for Western democracy. The biggest concern for him was that Western democracy could produce a great deal of chaos (like the Cultural

48 *The Dual Developmental State*

Revolution), sap the state capacity, and make economic development impossible. He believed "stability and unity" are the precondition for modernization and democratization.

The 1979 "Democracy Wall Movement" and the "Solidarity Movement" in Poland further strengthened Deng's apprehensions about Western style democracy. As a result, the decade of the 1980s started with the crack down on the "Democracy movement," the jailing of Wei Jingsheng for fifteen years, the rounding up and jailing of many other dissidents, and the deletion of the right to strike from the Constitution. The decade ended with the June 4th, 1989, shootings in Tiananmen Square. Judging from the developmental pattern of the past two decades, the West wind was never adopted as an official policy.

The Chinese leaders were searching for a formula that could lead to economic prosperity but not at the price of Communist rule. Disillusioned with Western democracy, China started to pay attention to two developments during the early Eighties: market socialism in Hungary (Ness, 1989; Halpern 1985) and the developmental state model in East Asia (Perkins 1986; White 1988, 1991; Vogel 1989). These two models had one thing in common that satisfied China's needs: the development of a market economy under one party rule. Therefore, their practices were potentially attractive to the Chinese leadership. China shared socialist legacies with Hungary as it shared Confucian traditions with the East Asian states. In terms of ideology, the Hungarian model, if it had succeeded, would have provided meaningful inspiration to China. But in terms of cultural affinity, the capitalist developmental state model in East Asia was more realistic. Because this model demonstrated that the Chinese in Taiwan, Hong Kong, and Singapore could modernize and at the same time help the Chinese on the mainland to restore self-confidence in their culture.

A coalition of Deng Xiaoping and Chen Yun started reforms by following the Market Socialism model of Hungary and other East European countries. The major theme of these reforms in Eastern Europe was to rationalize planning and the command system instead of destroying it. This rationalizing reform was based upon this assumption: if they could improve their plan, for example, through more accurate calculations and implementation, and at the same time, if they could introduce market mechanisms to supplement the central plan, then they could get the best of both worlds (Kornai 1995). The most important reason for the Chinese leadership to adopt the East European model was their shared ideological outlook. Because they followed the same Stalinist model--a command economy and Communist Party rule--China thought it might learn from the experience of the Eastern Europeans. Besides, at that time, the conservative forces were still powerful and stubbornly resisting reforms. The reformers for their part wanted to avoid the high transition costs of changing from one strategy to another. And they did not want to abandon the communist ideology since this would erode their own legitimacy. As a result, Deng formed an alignment with Chen even though he had disagreements with him over economic policy. In the early 1980s, Chen was in charge of the Chinese economy. His "bird-in-a-cage" economics (Chen described the relationship between the market and the plan as the relationship between a bird and a cage, See: Naughton 1995, 120), market socialism with Chinese characteristics, became the orthodox economic philosophy and the guideline for Chinese economic reforms.

To learn from Eastern Europe, China sent delegations out, invited foreign economists in, and translated many books.[1] China also paid special attention to the achievements in Hungary and sent several investigative groups there (Fewsmith 1994, 130). When Janos Kornai (1990b, Chap. 6) visited China, he was impressed by the frequent use of his ideas by Chinese economists when analyzing their problems. Before he moved to Beijing for the premiership, Zhao Ziyang, who was then the First Party Secretary in Sichuan, arranged to join a delegation headed by Hua Guofeng on a visit in 1978 to Romania and Yugoslavia. His trip to Yugoslavia greatly influenced his economic thinking. Upon returning home, with support from Deng Xiaoping, he started experimenting with enterprise reforms by giving enterprises more autonomy and exposing them to the price mechanism. These reforms were collectively dubbed as the "Sichuan experience" and recommended as a national model to be emulated (Shambaugh 1985, Chapter 6).

When viewed in light of later more radical reforms, the "bird-in-a-cage" economics was conservative since it regarded the relationship between the market and the plan to be antagonistic. However, it was at the time a pragmatic approach, as it rehabilitated the market within the context of a socialist economy and finally led China to a market economy. Besides, the idea of the coexistence of the plan and the market gave enough flexibility to the reformers to stretch harder to create more room for the market. It was quite natural then that in October 1984 the CPC adopted "The Decision on Economic Structural Reform" in which "a planned economy primary, a market regulation secondary" gave way to "a planned commodity

50 *The Dual Developmental State*

economy." This document broke away from the "bird-in-a-cage" economics, and moved to the radical type of market socialism found in Eastern Europe (Naughton 1995, 180).

Because the Chinese leadership was uncertain about the result of the Hungarian strategy at that moment, and to minimize the loss in choosing a wrong strategy, it followed a very pragmatic and eclectic policy and did not put all its eggs into one basket. Around 1980, the success of the Japanese economic development attracted attention from Chinese leaders and scholars. In 1978 and 1979, Deng Xiaoping made two trips to Japan. In 1980, Hua Guofeng visited Japan twice within one year. The top Chinese leaders had been curious about and were briefed on the Japanese developmental strategy. Under such circumstances, Chinese scholars translated Ezra Vogel's *Japan as Number One: A Challenge to the United States* into Chinese, and it was published simultaneously by two publishing houses. This book was widely read, even by some top officials (Vogel 1989, 6). Almost at the same time, Yoshida Shiegeru's small but influential book, *The Turbulent One Hundred Years* (*Jidang de bainianshi*), was translated into Chinese.[2] These two books told a successful story of a catch-up modernization, a rebirth of the phoenix from the ashes just next door, and aroused Chinese interest in the Japanese development pattern.

But at least two reasons prevented the Chinese government from emulating the Japanese model at that time: First, the resentment of Japan by the Chinese leaders and people was still strong. Second, the leaders were skeptical about the applicability and compatibility of a capitalist model to China within the context of the existing Communist rule. Since Hong Kong was at that time a capitalist colony, Taiwan was a renegade province, and South Korea and Singapore had no diplomatic relations with China, none of these followers of the Japanese model fitted China's ideological requirement. Meanwhile, some "democrats" at home used Taiwan to deny the achievements and the legitimacy of the CPC. The Chinese government did not want to associate China's SEZs with practices originating from these countries.

In a 1980 speech, Deng Xiaoping expressed his skepticism about the applicability of the models from these countries to the whole of China. He believed that what was crucial for the success of these countries was their small size, cheap labor, open markets, and continuous assistance and technological support from the United States. "For a large socialist country like China, no such short-cut is possible." Besides, he also worried that this

The Adoption of the Developmental State Model 51

path could lead China to a dependency on foreign capital, especially from the United States (Deng 1983, 242, 247). But his pragmatism did allow for a small amount of experimentation with this model. For Deng, this is the "tuition fee" China had to pay in order to find the best strategy for her modernization.

Deng diversified his options and chose two provinces (Guangdong and Fujian) as laboratories for experimenting with the East Asian strategy. In 1980, four SEZs in Guangdong and Fujian were established. Granted "special policies and flexible measures" in conducting their foreign economic activities, they were allowed to experiment with a market economy. Their governing principle, "the market is primary and the plan is supplemental" was in direct conflict with Chen Yun's strategy, which was in a peaceful competition with this market socialism (Crane 1990, 310). In contrast to Chen's "bird-in-a-cage" metaphor, the SEZs experiment was more like a natural enclave for the bird of the market economy. This is why Chen derided the SEZs capitalism. They were a "Hong Kong-ization," because "now all provinces want to establish SEZs, want to open a door" (*Sanzhong Quanhui* 1982, v. 2, 1063). For the conservatives, the SEZs had a hidden agenda to foster capitalism and then have it spread to the whole country to replace the socialist development strategy (Crane 1990, 35-48). These accusations were not paranoiac. The future development of the SEZs showed that that is exactly what the SEZs have done to China (see Chapter 7).

From the beginning of her reform, China was very selective in choosing different parts of different strategies. Its anti-Western attitude did not prevent China from relying on the West for sophisticated technology and capital. In most of the national economy, the more cautious East European model was adopted. In the SEZs, a flirtation with the capitalist developmental state model was initiated. In the countryside, a more radical liberalization was carried out. As Benedict Stavis (1988, 59-60) has observed,

> The Communist Party of China has always had a distinctive style of policy development and leadership. Social experiments play a major role. After theoretical discussions, social experiments are organized to test policy and to establish a demonstration that can be used for popularization....Experiments in political reform in a few localities will point the path to future national reforms in politics.

52 The Dual Developmental State

As for which strategy would become the optimal one, it was mainly decided by the results and performances of the experiments.

As China improved its relationships with these countries, the ideological taboo of learning from Japan and the East Asian "Four Little Dragons" was gradually removed. During the early Eighties, despite sporadic protests against the Japanese "economic invasion" in 1982, the Sino-Japanese relationship developed rapidly under the tenure of General Secretary Hu Yaobang. As the Chinese and Japanese governments established a "Commission for Sino-Japanese Friendship in the 21st Century" in 1984, and as more books about Japan were translated into Chinese--unimpeded by copyright issues--(for example, *Why Has Japan "Succeeded"* by Michio Morishima, *The Modernization of Japan and Russia* by Cyril Black, et al), Japan's image became distinctly favorable during the years between 1984-86. In many respects it was gradually offered as a positive model for selective emulation in the Chinese effort to modernize society and catch up with the advanced economies of the West (Whiting 1989, 92-93).

China also rapidly improved its relationship with Hong Kong. In 1982, when China and Britain started their negotiations over Hong Kong, finally concluding an agreement in 1984, Hong Kong became "a special gate to the outside." The "South Wind" brought changes, technology, capital, material goods, and ideas (Vogel 1989, 62-63). Although between Taiwan and China, there had been no direct channels, as the Hong Kong-China connections were deepened Taiwanese business got more access to the mainland. The Chinese government also implemented special policies favorable to "Taiwanese compatriots" to attract their capital. After 1987 the Taiwan government lifted its ban on Taiwanese visiting mainland China, Taiwan investors brought a large amount of capital to China, only second to Hong Kong (Hsing 1998).

The SEZs became a battlefield for the competition between the strategies of the market-oriented reformers and planed economy advocates. Despite strong opposition and some serious setbacks, the SEZs drew support from some important leaders, including Deng Xiaoping and Zhao Ziyang. To show his support, in 1984, Deng Xiaoping toured Shenzhen and Zhuhai, praising their achievements. He wrote in an inscription for Shenzhen that "The achievements and experiences of Shenzhen have testified that our policy to establish the SEZs is correct." Therefore, the SEZs could steer through dangerous waters and survive.

The Adoption of the Developmental State Model 53

The Shenzhen model had an immediate demonstration effect. Many provinces and cities asked the central government for the same "special policies and flexible measures." For example, Shanghai lobbied strongly (Crane 1990, 39). To meet these demands, and, as a result, to show the growing confidence in the SEZs, special status and policies were given to another fourteen coastal cities. Hainan Island also became a large special zone in 1984 after Deng's SEZs tour. The new policy was expanded along the coast from Northeast to the deep South, drawing into the market-oriented economy strategy the most vital part of Chinese economy (Yeung and Hu 1992, 4).

Meanwhile, some inland big cities were also chosen for a variety of experiments and innovations. In 1984, the State Council granted special status to thirteen larger cities. They enjoyed more freedom in making local laws and were allowed to initiate some policies for their own pilot economic structural reforms. In 1987, there were 74 cities experimenting with economic structural reforms, while 16 cities were conducting institutional reforms, 27 engaging in financial reforms, 79 experimenting with reforms of the production materials market, 5 instituting housing reforms, 9 reforming enterprise operations, and 2 upgrading scientific and technological systems (Gao 1987, 66). Following the emancipation of the countryside from the "bird-in-a-cage," more and more cities were being liberated. The new economic zones were expanding rapidly in the mid-Eighties from the countryside to the cities, from the coast to the inland regions. Given these developments, the coastal development strategy and market socialism finally had a showdown.

In 1986, Dwight Perkins argued that China's size and resulting lower ratio of foreign trade distinguished her from Japan, South Korea and Taiwan. "In terms of per capita income, human resources endowment, level of capital information, and degree of income inequality China has characteristics similar to those of its East Asian neighbors when they entered into sustained periods of rapid growth" (Perkins 1986, 57). He concluded: "If the political environment does remain supportive, there is every reason to believe that China will undergo an economic and social transformation with many features similar to those that occurred elsewhere in East Asia" (Perkins 1986, 85). But exactly in that year, Chinese politics became volatile, and China's development faced a crossroads.

54 *The Dual Developmental State*

Transition to a Neo-authoritarian Program for Reform

In 1986, Deng Xiaoping still had not decided on a comprehensive strategy for reform. This was especially so in the political field. As he said, "Since our country is very large and the situation is very complicated, reform is not easy. Therefore, we must be prudent when making policy decisions. Because we lack experience in this regard, we are still groping our way forward" (Stavis 1988, 85). However, two large-scale student movements in 1986 and 1989 challenged the "muddling through" strategy and forced Deng, the "chief architect of China's reforms," to point out a clear course for these reforms.

After the 1986 student demonstrations and before the convening of the Thirteenth Party National Congress, Deng systematically reiterated his ideas for reforms, which were first put forward around 1980 when his program for China's reforms gradually took shape: (1) In the coming 50 to 60 years, "the major goal for China is development, to lift us out of backwardness, to strengthen national power, and to gradually improve people's life." The goal is: "At the end of this century, to achieve a comparatively well-off standard of living, namely, per capita GNP of $800 to $1,000. Then, within 30 to 50 years into the next century, to achieve the standard of living of a moderately developed country." (2) To achieve these goals, a stable political environment is required. China must keep the strong state capacity, or "the general efficiency" of the system. He argued, "A socialist country has one great advantage: once we make up our mind, a decision is made, and it is implemented immediately without foot-dragging…. In this respect, the efficiency of our system is high." (3) China should not adopt a separation of powers, a multi-party system, a bicameralism, nor direct parliamentary elections. He said, "Democracy shall only be developed gradually. We cannot transplant Western ideas. To do that would be to make China chaotic." As for direct elections at the national level for one billion people, it would certainly produce "chaos like the Cultural Revolution," "a complete civil war." Therefore, China has to wait for another 50 years. (4) To guarantee stability and to prevent China from going astray into "bourgeois democracy," the government must have a tough policy towards student demonstrations. "When necessary, we must deal severely with those who defy orders. We can afford to shed some blood. Just try as much as possible not to kill anyone." In case of an emergency, it is advisable to resort to "the methods of dictatorship." (Quotes from: *Sichuansheng Renda* 1991, 136-140; Zhou 1995; Stavis 1988, 113-114; Baum 1993, 397-399).

Guided by these principles, the blueprint for political reforms adopted by the 13th Party Congress in its Political Report defined a neo-authoritarian strategy for China's political development. Its major goal was to develop the economy, more specifically, to speed up the establishment and improvement of a socialist market system. "Helping to expand the productive forces should become the point of departure in our consideration of all problems, and the basic criterion for judging all our work should be whether it serves that end" (Zhao 1987, 27). This document later made it easier for the CPC to abandon a great deal of its old ideology and converge with capitalist developmental strategies. But this document was also neo-authoritarian, pragmatic as well as conservative. It emphasized that reform would be a top-down process of self-improvement guided by the Party and proceeding "step by step in an orderly way" (Zhao 1987, 28) As Richard Baum (1993, 414) commented, this was a "transitional neo-authoritarian manifesto;" it "had a decidedly illiberal edge to it."

Undoubtedly, the political report was a brainchild of Deng Xiaoping. However, it was also introduced against the big backdrop of the ongoing theoretical debates in the think-tanks and academic circles at that time. During mid-1980s, when Park Chung Hee's *To Build a Nation* (*Women Guojia de Daolu*) and Samuel Huntington's *Political Order in Changing Society* were translated into Chinese, a heated debate was carried out among Chinese scholars on the successful experiences of the "Four Little Dragons," as well as on neo-authoritarianism, and the applicability of the developmental state model to China. The Economic Structural Reform Institute in Beijing, a think-tank for Zhao Ziyang, proposed a "hard government, soft economy" strategy to Zhao in 1988. It argued that a market economy under a highly centralized political authority could satisfactorily meet the special demands of transition in the developing countries. The "hard government, soft economy" model, namely, a market economy with a strong government as in the East Asian "Four Little Dragons," had been very successful in transforming backward countries. Therefore, it proposed that the development of China "requires the concentration of political power and the dispersion of economic power, to place in leadership positions minority elites who represent the interests of the majority and control the direction of the state, and to realize by the middle of the next century the goal of a market economy and democratic politics" (Ruan 1994, 205; Qi 1991, 258). In March 1989, when Zhao informed Deng about the neo-authoritarianism

56 The Dual Developmental State

debate, Deng said "I quite agree with this notion." Actually, he said he had practiced it himself (Ruan 1994, 194).

Despite a predominant authoritarianism in Chinese Communist rule, young Chinese intellectuals have demonstrated a strong anti-establishment mood. In the developing countries, students are a permanent political opposition force and active agents for modernization (Huntington 1968, 369). In China, this is even more the case. As Stavis (1988, 90) observes, "Chinese youth has a long tradition of concern for national development." In 1989, they once again exploded. Here I do not want to discuss the 1989 student movement per se but to emphasize that the 1989 Tiananmen Square crackdown was a decisive step in the application of the neo-authoritarian principles to political practice.

For many Western observers, the 1989 crackdown was Deng's Waterloo. It doomed his political career, diminished his image as a reformer, and permanently destroyed his place in history. In Samuel Huntington (1991, 130)'s words, Deng did not die in time. Contrary to many arguments, the brutal handling of the student riots was neither a mistake nor a regression, but should be taken as an integral step towards the establishment of the developmental state model. When the military was ordered to implement martial law in Lhasha (Tibet) and Beijing, the theatrical use of the military served the long-term goal of political deterrence. It demonstrated that the central government was willing and ready to resort to force to suppress localism (as in Tibet) and liberalism (as in Beijing).

For a set of rules to be an institution, the members of the relevant community or society must share knowledge of these rules (Knight 1992, 2-3). From this perspective, the Tiananmen Square crackdown was used as a shocking political commercial by Deng to socialize Chinese cadres as well as the whole nation into accepting his strategy. It was rumored that before he made his decision Deng said: "It is worth sacrificing twenty thousand students for twenty years of stability." Even if it is uncertain whether these are Deng's own words, they to some extent reflected his state of mind. What worried him was this scenario: "If we allow these people to go into the street, one year has 365 days, China has one billion people, then everyday there are troubles" (*Quanguo Renda* 1990, 139). He also believed that compromise could not solve the problem but would whet the students' appetite and escalate the conflict. Even if this time compromise could ease the conflict, the problem would be that they would come back at unexpected moments in the future, as was the case in the turmoil that occurred in 1985,

The Adoption of the Developmental State Model 57

1986, and then in 1989. He not only wanted to end the current crisis, but also the recurring pattern of student demonstrations. Therefore, he might have had some opportunities to de-escalate the crisis, especially when many young scholars and faculty members started persuading students to give up, and many students did start withdrawing from the hunger strike. Deng did not try to capitalize on these opportunities to bring the crisis to a less tragic end. The soldiers were ordered to enter Beijing, especially Tiananmen Square, in an exaggerated, theatrical manner.

It is clear that the actual death toll was lower than what people perceived. This is exactly the theatrical effect Deng wanted to create. According to his logic, the actual cost of the June 4th crackdown was lower than if China spun out of control and lost its opportunity to develop. The theatrics made the cost even lower and his great lesson to the Chinese people even more unforgettable. For the Chinese leaders, this might have been a rational investment in creating a long-term reputation as tough disciplinarians (Solnick 1996). Indeed, one decade later, Liu Ji, advisor to Jiang Zemin, did say openly: "The way to handle the June 4th incident conforms to the principle of economics," namely, it used "the least price" to exchange for the "maximum interest" of social stability and continued reform (Xiao 1997, 224).

Early when Gorbachev encouraged the East European countries to move further away from the old system, especially towards a Western style democracy, China became suspicious of reforms in Eastern Europe. After the Hungarian reforms failed, the Communist regimes collapsed. While, in contrast, China maintained a high economic growth rate without simultaneously producing a Western style democracy or changing the one-party rule as in East NIEs. The Chinese leadership was convinced that the developmental state model was a potion for boosting the economy as well as preserving a one-party rule. Zhao Ziyang was fired, even though his advisors advocated, and he himself accepted, neo-authoritarianism. The conflict between Deng and Zhao was not over whether or not to follow the neo-authoritarian strategy, but over who shall be the benevolent, enlightened, and developmental dictator.

China's Strategic Move to the East Asian Model

In his political career and also during the last twenty years of reform, Deng Xiaoping demonstrated his excellent skill in simultaneously juggling an

58   The Dual Developmental State

authoritarian politics with a liberalized economy. But it has taken time for his successors with lesser ability to master this craft. Actually, in the first two years after the 1989 crackdown, his successors failed to understand their master and almost spun China's reform out of control. Facing the counterattack from the conservatives in the form of a campaign against "bourgeois liberalization" and hidebound "leftism" in academic and theoretical circles, the need to maintain stability became the highest goal for the new leadership, even at the price of reforms. To be called "socialist" or "capitalist" became the criteria for politics and the economy. Even growth was less important. China returned to economic retrenchment and political repression. Deng had to fear that the reforms he initiated ten years earlier were losing momentum and becoming moribund.

Even though the CPC survived its largest crisis since it took power, all the Communist regimes in Eastern Europe and the Soviet Union were swept out like dominos. Deng did not believe that the shooting alone made the difference. Rather the Chinese economic development was the fundamental reason for the survival of the CPC. Therefore, he concluded, stability is necessary for development. Only development is the hard truth. Without development, there would be no stability (Yuan and Han, 1992, 56). Only sustained development can provide performance-based legitimacy to a dictatorial regime. In 1992, at the age of 88, Deng resorted to another theatrical way to teach his successors a small lesson. This was his famous "Southern Inspection Tour" (*nanxun*) It was also called by the foreign media "the Deng Whirlwind." It was the swan-song of Deng Xiaoping as a statesman in Chinese politics.

Along his tour, Deng Xiaoping stated a series of important ideas: (1) The plan and the market are two instruments to organize the economy. The plan is not equivalent to socialism, neither is the market to capitalism. (2) To judge whether something is "surnamed socialist or capitalist," there are three criteria: is it conducive to the forces of production, to strengthening the national power, or to improving the people's standard of living (his "theory of three conducives"). If a policy or a system meets these three requirements, it is socialist. (3) Stability is for development. The speed of economic development should be accelerated. Stagnation is like moving backward. Only development is the hard truth. The leaders who cannot develop the economy will be forced to step down. (4) The strategy of developing SEZs has proven correct and has been a success. The successful experiences should be instituted in other localities. (5) China should learn from the Asian

The Adoption of the Developmental State Model 59

"Four Little Dragons." Some provinces, like Guangdong, should surpass them within twenty years. Shenzhen should be the next Hong Kong and more "Hong Kongs," and "Singapores" should be created in China (Yuan and Han 1992; Lam 1995; Deng 1993, vol.3, 370-383).

Deng told the leaders of Guangdong province: "the Asian 'Four Little Dragons' developed rapidly. You also developed rapidly. Guangdong shall catch up to the 'Four Little Dragons' within twenty years. Not only the economy shall develop, the social order and mood also shall improve.... The social order in Singapore is good. They manage strictly. We shall borrow their experiences and do a better job" (Yuan and Han 1992, 33).

In 1992, the provinces that accelerated their development, asked for favorable policies from the center, and demanded that they be decentralized and given local autonomy. China's development, having become comprehensive, was no longer limited to coastal areas. The whole country started applying the SEZ model, namely, the East Asian developmental state model. In November 1993, the CPC passed the "Decision of the CPC Central Committee on Some Issues Concerning the Establishment of a Socialist Market Economic Structure." This document finally marked the official acceptance of the market economy in China. This change to a market economy was so inevitable that even the father of "bird-in-a-cage economics," Chen Yun, climbed onto the bandwagon. [3]

The reforms under Deng's two decades accomplished more than had occurred in the previous one hundred years, with the most fundamental changes happening in the five years from 1992 to 1997 -- that final year being the year that Deng Xiaoping passed away. Jiang Zemin showed his respect to the "Chief Architect" by choosing this role for himself as the "Chief Engineer" for Chinese modernization. [4] This title for Jiang is appropriate, not only because he was trained as an engineer, but also because it indicates that the strategy for the future of Chinese development had been set. The main task for Jiang is to enforce it, to guarantee its smooth operation, and to see to its fruition So far, Jiang and the third generation leadership with him as the core have proven themselves not like the successors to Bismarck who were with much less ability and spun off his demanding legacy. Jiang and his colleagues have carefully maintained a "balanced tripod of political discipline, economic expansion, and dissident repression" and taken care of the "developmental dictatorship" (Gilley 1998, 291). Partially this success is attributed to the personal character of Jiang, who is a social conservative as well as an economic reformer. Besides, the core members of political elite have shared Jiang's

60 *The Dual Developmental State*

view. For example, one of Zhu Rongji's entourage told the press about the direction China was moving towards during Zhu's visit in the United States in April 1999, "Either we look like Singapore or we look like Russia. And that's not a choice."

Polanyi (1975, 57) argued "that a market economy can function only in a market society." A market economy indicates an emergence of the economy as a separate complex institution. Moreover, its function depends on many supporting institutions, for example, a legal framework and a system of private property. "Making markets" requires a package of achievements. According to Islam and Mandelbaum (1993, 183), in a Communist command economy, "marketization" has "three wheels": (1) Liberalization, which includes freeing the prices, devaluing the currency and making it convertible, integrating with the world economy, and reforms in the labor and financial markets. (2) Privatization of the economy, which involves the development of the private sector, the reform of the ownership system and state enterprises, and the protection of property rights (housing and land). (3) Development of a market-supporting institutional infrastructure, which requires "constitutional, legislative, legal, accounting, regulatory, fiscal, monetary, and social insurance reform." Therefore, the change from a command economy to a market economy is a structural transformation that minimally requires an exchange mechanism as well as accessory institutions, norms and rules to guarantee sellers and buyers the proper status within the market. Its development requires a triple process: dismantling the command economy, creating markets, and then governing the market. Because of the nature of fundamental change, once the market economy is pursued, it causes a chain reaction in the whole system of Chinese political economy. Many of them are beyond the imagination and the control of the Chinese leadership.

As a result of marketization, capitalism has been introduced into China by stealth. State socialism as an economic system and ideology has withered away. From 1981 to 1991, the share in the industrial output by the state-owned sector declined from 78% to 53%. By 1996, it dropped further to 28.8%, which, in 1992, the Chinese government anticipated would not happen until the year 2000. In contrast, the share of collectively-owned and privately-owned sectors climbed respectively from 21% and 1% in 1981, to 36% and 11% in 1992, and finally to 44.4% and 30.8% in 1996 (Kristof 1992; Ru, et al, 1998, 26).

The Adoption of the Developmental State Model 61

Deng left a systematic model of development for China: a developmental state. His behavior also has become a legacy for his successors to emulate: his commitment to economic modernization coupled with political stability and gradual change. China has demonstrated two basic characteristics of a developmental state: a developmental dictatorship (hard government) and a market-oriented economy (soft economy). As Steven Solnick (1996, 237) argues, "The hidden hand behind the Chinese market wielded a bloody bayonet." In contrast to Mao who was an idealist and populist, Deng was a realist and elitist, a developmental dictator. "(H)e has had a simple agenda for China since at least his work-study days in France during the early 1920s: to contribute to making it a strong, wealthy, and unified country" (Lampton, in Deng 1995, xii). If he had not been sent to a farm for manual labor during the Cultural Revolution, but instead had started reforms in the late 1960s, Samuel Huntington might have chosen him as an icon for his *Political Order in Changing Societies*. Unfortunately, as the zeitgeist changed, Deng, like Park Chung Hee in history, was not loved when alive, but will be remembered now that he is dead.[5]

Uncertain Start, Coherent Logic

The Chinese state has traversed a long, difficult journey to search for political institutional arrangements that would allow flexibility while maintaining stability. At the beginning of this search process, the Chinese leadership had lost faith in the efficiency of the classical Stalinist system. On this model, China had, for 30 years (especially in the later ones), experiences of low efficiency, low incentive, bureaucratism, waste, shortage, and political risk (irrationality and brutality). They knew the problems of the classical Stalinist system very well and they had to give it up. Based on their historical experiences and through comparison with other countries, the Chinese leaders did not think that their economy should have a complete laissez faire market system as its goal. They believed this strategy would cause chaos and delay or even destroy the possibility of economic development. Therefore, the Chinese leaders knew what they did not want, but they did not know where they should go to get what they did want. They did not have a clear blueprint in mind at the beginning.

The Chinese leaders tried to find a middle path, or a hybrid of market economy and state intervention. The chief architect of China's reform, Deng

62　The Dual Developmental State

Xiaoping, adopted a cautious strategy--"crossing the river by groping the stone"--to guide China's explorations. This gradual, cautious strategy for development left a great deal of leeway to localities to experiment with a variety of innovations within a limited geographic area.

Basically, three kinds of experiments were conducted in different areas: "a household responsibility system" in the countryside, a market socialism in most other parts of the country; and the East Asian model (a Hong Kong style market economy) in the four SEZs (Shenzhen being the most famous one). They tried market socialism in which the plan is primary and market mechanisms supplemental. But the severe contradictions between the plan and the market could not be resolved. They also tried the developmental state model in which a market economy is primary and state intervention (for example, administrative guidance) is supplemental. The various experiences proved that this was the best model for China if it meant to maintain a high economic growth rate and political stability as it meant to transform the society.

Despite "China's Rise and Russia's Fall," China faced jeers but Russia received cheers for choosing different strategies, even as Russia is still swirling in chaos and still unable to see the dim light of capitalism. Certainly, China's successful institutional transition from state socialism to capitalism has been quite amazing.

Some critics of Deng Xiaoping insisted that Deng did not have a strategy, or that at best his strategy was "muddling-through." This is totally wrong. In the last two decades, China's vigorous economic growth has not taken place in a political vacuum. Deng's experiments with different models stand out as a living edifice of Deng's strategic thinking and planning for institutional design and institution building. Deng's modernization strategy compared the transaction costs of different systems for the economy, leading him to abandon Stalinism and to embrace the market economy. Deng had always been a committed nationalist and patriot. The three purges turned him into a pragmatist who was concerned with holding power. For these reasons, he also wanted to avoid the high transition costs arising from the sudden transformation of Stalinism into a market economy. If the transition costs were too high, they could make the already devastated economy worse and ultimately destroy his own power. Under such constraints, Deng found the wisdom of choosing carefully between what is best and what is possible, and transformed the Chinese political economy by following a middle ground, a network strategy that

The Adoption of the Developmental State Model 63

maintained characteristics of both a market and a bureaucracy. By following this strategy, China experienced a gradual accumulative change (Chen 1995; Su in Lyons and Nee, 1994; Qian and Xu 1993).

In Coase's and Williamson's theory of the comparative transaction costs, the major concern is how the movement from a market to a hierarchy, or from a contractual relationship to a vertical integration can minimize transaction costs and improve efficiency. It presupposes a pre-existing market and the reality of "market failure." In economizing the costs of using markets, or remedying the market failure arising from high transaction costs, the firm as a price-suppressing mechanism is introduced to improve efficiency. Put differently, the firm chooses the strategy for the internalization of activities that used to be provided by the markets. But in the case of China, the image is completely reversed. The issue is how the state has chosen a strategy of externalization; namely, the shifting of many functions from the state-controlled realm to the markets to reduce the costs of resource allocation by the state (Pitelis 1993).

With respect to the economy, China had long been a Stalinist command economy, and as a result, under a hierarchy that placed an emphasis on control and vertical integration. As a result, the major problem for China's system (and also other former Communist countries) was the state's failure, as indicated by the organizational costs (overhead and coordination) arising from an inflated bureaucracy as well as by a lack of innovation and incentives. To improve the efficiency of the national economy, the reform leaders in China resorted to market mechanisms. By loosening bureaucratic control over the economy and increasing autonomy and competition, the leadership expected to lower the organizational costs. In politics, rigid administrative control and high centralization also greatly increased the cost needed to maintain the system. To reduce organizational costs and increase efficiency, the Chinese leadership has implemented a variety of policies, such as decentralization, and the differentiation of state organizations and functions.

As has been the case with the economy, the Chinese political system also has moved from a hierarchical control and vertical integration to a kind of contractual relationship. Therefore, the Chinese leadership has had to calculate the advantages and disadvantages of state control and market mechanisms. There are organizational costs with the former and transaction costs with the latter. The economics of transaction costs has provided us with the rationale and criteria to compare different institutional modes of governance. But considering that all modes of governance are

64 The Dual Developmental State

institutionalized, shifting from one to another makes this a process not without friction. In other words, while the old mode will resist this change, the new mode may not be ready to take over and function effectively. Therefore, while the capacity of the organization is necessary for the choice of one specific mode of governance, the strategy to overcome the resistance and build coalitions is important, too. We cannot neglect the strategy to change from one mode to another. Therefore, it has become quite understandable and even wise that the Chinese government has chosen a strategy of "growing out of the plan" (Naughton 1995) into marketization and "growing out of the hierarchy" into political institutionalization.

Using a decision-making tree model sheds light upon our understanding of the formation of the development strategy in China. Starting at the root and looking at the branches, the choices are infinite. Once you have arrived at one point on any branch, the path always becomes linear when you look back. But this is not determinism. Looking back, a logical evolution and coherent strategy can be identified, despite the uncertainties of the Chinese leaders at the beginning. Essentially, these social experiments are a comparative process for the Chinese leadership to determine which is the most efficient way, in terms of economizing transaction costs and transition costs, to organize economic and political transactions. As Coase (1988, 155-156) has emphasized:

> It would be clearly desirable if the only actions performed were those in which what was gained was worth more than what was lost. But in choosing among social arrangements within the context of which individual decisions are made, we have to bear in mind that a change in the existing system which will lead to an improvement in some decisions may well lead to a worsening in others. Furthermore, we have to take into account the costs involved in operating the various social arrangements (whether it be the working of a market or of a governmental department) as well as *the costs involved in moving to a new system*. In devising and choosing among social arrangements we should have regard for *the total effect* (emphasis added).

Putting it another way, even if the Chinese leaders did not intentionally and systematically follow the comparative transaction costs approach, their decisions did follow after a comparison of the effectiveness of different models to organize the economy and the political realm. And they did "take into account the costs involved in operating the various social arrangements... as well as the costs involved in moving to a new system." They then had to consider the trade-offs among the different choices.

Deng's thinking nicely coincides with R. H. Coase's theory of comparative transaction costs. The only difference is that Deng certainly did not study Coasian economics. He used his own terminology. For Deng, his primary concern was "the total efficiency" (*zhong xiaolu*) which is, to some extent equivalent to the "total effect" in Coase's writing. In Deng Xiaoping's deepest reflections on the subject, this total efficiency included three parts: a sophisticated technology, an efficient management, and a stable and effective government. Clearly, his concerns for productivity mainly targeted the production costs. His attack on bureaucratism, the lack of incentive, and the decoupling of responsibility with obligation generally was in the service of reducing the transaction costs. And his paranoiac concern about "chaos" (*luan*) and "costs" (*daijia*) indicated his calculation of the transition costs, or in Coase's writing, "the costs involved in moving to a new system."

In this period of two decades, the Chinese political system demonstrated its remarkable resilience, flexibility and receptivity. Deng Xiaoping also demonstrated his skillful leadership in building a coalition and steering his reforms through all kinds of challenges. Ultimately, China gradually jettisoned its rigid Communist ideology which is against economic development, embraced pragmatism as the highest standard, learned constructive lessons from foreign countries, quickly adopted their experiences, and selectively applied foreign models with great innovation and ingenuity. The formation of a dual developmental state is an example. Without these virtues, China could not shift from a Stalinist system to a market socialism, and finally to a developmental state. Also, without this transformation, the Chinese economic performance could not be sustained.

The evolution of the development strategy gradually improved the political environment in China and created a hospitable, market-facilitating institutional arrangement that had provided for economic growth. Even if we can argue that the Chinese political system was not very democratic, we cannot deny it was supportive to the economy. There is no reason to believe that the Chinese economy had been implemented under a dysfunctional, anti-developmental political system. In the next chapter, I will discuss how the developmental state model had structured the choice-set of Chinese political institutions and how these institutions in turn had further provided a political foundation for the operation of this model.

66   *The Dual Developmental State*

Notes

1   For example, books written by Hungarian economist Janos Kornai, Czech economist Ota Sik, Polish economist Wlodzimierz Brus were translated into Chinese.

2   It was published by the World Affairs Publishing House (*Shijie Zhishi Chubanshe*) in Beijing, 1980.

3   In his July 1992 "Eulogy for Comrade Li Xiannian," Chen wrote: "Although Comrade Xiannian and I have never been to the SEZs, we have always paid attention to the construction of SEZs. We believe it is necessary to establish SEZs." See: Yuan and Han 1992, 80.

4   Liu Ji, Jiang's close advisor, revealed that Jiang claimed himself as the "chief engineer." See: Zhang Wenmin, et al, 1998, v. 3, 6-7; Gilley 1998, 321.

5   Indeed, when Deng died, the China News Digest (CND) website received hundred of e-mail messages to mourn his death, many with praising words.

4 The Pillars of the Chinese Developmental State

For most countries of late-modernization, the emergence of the market as a spontaneous order is a history that cannot be easily repeated. The experiences in East Asian countries clearly demonstrated that the state can be a major actor in pushing forward modernization. As some scholars have noted, the relationship between the economy and the state in this region has involved "a market that is the engine of economic growth and an authoritarian state as the driver of the engine" (Simone and Feraru 1995, 163). Chinese scholars agree that this development has not been spontaneous, but induced and guided by the state (Cheng 1998, 93-100; Wang and Hu 1993; Rosen 1990-91). Since the state has been an indispensable partner with the market forces in driving forward the Chinese economic engine, it is justifiable to discuss the impact of the institutional arrangements within the state and the state's policies upon the economic development of China.

With regard to the relationship between the state and the economy, there have been two predominant arguments. One group of scholars believes that the Chinese state was too dysfunctional and antiquated to have played an important role in the country's economic development. If the Chinese economic development had not been achieved within a political vacuum, it certainly had done so despite the adversities created by the state. In the preceding chapters I have already discussed these viewpoints. A second group of scholars, mostly Chinese, believes that despite changes within the state, a time lag certainly has existed between the economic and political reforms. Put another way, economic reforms and political reforms in China have been on two-tracks; the track for the economy has been much faster than that for politics. If either of these two arguments stands, the image of the Chinese state as an initiator or primary mover will be cast in doubt. Instead, the state will be seen as a drag on the economy, something that should be cleared away rather than something to be counted on.

68   The Dual Developmental State

However, to review the past two decades, the "general design" (*zhongti sheji*) of the political system has always been a main concern for the top Chinese leaders from Deng Xiaoping to Jiang Zemin because their own political survival as well as the economic development of the country depended on doing this task well. Through constant changes, the Chinese state has made efforts to maintain at least a role of catalyst to development, or a partner to the business, if not an initiator.

The fever for political reforms (in the form of heated discussions and consequent actions) has swept over China in three waves. From Deng's 1980 speech "On Reform of the Party and Government Leadership System" to the adoption of the 1982 Constitution was the first wave (Hamrin and Zhao 1995, 133-152). The "anti-spiritual pollution" movement in 1983 disrupted it. Later, in early 1986, a brief lively debate on political reform occurred, but it was soon quenched by another "anti-bourgeois liberalization" movement at the end of that year when student demonstrations died out. A period of low ebb followed. The second wave of political reform came in 1987 when the Thirteenth Party's National Congress convened, its political report systematically presented a blueprint for China's political reform. The ensuing two golden years for political debate in modern Chinese history ended with the shootings in Tiananmen Square in 1989. A long, dark, and cold political winter followed and lasted for almost a decade.

Finally in 1997 after Deng passed away and Jiang Zemin consolidated his power, Jiang started flirting with the issue of political reform. In that year he first sent a trial balloon in his May 29th commencement speech at the Central Party School. The political report he later delivered in September to the 15th National Party Congress reiterated his ideas for the continuation of political reforms and the establishment of a state under the rule of law. It worked as a "cardiac stimulant" (Dong and Shi 1998, 109) and revitalized the debate on political reform. As before, the Chinese intellectual community immediately understood this political message and responded quickly. The third wave of political reform was generated.[1]

Generally speaking, each of these three waves of political reform defined certain boundaries, or laid out certain taboos. They ruled out the consideration of separation of power, bicameralism, federalism, free elections, a multiparty system, and freedom of press and speech. Since these fundamental features of the Western political system are absent from the twenty years of political changes, it is small wonder for many Western observers that nothing really has changed in the Chinese political structure.

The Pillars of the Chinese Developmental State 69

Thus, in this chapter I will leave aside these taboos and discuss what else has changed in the Chinese political system. I will focus on the changes that have occurred at the different levels of political system. Specifically, I will discuss the ideology, structure, personnel, and policy, as well as their significance to the creation and maintenance of a developmental state in China. I will then evaluate these changes in order to learn whether these changes are optimal or even sufficient for the Chinese political and economic transition. If not, I will consider what problems persist and where possible solutions lie. Finally, I will discuss how these problems and solutions will have an impact upon the existence and the future of the Chinese developmental state.

Changing Ideological Orientations

Nothing is more striking for showing the fundamental changes within the Chinese political system than the abandonment of communist ideology by the Chinese leadership. It is true that the Chinese leadership still gives lavish endorsement to the so-called "four fundamental principles." However, everyone knows that among them, only the Communist leadership matters. From his "theory of the cats" to his "theory of the groping stone," to his "theory of three conducives," Deng Xiaoping had successfully finished his revolution of de-communizing China before his departure in 1997 (Liu 1993; B. Yang 1998). Today, China is a proto-capitalist nation, or a "capitalist country with Chinese characteristics." The only characteristic remaining is the CPC leadership. This has long been concealed from the ordinary Chinese: "Under the leadership of the Communist Party, we're advancing from socialism to capitalism" (Kristof 1992). If we say that nobody knew China better than Deng Xiaoping, then nobody knew Deng Xiaoping better than Mao Zedong. Mao was right in his judgment that Deng was "an absolutely unrepentant capitalist-roader."

The radical movement from communism to commercialism, from Marxism-Leninism to Market-Leninisim, from Marxism to mercantilism by nature is a shift away from socialism to capitalism. It has happened in the process of building up a developmental state in the guise of a three-staged jump, or in the guise of the so-called "three emancipations of the mind." According to the official mass media, China has experienced three emancipations of the mind. In 1979, Deng Xiaoping successfully guided

70 *The Dual Developmental State*

the debate on the criteria for truth, abandoned the ultra-leftist Maoist ideas, established the authority of "seeking the truth from facts," and shifted the focus of the CPC from class struggle to economic development. What Deng called the "second revolution," official propaganda called "the first emancipation of the mind."

In 1992, when the Chinese economy was in stagnation and the debate on "Is It Surnamed Socialist or Capitalist" suffocated any new idea, Deng, at the age of 88, toured Shenzhen and other cities. In his legendary "Southern Inspection Tour," Deng made a series of speeches. Later his ideas were amplified through the newspapers in Shenzhen, sending a clear message to other parts of the country. The central theme of all these speeches was that the debate on whether a policy is surnamed socialist or capitalist was useless and should be ended. The sole criterion for a correct policy is the "theory of three conducives." Accordingly, the market economy was not taken to be a patent solely owned by capitalism. The plan and the market are two instruments that a socialist country can use to organize its economy. This was the "second emancipation of the mind."

In 1998, Jiang Zemin consolidated his power after Deng's departure. His advisors circulated a message that China needed a "third emancipation of the mind," and the decision allowing for all forms of ownership symbolized it. In the resolution passed by the 15th National Party Congress, the stock sharing system and private ownership were endorsed, and the debate on whether "private-ownership" or "state-ownership" matters was ended.

Capitalism has been introduced to China by stealth. Since it does not want to advertise the capitalist nature of its development, the CPC likes to say in a more euphemistic way: Chinese socialism has successfully adopted the "capital system," or the mechanisms of capital operations that are also commonly used by capitalism. To compound the confusion, new terms such as "Market-Leninism" were coined (Kristof and WuDunn 1994). But an anecdote tells everything: President Clinton, President Yeltsin, and Deng drove their cars to a fork in the road which was leading to two directions: capitalism and socialism. Of course, Clinton chose the road to capitalism right away. Yeltsin hesitated for a few seconds then he followed the road to capitalism, too. Deng pulled up his car, stepped out, and turned the road sign arrow of socialism toward the direction of capitalism. Then he followed the arrow pointing toward socialism with full speed. Deng's way to deal with socialism and capitalism incarnates the

The Pillars of the Chinese Developmental State   71

apex of Chinese political wisdom: Something you can do but not say, something you can say but not do (Li 1989, 37).

The erosion of communism as an ideology in China has left the door open for some new myths to justify the Communist rule. The CPC has returned to nationalism where its original success lay. Nationalism and patriotism have a great appeal to the Chinese, even for the most educated youths. This is indicated by the publication of a large number of books on the rise of China and the coming of the Chinese century, or, in a more modest version, the Asian Century. Among them, *China Can Say No* is the most notorious one (Tyler 1996).

In addition to the intentional use of nationalism by the CPC to integrate the nation, the fever of nationalism in China has also been fanned by a series of factors. First, the economic take-off in most East Asian countries gave the people there a new sense of pride and confidence in their culture, and produced a revitalization of "Asian values", or "an Asian Renaissance" (McCord 1991). Second, the sustained economic growth in China for the past twenty years against the big backdrop of the collapse of the Soviet Union has enhanced the mutual sensitivity of the United States and China to each other. The Chinese reacted strongly to the bullying policies from the United States, such as blocking China's entrance to the WTO, chasing Chinese submarines in the Yellow Sea, stopping and inspecting Chinese ships for chemicals in the Persian Gulf, voting against Beijing's application for hosting the 2000 Olympic Games, and sending aircraft carriers to the Taiwan Strait. Third, the praise for the Chinese economic success from foreign observers and international organizations (including the World Bank and the International Monetary Fund) has created an illusion and euphoria among the Chinese. Many of them have confused their wishful thinking with reality and fantasized a "Chinese Century" in the new millennium only twenty years after they could barely feed themselves. As communism has completely lost its credibility worldwide in recent years, the CPC leadership has also shifted its ground to nationalism. Since all developmental states in East Asia have done so, and nationalism has been a convenient excuse for political authoritarianism, the erosion of the communist ideology and the embrace of nationalism have created one more favorable condition for China's move to an East Asian developmental state model.

To argue that China has been in a process of de-ideologization seems to be unsound because "Deng Xiaoping Thought" was just apotheosized in

72 The Dual Developmental State

the 15th CPC National Party Congress and added to the Constitution. This is ironic, for the essence of Deng's ideas is that nothing should be defined and rigidified as holy. As Benjamin Yang (1998, 282-283) remarks, "It has been conventional for Western observers to label Deng's political philosophy as 'pragmatism.' To a large extent this is a just and fair description, and Deng was indeed a pragmatist politician. Yet, the problem, of course, is that as much as pragmatism can be called a theory without theory, Dengism can be called a philosophy without philosophy!" Therefore, Deng's ideas defy theorization and apotheosis. Because Jiang Zemin was personally anointed by Deng, Jiang's legitimacy relies on the wisdom of Deng's decision. Jiang, like Hua Guofeng, established a new "whatever doctrine" that completed an ironic circle back to what Deng was against. Also considering Jiang's call for a return to Confucianism--a revival of communist commitment in the form of self-sacrifice--the current Chinese leadership has lost a coherent ideology. However, they do juggle a hodgepodge of ideas to justify their rule.

Is the loss of ideological purity and coherence a danger to the current regime? Does it mean the loss of the party strength? Not necessarily so. Without doubt, communism used to be an effective ideology to mobilize and integrate Chinese society when it was still under the Stalinist political and economic system. Once this system was destroyed and replaced with a developmental state, communism became an obstacle to economic development as well as an obstacle to the way in which the state rearranged its relationship with the economy. A developmental state can be either socialist or capitalist (G. White 1984; White and Wade 1988; Johnson 1995; Castells 1998), and the Chinese state under Mao was in some sense developmental. However, in the long run, only a developmental state based on a capitalist economy, namely the market economy, can sustain itself and eventually succeed. The dilution of orthodox communist doctrine removed the ideological hurdle that had prevented the Chinese socialist developmental state from converging with the capitalist developmental state commonly seen in East Asia.

Furthermore, the dissipation of rigid ideology has created a new possibility for the CPC: to convert itself into a "catch-all party." A single-dominant party system, as all East Asian countries have experienced, might be the future scenario for the CPC. Considering the experiences in these East Asian countries, a single hegemonic party still can hang on to power for decades, even possibly for a century as the Mexican case indicates. Therefore, the immediate danger for the CPC rule is not its

The Pillars of the Chinese Developmental State 73

ideological dissolution. The real problem has arisen from the tension between the public domain and private discourse of the Communist rule. On the one hand, the CPC and its ruling class have lost their commitment to communism and their zeal to serve the people; on the other hand, they still desperately try to instill communist values into their people, trying to put their ideological Humpty-Dumpty back together. It has created a double-think, a hypocrisy that is so prevalent in the Chinese society.

Some people who believe in the official propaganda really have a difficult time adapting to the process of marketization. Many laid-off workers who refused to change are still living with the illusion that "Socialism will not allow people be hungry and die." The hypocritical propaganda coupled with a population that once benefited from the socialist system have together further compounded the chaotic situation of the value system and have provided rich soil for phantoms of Maoism, populism, and egalitarianism in China. This is detrimental to a market economy and to the adjustment of the state behavior in the process of marketization.

As the orthodox ideology lost ground in Chinese society, many important principles and norms have taken root there. In the past two decades, the Chinese leadership has struggled with itself and the society but finally has accepted two fundamental principles unknown in the history of the people's republic: the market economy and the rule of law. As everyone had already known, Mao's China banished the market economy. Even the selling of several eggs by an old grandma in the market was banned as a "tail of capitalism." Many leaders and scholars suffered dearly during the Cultural Revolution for their advocacy of the supplemental role of the market to a socialist planned economy. Until 1979, Chen Yun and Li Xiannian, two leaders in charge of the economy, supported the idea of "A planned economy primarily, a market adjustment supplementary." In 1980, some economists suggested to the leadership that they use the concept of a "commodity economy." They were immediately attacked and faced strong resistance.

Until 1984, the 12th National Party Congress accepted the concept of a "planned commodity economy." Then, in 1987, the 13th Party Congress endorsed the doctrine that "the state regulates the market, while the market guides enterprises." It was only a short distance to the concept of a market economy. However, the 1989 political events in China turned the clock back and marketization was labeled by orthodox officials as "capitalism."

74 The Dual Developmental State

Until 1992 Deng Xiaoping stood out as a defender of the market. Following Deng's speeches during his Southern Inspection Tour, the 14th Party Congress in the same year endorsed "the socialist market economy" as their goal (Dong and Shi 1998, 196-215).

The idea of the rule of law has also traveled the same long, rugged distance. First in 1979, Deng Xiaoping and other victims of the Cultural Revolution realized the tragic side of "rule of man" and started the process of "legalization," which basically meant to pass more laws, to reconstruct the legal system, and to deal with the population by law. After many years, "rule by law" was accepted by the leadership. This principle was limited to the claim that law is a tool for the rulers to govern, and the rulers should follow their own laws to govern. But it did not change the fact that the state was above the law.

In the late 1980s, the "rule of law" was still an alien and radical idea. It took almost another decade to take hold. In 1996, the concept of "the rule of law" started to appear in official documents. But problems persisted. The Chinese leadership tried to practice "rule by law" or establish a "law-based state" without fully committing to the true meaning of "the rule of law" commonly understood in the West. The legal scholars and political scientists now are pushing the Chinese government to further clarify their commitment to "the rule of law." In other words, the state and the party should accept and follow the law instead of standing above the law, and the law should embody some universal principles, such as justice, equality, due process, and civil rights (Dong and Shi 1998, 233-266; Xiao 1997; Liu 1997). Although the market economy is still prefixed with "socialist," and the leadership tries to play a word game with "rule by law" and "the rule of law," the Chinese leadership has endorsed the two most important principles of Western civilization. This may lead the Chinese regime to some new institutional break-through.

It is noteworthy that the continuous, multistage development of de-ideologization was carried out by way of "hollowing out."[2] The old value system has never been fully refuted or discarded. Many old shells remain. What is absent is the substance of the old ideas and values. The problem with this "hollowing out" process is that confusions abound. The merit of it is that a gradual process can be conducted, and any old ideas and institutions can be chipped away bit by bit. Instead of a democratic revolution, the "hollowing out" phenomenon points out a direction for a democratic evolution in a system in transition. Actually, if we take a close look at the Chinese Communist regime as a whole and many institutions in particular, we can also see that a phenomenon of "hollowing out" is happening to the authoritarian system in China

Restructuring the System

When Deng Xiaoping initiated economic and government reforms in the late 1970s, he faced the dilemma of the state as a solution as well as a problem. His 1980 speech was a classic indictment of bureaucratism within the Chinese political system. He was pretty sure that without first changing the state itself it would be impossible for the state to initiate and guide the economic development. Starting from the beginning, political reform was deemed necessary not for its own sake, but for its instrumental value for economic development. Therefore, the highest goal in his political agenda was the increase of "the general efficiency" of the Chinese state. The criterion for this general efficiency lay in the suitability of the state for the improvement of the performance of the economy (Dong and Shi 1998, 3-14). This guideline for political reform had been confirmed repeatedly in the 13th and the 15th Party Congresses, respectively, under Zhao Ziyang and Jiang Zeming as the General Secretaries. According to Wang Huning, Jiang's political advisor and a participant in the drafting of the political report for the 15th Party Congress, the political reform must follow these five principles: "To proceed, political reform must be conditioned on improving the vitality of the Party and the state, safeguarding the characteristics of socialism, and best using its advantages; maintaining the national unity, solidarity of nationalities and social stability, bringing the people's initiative into a full play, and improving the production and social development" (Dong and Shi 1998, 15-18; Liu 1998, 13-15).

The so-called general efficiency depends on two factors: state capacity and rationality. On the one hand, the state must have the resources and the ability to allocate them in order to make effective policies. The state also must be able to transform theses policies into reality. In other words, the Chinese government must have a strong state capacity (Wang and Hu 1993; Migdal 1988). On the other hand, a strong state that often makes irrational decisions cannot be developmental. Therefore, only a strong state able to make rational policies can achieve general efficiency.

76   The Dual Developmental State

In order to do that the Chinese state had to resort to structural changes and new policy tools.

Transformation of the State Function

For a developmental state to work, the critical issue is not whether the state should intervene in the economy, but in what way, to what extent, and upon which sector of the economy the state should intervene. The failure of Mao's development scheme was due precisely to the excessive and comprehensive intervention of the state into the economy. Thus, the key to success is to know when and where the state can be a solution, or a problem. It also depends on the selective targeting of the state. As Dietrich Rueschemeyer and Peter Evans have argued, "Increasing intervention makes the state more clearly an arena of social conflict and makes its constituent parts more attractive targets for take-over." "Selectivity" has become a "general feature of developmental states" (Evans, et al, 1985, 69; Evans, 1995, 58).

During the first decade of reform, the Chinese government, to use a metaphor here, tried to use 10 fingers to control one billion people. This was reflected in the number and name of governmental ministries. Just in recent years, the state has become less ambitious. It now only wants to use its 10 fingers to target a couple of highly important issue areas and crucial personnel. Accordingly, the state has abandoned totalism and embraced new doctrines, such as "Small Government, Big Society," and "Small Government, Big Service." This transformation is, of course, timely as the Chinese economy has become more complicated and the market is now playing a larger role.

The shrinking of the state function happened only after several rounds of failed attempts to streamline the government; it was made possible by the introduction of the market economy. Chinese scholars have identified several vicious cycles of governmental reforms. In the first cycle (1949-59), the number of ministries and bureaus directly led by the State Council changed from 35 in 1949, to 42 in 1952, to 64 in 1954, to 81 in 1956, and finally to 60 in 1959. In the second cycle (1960-70), this number changed from 60 in 1960, to 79 in 1965, then to 32 in 1970. During the third cycle (1971-82), this number changed from 52 in 1975 to 100 in 1981, and to 61 in 1982. In the fourth cycle (1983-93), this number changed from 72 in 1986 to 68 in 1988, to 86 in 1992 and finally to 59 in 1993 (Xin 1998, 273-302; Liu 1998, 289-314). Despite several rounds of cutting and

The Pillars of the Chinese Developmental State   77

downsizing, the government showed a strong ability to bounce back and even to expand further.

Parkinson's Law is well supported by the behavior of the Chinese bureaucracy. In 1997, some scholars did a calculation that showed that the current ratio of cadres (all state employees on the state payroll) to the population was 1 to 30. In contrast, under the Qing Dynasty (1644-1911), it was 1 to 911. Under the Tang Dynasty (618-907) it was 1 to 3927. The state had clearly become parasitic upon the national economy. For example, 20% of the GNP was consumed by the state employees in the form of payroll and other spending (Liu 1998, 22-24). Moreover, an overblown bureaucracy had two additional negative effects upon the economic development: First, when officials are many and have no real work to do, they tend to engage in infighting over the distribution of power and resources. Second, if the officials want to seize power over the economy, the marketization of the economy suffers. Even for Jiang Zemin, the state bureaucracy had become intolerable. He told the 15th National Party Congress in his political report, "The oversized government, overstaffing, the fusion of government and enterprises, and rampant bureaucratism have become an obvious obstacle to the deepening of reform and economic development, and also have poisoned the relationship between the Party and the masses." Under his call, in the year of 1998, a new round of government reforms was carried out across the country.

The 1998 reform enjoyed one distinct advantage over the previous reforms: The market economy had been formally accepted. The market economy acted as an Ockham's razor shaping the government into one that was small but efficient. In the middle 1980s, the political report of the 13th Party Congress also envisioned a small and efficient government. It stated, "To avoid repeating the old practice of 'streamlining, swelling, re-streamlining, re-swelling,' we must concentrate on a change of functions, which is the key to structural reform" (Zhao 1987, 39). The reduction of government functions, especially in the economy, was also suggested and included in the reform agenda.[3] But under the old planned economy, it was impossible to relieve the government from many of its economic and social functions. Functions create institutions. This was why the good intentions failed to prevent the government from getting larger. But in 1998, totalism and statism faced fierce attacks from the scholars and entrepreneurs. Drawing historical lessons, the Chinese government had

78 The Dual Developmental State

decided to implement the following principles: The government should be decoupled from enterprises. The government should give up its functions of production and only focus on limited roles. The market and other institutions within the society should be fostered to take these functions from the government. The optimal goal of reform was to achieve "*lianzheng*"--clean and cheap government. Under these guidelines, the relationships between the state and the market, between the state and enterprises, between the state and society, and between the central and local governments were to be completely restructured (Liu 1998, 81-82). The central ministries for economic macro-management had been strengthened; those for specific industries had been downgraded or abolished, except for those pillar industries and infrastructures. Those for social welfare, education and scientific affairs had been consolidated and streamlined. The traditional ministries for political affairs, such as defense, foreign affairs, justice and state security, had not been changed very much (Liu 1998, 91-94).

Judging from these changes of ministries in these four functional areas, the Chinese government seemed to have stipulated five roles for itself: regulator of macro-economy, umpire for social and economic conflicts, propeller for the targeted pillar industries, life-saver for the weak and disadvantaged, and finally a stabilizer for the whole society (Xing 1998, 200-204). Now it is hard to predict that these goals will be achieved, but certainly they have a better chance than ever.

Dual Structure: Political Stewardship and Technocracy

Deng Xiaoping was never shy of admitting that he was a "layman" with regard to the economy (Dong and Shi 1998, 8; B. Yang 1998, 231). But the Chinese economy did take off under his leadership and he, "more than any one else, should be given the credit" (B. Yang 1998, 266). This strange phenomenon can partly be explained by Deng's realization that economics was beyond his expertise. It was rumored that when he was pondering over choosing a premier, he said in 1992: "Zhu Rongji really knows economics, but he was not used properly. I do not know it, but I can understand. As for some leaders in charge, they neither know nor understand. In the future when we select successors, we should not neglect this qualification" (Su 1995, 34; Liu 1998, 78; Cheng 1993, 14-15). Inevitably, Li Peng was eased away from managing the economy even while he was still the Premier. Zhu was given the power to manage the economy and ultimately became

The Pillars of the Chinese Developmental State   79

the Premier. The reason for the economic success under a leader without expertise in economics was that Deng created a structure to allow the officials with economic expertise to take care of the economy.

In the whole process of twenty years of reforms, the Chinese leadership had been roughly divided into two categories: party officials and state functionaries. All of them were politicians, but the primary responsibility of the party officials came from the party organization. The state functionaries of course wore hats within the party apparatus, but their primary responsibility was to work within the state institutions (Zheng 1997, 19-20). Usually, the party officials were also involved in the consideration of important economic decisions and providing guidelines through the Annual Central Economic Work Conference and the Annual National Planning Work Conference. They often restrained themselves to the political stewardship, which means they had control over the direction they went, but the mundane job of running the economy was often left to the state functionaries, particularly the technocrats within the State Council.

Starting from the beginning of the reforms, Deng Xiaoping respected Chen Yun's expertise in running the economy (B. Yang 1998, 231-239). When Hu Yaopang and Zhao Ziyang formed a partnership, the former concentrated more on party affairs and ideological issues. Zhao was left a free hand to deal with the economy. After Li Peng became the Premier and took charge of the economy in 1989, the Chinese economy became rudderless because Li, as Deng hinted, had no economic expertise. He was assisted by Yao Yiling who was a believer in a planned economy. This period ended in 1991, when Zhu Rongji was promoted from the Mayor of Shanghai to the first Vice Premier. He was given a mandate to fix the troubled economy. Even before Zhu Rongji was finally appointed as the Premier, a dual structure was formed. Jiang Zeming and Li Peng spent more time on political, ideological, organizational and foreign issues. Zhu was in charge of economy. Now, assisted by the first Vice Premier Li Nanqing, another technocrat, Zhu has enjoyed relative autonomy in managing China's economy.

The Chinese practice of "party leaders steering, the state technocrats rowing the boat" is comparable to the distinction between the "reigning" and "ruling" in Japan. As "reigning" was a domain reserved to the elected politicians and partisans, it was often conducted in the form of political confrontation and compromise. "Ruling," namely, the orchestration and

80 *The Dual Developmental State*

guidance of the national economy, was carried out by the technocrats who had expertise in economy (Johnson 1982; Simone and Feraru 1995, 163). The chief merit of this division of roles is that it tended to safeguard the authority of party leaders as well as guarantee the efficiency of technocracy.

Normally, the decision on important guidelines with regard to the economy was deliberated, debated and formulated at the Annual Central Economic Work Conference, where the politicians had an institutionalized forum that enabled them to have an impact upon the economy. Occasionally, one top leader might violate this convention and exert his personal influence upon the economy by other means. For example, the technocrats complained that both Hu Yaobang and Zhao Ziyang, two party General Secretaries, over-stretched their power to intervene into the economy. These complaints reportedly became part of the reason that both of them were removed from office. In 1987 Deng initiated and pushed hard for price reform. After the social and economic consequences became troubling, he retreated to the background and scapegoated Zhao Ziyang who was at the front stage "ruling" the economy. The negative political impact doomed Zhao's political future but did not hurt Deng's authority (Hamrin and Zhao 1995, 62, 189-204).

As these cases show, the authority of party officials and the concern for efficiency by the technocrats sometimes came into conflict. To some degree, the choice of Li Peng as the Premier in charge of the economy blurred the division of labor between the officials who knew economics and those who didn't. It is true that both Jiang Zemin and Li Peng had a common technocrat background, but once the technocrats themselves were divided into two groups with different orientations towards reforms, those who were more ideological were assigned to the party positions, while those who were pragmatic were assigned to state positions.

To some extent, the formation of this dual leadership was facilitated by Deng's idea of separating the party from the government. In his 1980 speech on "The Reform System of The Party and State Leadership," he realized the urgency and pushed forward the efforts "to distinguish between the responsibilities of the Party and those of the government, and to stop substituting the former for the latter" (Deng 1984, 303). He also persuaded a large number of party leaders to give up their positions in the government by first doing so by himself. In 1986, he further proposed to carry out "the separation of the party from the government" (*dangzheng fengkai*) as the primary goal of political reform. The political report of the

The Pillars of the Chinese Developmental State   81

13th Party Congress reflected this idea. Although many proposals in this report later were aborted, concrete steps were taken to implement the separation of the party and the government (Hamrin and Zhao 1995, 153-168).

Although Deng did not allow the economic liberalization to proceed at a pace and to a point such that the political authority was threatened, he also did not want political stability used as an excuse for putting his economic reforms on the back burner. Several examples illustrate how this structural design had shielded the economy from the negative impact of ideological disagreement among the party leaders. Deng Xiaoping once encouraged premier Zhao Ziyang to explore bold economic reforms. He would take care of any political resistance that might ensue. In the notorious "anti-spiritual pollution" campaign, Zhao quickly declared that in the economic field there was no "spiritual pollution." Hu Yaobang respected this.

Immediately after the 1989 crackdown, Deng summoned both Li Peng and Yao Yiling and clearly told them, even under these special circumstances, the economy could not be sidelined. The reform-minded officials must be promoted to take charge of the lead work of the economy. However, he did not stop another ideological debate that stalled the national economy. Deng stood out by laying down his "theory of three conducives" and stopped the spillover of ideological debate to economic issues. Due to his insistence, the reshuffling of the leadership at the 14th Party Congress further strengthened rather than weakened the pragmatic reformers' control of economy. As one Chinese political analyst wrote, "The leading body produced by the 14th Party Congress is very neat. All are reformers. No one who does not support reforms is included" (Xiao 1996, 170). This is one positive structural factor that guaranteed that the economic development was to be the central task of the government work.

Meritocracy and the Rise of "Think Tanks"

Thomas Hobbes (1968, Intro., 81-82) said, the state is "but an artificial man" with the "matter" and "the artificer" both being man. Deng Xiaoping clearly realized that to reform China's institutions, the first thing to handle was the problem of man. He believed that to reform institutions, overhaul the aged cadre team, and bring in new blood would constitute a "revolution." "If this revolution is not carried out, and the aged and sick

82   *The Dual Developmental State*

continue to block the road for the younger, more energetic and competent, not only the Four Modernizations are doomed, but it may lead to the death of the Party and the state" (*Sanzhong Quanhui* 1982, 1036). Under this guideline, the government and the party experienced significant personnel changes since the early 1980s. The two most important ones were the change of state personnel from the revolutionary cadres to technocrats, and the establishment of the civil service system. Coupled with the use of think tanks on a large scale, they greatly enhanced the quality of decision making within the Chinese government.

Around 1982, a large number of veteran cadres stepped down from their positions in the party and government organizations. After 1984 as the retirement system became institutionalised, many cadres in the government and party branches became relatively younger. Noticing that health considerations left loopholes for some older leaders to exit into the PCs and to avoid a complete retirement, the CPC Central Committee issued a new document around 1984, reiterating that "no organization was to be used as a substitute for full retirement for cadres who were too old or unwell actually to do any work—even if these cadres were leaders" (Manion 1993, 67).

As a result of Deng's aggressive retirement policy, the leaders in various institutions became younger and their level of education also improved. For example, from 1982 to 1984, the average age of ministers and vice-ministers dropped from 65.9 to 62.8 and that for directors and deputy directors dropped from 59.6 to 54.3. In contrast, the percentage of those having college-level education increased respectively from 43% to 53.5%, and from 40% to 55.6%. For the leaders of the State Council, their average age dropped from 65.7 to 59.5, and the percentage of college graduates increased form 35.5% to 52% (Tang 1997, 224). Many of them were born in the 1930s and joined the Party after 1949. They had not served in the army, but moved up through administrative and party bureaucracies.

Personnel shifted from the revolutionary cadre to the party technocrat (Lee 1991; Li and White 1988, 371-99; Zang 1991, 512-525). Prominent among these were many graduate students from China's prestigious universities and returned students from the Soviet Union, Eastern Europe, and now even from the United States and other Western countries (Li 1994). Because government work was often regarded as the "first front work," the quality in terms of education, age, and expertise of the government officials were further improved in the Zhu Rongji cabinet

The Pillars of the Chinese Developmental State 83

formed in 1998. The average age of 29 ministers was 57.45, and all had had a college-level education. The average age of the 136 deputy ministers was 54.62. Of these, 34 had had a college-level education, while 23 had had a post-graduate education (*PD* May 15, 1998, 1).

To assist the government in its work, two important systems were also introduced in the late 1980s: the state civil service system and the consulting and research institutions. The civil service system was proposed in 1987 at the 13th Party Congress. Its main purpose was to distinguish the elected and appointed politicians from the bureaucrats who were recruited based on competitive examinations. But soon after it was proposed, the advocate for this reform, Zhao Ziyang, was forced to leave power in disgrace. And any reform of the civil service became impractical. However, in 1993 this reform picked up momentum, and the State Council passed the Provisional Regulations for the National Civil Service. The National College of Administration was later established and even worked with the Maxwell School of Syracuse University to improve its training programs.

Comparing the 1987 reforms to the current practice, it seems that the Chinese leadership had shifted its primary emphasis from stability and efficiency to liveliness and efficiency. Permanent employment was not guaranteed for state civil servants. As Zhu Rongji told the students in the National College of Administration, workers may be laid off, and so too the state civil servants (Liu 1998, 70). Even though the current civil service system was not perfect, it was a step forward relative to the old cadre system which put too much emphasis on "being red." According to Song Defu, Minister of State Personnel, the percentage of state cadres with professional knowledge increased from 33% in 1979 to 70% in 1999. Meanwhile, those with a college level and above education increased from 18% to 44%, and people under the age of 45 increased from 68% to 76% (*PD* Jan. 11, 1999, 4). As Zhu Rongji's downsizing has been directed more at those without professional knowledge, it has become impossible to enter the government without a college degree.

During the Zhao Ziyang era, many think tanks came into being. Some of them were affiliated with the government: for example, the Institute of Economic Structure Reform, the most famous think tank for Zhao Ziyang. Many important and influential research institutes affiliated with the State Council, such as the Research Center for Rural Development, the Center for International Studies, and the Research Center for Economic Law and

84   *The Dual Developmental State*

Statutes, were established during Zhao's tenure. Some were independent; for example, the Stone Company's Institute for Development, and the Beijing Institute of Social and Economic Research, headed by Wang Juntao and Chen Ziming, two leading intellectuals in the 1980s.

In 1986 when Zhao Ziyang was assigned to organize the design for political reform, he heavily relied on in-house and outside scholars for this task. For the purpose of drafting a blueprint for political reform a five-member Political Reform Research Group was formed, which was headed by Zhao himself and included top leaders from the Party Secretariat, the State Council, the NPC Standing Committee and the CPC Advisory Commission.

Under the Political Reform Research Group, the Political Reform Office led by Bao Tong was set up and included 20 members. Among them were many leading intellectuals. This office then coordinated seven forums that consisted of more leading scholars who were each assigned one specific topic (The seven topics were: the separation of the party and the government, the development of an inner-party democracy, decentralization and administrative reform, party organization reform, personnel reform, the expansion of socialist democracy, and the perfection of a socialist legal system). Each forum recruited legal scholars, political scientists and other researchers from universities and research academies nationwide.

Parallel to this, the Central Party School also organized seven forums so that they could conduct their own independent study in order to provide different perspectives for the purpose of comparison. As a result, 400 experts wrote in their reports 40 million words on political reform. Based on all these reports, the "General Program for Political Reform" was written. Later it was incorporated into Zhao's political report to the 13th Party Congress. This decision-making process showed as one insider, Chen Yizi, said, that "[f]rom Mao Zedong to Deng Xiaoping to Zhao Zhiyang, the nature of the 'ideas' that initiate policies shifted from idealism to utilitarianism, and then to rationalism" (Hamrin and Zhao, 133-152; Wu 1997).

Jiang Zeming has his own think tanks. In the Zhongnanhai compound, The Policy Research Office of the CPC Central Committee and the Policy Research Office of the State Council are the two most powerful institutions assisting the leadership in the decision making process. Both are headed by people with post-graduate degrees. Many other members have doctoral degrees and professorships, and some have studied in the

United States, Japan and other countries. For example, one prominent member, Wang Huning, the Deputy Director for the Policy Research Office of the CPC Central Committee, was brought in by Jiang from Fudan University in Shanghai. Wang was a political science professor and later the Department Chair of International Politics and Dean of the Fudan University Law School. Now he plays an important role in influencing Jiang's decision-making. It is also said that Wang Daohan, a former Shanghai mayor, is a "private advisor" (*shiye*) to Jiang Zemin. Wang Daohan organized several research centers in Shanghai, such as the Center for International Affairs, to generate policy study reports and proposals. Through this coordination, a large number of social scientists in the Shanghai Academy of Social Sciences, Fudan University, and the Shanghai Institute for International Studies have been involved doing policy-oriented research (Gao 1997). In addition, several economists have access to the central decision-makers to whom they are able to give their policy suggestions (Xiao 1997).

Even before the reforms started, the Chinese leaders did consult their assistants when they made decisions. But there were some fundamental differences in the way they went about this. Traditionally, the leaders relied on their "secretaries" (*mishu*) to acquire, process information, and make their decisions (Li and Pye 1992). The secretaries tended to be "effective writers" (*biganzi*) with educational backgrounds mostly in literature, history, or philosophy. Because they were dependent upon the officials, they always tried to "read the minds" of their leaders. The best secretaries were those who were able to understand their leaders and formulate their ideas in a systematic way. In contrast, the think tanks are more institutionalized and have more autonomy. They examine policy alternatives from different angles and present recommendation with more objective evidence. This change from "*mishu* politics" to the role of "think tanks" in policy-making, or more accurately, to complement the former by the latter, was a laudable achievement that marked a move towards a more rational and scientific administration.

Macro-Management and Economic Control

One scholar has summarized the lessons China learned from other East Asian countries as follows: "In addition to the absolute necessity for a

86 *The Dual Developmental State*

coalition of reformers, for China, the most important lesson from the Asian experiences is the need to implement economic reform prior to political reform. The Chinese leaders have keenly realized that the state cannot function properly without first having a powerful Ministry of Finance, an effective central bank, a modern army and police force, and so forth" (Cheng 1998, 98).

What this author omitted, but should have included, is the State Planning Commission, now the State Development Planning Commission (SDPC). These institutions to some extent can be regarded as four wheels for the developmental state machinery. Since the military and police force have gained enough publicity, particularly after the bloody clamp down in 1989 and actions against political activists in the later years, I will only consider the macro-economic control of three institutions.

The SDPC, as its name indicates, is responsible for the general overseeing, forecasting and coordinating of long-term policies of the national economy through its control over the supply of materials, funds, and human resources. Since the 13th Party Congress, it has given up its role in micro-managing the economy and in managing specific industries. Now it solely focuses on macro-economic coordination. Because its members often include the ministers from the Ministries of Finance, Labor, the State Commission for Science, the President of the People's Bank of China and the directors of the State Bureau of Statistics and the State Bureau of Prices, this Commission is the "largest, most powerful, and most comprehensive Chinese economic policy-making organ," often referred to as "the Little State Council" (Hamrin and Zhao 1995, 52; Pu 1990, 196).

Because its central concern is the general healthy equilibrium of the national economy and its stable growth, it plays more the role of a stabilizer rather than a dynamo to the economy, more a brake rather than a gas pedal. Not surprisingly, it was often regarded as being associated with the conservative leaders and their policies. But if it is agreed that several rounds of "overheating" of the national economy was dangerous if left uncontrolled, this Commission deserves credit for its contribution to the overall health and stability of the national economy.

But the role of the SDPC in Chinese macro-economic control should not be exaggerated. Its power and influence fluctuated dramatically during the Great Leap Forward and the Cultural Revolution. It has never reached the status of an "economic general staff" which its East Asian counterparts enjoyed in their countries: for example, the MITI, the Council for

The Pillars of the Chinese Developmental State   87

Economic Planning and Development in Taiwan, and the Economic Planning Board in South Korea. Liu Sunian and Xue Muqiao, two economists for the State Planning Commission, complained in 1986 that they could not control the scale of investment in China that resulted in an overheating of the economy and redundant projects. For example, 112 color TV production lines were set up--72 were imported, 50 from Japan. According to Liu and Xue, the central plan did not increase its investment, but many top leaders "signed notes" to make decisions on investment. The local governments also found their own funds for new projects (Gui 1987, 5-13). In other words, "*guanxi* (connections) politics" and local developmentalism often are intertwined in that local leaders always seek patronage from some central leaders with whom they have connections. This has made it more difficult for the State Planning Commission to coordinate the pace and scale of development.[4]

The SDPC was vulnerable to its political environment. Once the national environment changed--for example, the introduction of the market economy--this commission also quickly adapted to it. So far, it has acted as a match-maker to help the merger of enterprises into large industry groups. It helped Hubei Province establish the biggest automobile group, Shandong Province the biggest heavy-duty truck group, Shanghai the biggest bicycle industry group, Jiangsu the biggest electronic industry group, and Shanxi the biggest sewing-machine group. It also helped Baoshan Steel and Iron Mill acquire other steel mills to consolidate into a competitive trust (Cheng 1998; 138-139; *PD*, Jan. 22, 1998, 1). Thus, in the process of marketization, the SDPC did not lose its relevance to Chinese national economy.

Coordinated with the SDPC, the Ministry of Finance takes primary responsibility for making annual budget plans and long-term financial plans. Through the distribution and redistribution of national wealth, the Ministry of Finance has important leverage with which to macro-manage the national economy. However, four serious problems compromised the effectiveness of this leverage. First, the "soft budget constraints" under the socialist economy was a persistent problem in China. Because the resources were allocated by the central government, the state-owned enterprises and local governments had a strong incentive for more investment, the so-called "investment hunger disease." But, meanwhile, there was no distinction made between taxes and profits as everything went to the central authority. Moreover, the enterprises lacked

88   The Dual Developmental State

responsibility for the efficient use of state funds. Projects were duplicated, and thus, wasteful. Second, since the reforms started with "the devolution of authority and the granting of profits" (*fengquan ranli*), the fiscal capacity of the central government declined after the reforms were initiated. The proportion of financial receipts in the GNP dropped from 31.2% to 15.8% in 1990 and to 10.8% in 1995 (Wang and Hu 1993, 29; Xin 1997, 51). Third, in contrast to the decline of the financial capacity of the central government, the rise of the extra-budgetary fund at all levels was also staggering. For example, in 1955, the extra-budgetary fund accounted for only 5% of the budget. In 1981, it increased to 60%, and then to 90% in the early 1990s (Zhu 1997, 330, 344). Fourth, as many state-owned enterprises became money-losing ventures and the state financial subsidies increased accordingly, the budget deficit became larger and larger during the Deng era. Before 1978, the average annual budget deficit was 0.757 billion yuans. From 1979 to 1990, it rose to 21.656 billion. In 1995 and 1996, the budget deficit was 58.2 and 54.8 billion yuans, respectively (He 1998, 18). The central government had less leeway to spend money on some important issues, such as the alleviation of regional disparities or the widening gap between rich and poor.

Because the central government could directly control only 19% of entire investment in 1994, it had only limited resources (*Xinzhen Tongquan*, vol. 3, 94). The investment by the local governments and other sources of investment (e.g., foreign direct investment, self-generated funds within the society) produced an overheating of the economy (e.g., in the early 1990s) and the central government had to resorted to administrative means to achieve its "soft-landing." These problems hampered the state capacity to regulate and steer the national economy.

To address these economic problems, the Chinese central government introduced some fundamental reforms. The first thing the government did was to force the state-owned enterprises to face financial discipline. The old appropriation was replaced by loans from the government, with the profits going to the central authority via taxes. The central government only took care of 1,000 key state-owned large enterprises--all others were encouraged to privatize, consolidate through mergers, or restructure through stock-sharing systems. The most important one was the establishment of a modern tax system, the so-called tax separation system, which aimed to increase the percentage of the budget to 20% of the GNP and the percentage of the central government budget to no more than 60% of the total budget (Xin 1997, 52-53). Moreover, the central government intensified its supervision over the budget of the state-owned enterprises through irregular "financial inspection" campaigns. And in 1998, the State Council also appointed "special inspectors" at the ministerial level to monitor the large state-owned enterprises. Through January 1999, there were 38 such inspectors (*PD*, Jan. 9, 1999, 1).

As we know, many financial and budgetary problems in China can be attributed to the structural decoupling of responsibility from obligation. The relationships among the SDPC, the Ministry of Finance, the banks, and other ministries did not avoid this problem. For example, the loans for capital construction were primarily decided and arranged by the SDPC and other ministries. The banks (primarily the Bank of Industry and Commerce) merely acted as cashiers to dispense money. Some Chinese summarized this situation as: "The SDPC sends out invitations, the ministry (any one) takes orders, and the banks pick up the checks" (Zhu 1997, 297).

Because the governments at different levels controlled the banks, they lacked the independence and autonomy to decide whether, and to which enterprises, they should give or take back loans. Many times, the size of investment from the central government was larger than the financial assets of the banks. And because many loans were given out based on the connections of the borrowers with the leaders and not on their future profitability, the banks in China had a large amount of dead debts and bad loans and faced the danger of bankruptcy. The financial crises in East Asia alarmed the Chinese leadership, made them to realize these problems, and also prompted them to take strong measures to fix them.

After the State Council passed a decision to reform the monetary system in 1993, reforms of the banking system in China started in 1994. That year, the leadership position of the People's Bank of China (PBC) as the central bank was strengthened. The commercial banks were separated from the three policy banks, the State Bank of Development was established, and other monetary institutions were allowed to exist. In 1998, by emulating the American Federal Reserve system, the PBC had another overhaul. Under the old system, the PBCs were established at the provincial level, and the provincial governments dictated their decisions. However, the Chinese government abolished all People's Banks at the provincial level and established nine regional banks. This was done to "strengthen the authority of the central bank to implement monetary policies; to strengthen its independence, uniformity and effectiveness of

90 *The Dual Developmental State*

monetary supervision; to coordinate and use the manpower for cross-provincial regulation; to get rid of interventions from all directions; to seriously deal with monetary institutions and their leaders that violate regulations, and to improve the efficiency of monetary regulation." This system started to function on January 1, 1999 (*PD*, Nov. 16, 1998, 1, 4).

Macro-Management: Industrial Policies

Chalmers Johnson (1987, 159) argues: "One of the characteristics that distinguishes industrial policy from general economic policy is its penetration to the micro-level, meaning government attempts to influence economic sectors (agriculture, high technology), whole industries (advanced electronics), and individual enterprises within industries (Lockheed, Chrysler)." In terms of industrial policy, China had had less flexibility to move in or out of this or that industry. In the 1980s, the government's attention to industrial policy was very insufficient. The Chinese state had tried to interfere with too many industries. The number could easily be counted from the name of the ministries in the government in the Eighties. One World Bank report commented in 1990: "The present system involves setting too many priorities, which is as good as not having any priorities" (Singh 1992).

As a result, the lack of effective central coordination over the national economy and important industries produced chaos. One example was the overheating economy and hyper-inflation in 1994 that caused the central government to strengthen its macro-management and regulation over investment and the economy. Another example was China's automobile industry that had 125 automobile factories, more than 600 auto refitting factories, and about 2,300 auto parts factories in the early 1990s. The annual production of all combined was less than one month's production of any one of the American "Big Three" auto companies.

As the developmental state model was adopted, China changed its policy from a regional development strategy--"the policy stressing some geographic areas" ("geographical sliding policy")--to "the policy of stressing some policy areas" ("product sliding policy"); namely, an industrial policy strategy and "a comprehensive opening-up strategy" (Lam 1995, 60). In 1994, the State Council passed "An Outline of the State Industrial Policies in the 90s," in which the machinery-electronic, petrochemical, automobile, and construction industries were chosen as "pillar industries." "The Industrial

The Pillars of the Chinese Developmental State 91

Policy for the Auto Industry" that was passed later was the first document for a specific industrial policy.

In terms of the state-industry relationship, the Chinese government intentionally tried to learn from other East Asian countries. They especially tried to learn from the experiences of South Korea (*Economist* June 7, December 20, 1997). Generally speaking, the restructured state-industry relationship had consisted of three major components: First, the state should take a lead in investing in basic industries and infrastructure, e.g., energy, transportation, communication, and the development of new materials. When the East Asian financial crises caused a negative impact upon the Chinese economy after 1997, the Chinese government took a more active role in establishing fiscal policy and issued 225 billion in government bonds to boost the national economy by investing heavily in these industries. Second, the state should provide favorable policies to the chosen four "pillar industries." These favorable policies included more investment, subsidies for research and development in crucial technological areas, tax remittance, favorable loans, price support, trade restrictions with high tariffs (180-220%) on foreign competitors, etc. (Xin 1997, 103-114; He Yiqun 1998, 105). Third, the state should follow the policy of "targeting the big ones and freeing the small" and pay more attention to 1,000 large state-owned enterprises while at the same time giving up its control over the smaller enterprises. The central government should take actions and support the enterprises to consolidate their competitive advantage at home as well as in the international economy through mergers and acquisition of smaller enterprises. The goal was to help Chinese enterprises form industry groups, or the so-called "national teams," which, by taking advantage of economies of scale, could become members of the top 500 multinational corporations.

Just when the Chinese government started enforcing its industry policy, the East Asian financial crises broke out and destroyed or paralyzed many famous South Korean "*chaebols*," the model for emulation in the eyes of the Chinese. Although there was no indication that the Chinese government had given up the strategy of developing industry groups, this policy needs to be re-evaluated and more lessons need to be drawn from the South Korean experience. Based on the studies of the automobile industry and the electronic industry (Harwit 1994; Naughton 1997), the Chinese central state lacks "the embedded autonomy" which has been recognized as a key to successful industrial policies (Evans 1995). As we

92 The Dual Developmental State

have seen before, the autonomy of central commissions and ministries has often been overridden by the connections to higher leaders. Local property ownership and development also prevented the central ministries from effectively getting involved with specific industries at the local level.

Difficulty for effective industrial policies comes from the local protectionism and developmentalism. Because many provinces wanted to get investment from the central government, they pronounced these pillar industries as their own key targets in local social and economic development. Sichuan, Hubei, Anhui, Jiangsu, Zhejiang, Shanghai and Chongqing all had included the automobile industry as their primary pillar industry. Liaoning set the petrochemical, metallurgical, machinery, and electronic industries as its own pillar industries, overlapping the national target (He Yiqun 1998, 112; Xin 1997, 485). If all local governments embraced the limited pillar industries, the intention of concentrating limited resources on a few sectors and increasing the scale of economy would become impossible.

In terms of the commercial airplane industry, the opposite was the case. Even though the central government invested a large amount and tried several times to target 100 and 150 passenger airplanes (Yun-7 and Yun-10), it failed miserably. One major problem was that without effective central coordination and leadership, tensions between the military and the civilian industry, and the center and local governments became unmanageable. For example, even though Shanghai had the best conditions for producing passenger airplanes, the city government shunned this opportunity because it had no power to coordinate the production with other airplane factories in other provinces (Xi'an, Shaanxi; Harerbin, Heilongjiang; Chengdu, Sichuan; Nanchang, Jiangxi) (Hu 1997; interview, June, 1997). Therefore, the distance from the making of industrial policies to the implementing of them as intended is still great. The Chinese central government has a lot to learn if it is to govern the market. The central-local tension has to be taken into consideration in analyzing the success or failure of the developmental state in China. In the later chapters, when local developmentalism is discussed, we will see that the Chinese state has been done better in "regional inclining strategy" than in industrial policy.

Built-in Tensions within the Chinese Developmental State

It has never been easy for the Chinese leadership to create and then to maintain a developmental state. Its communist background (cultural factor) and sheer size (ecological factor) have created tensions within the developmental state. From the buildup to the maintenance of the developmental state, these two factors have played an important part, sometimes stronger, sometimes weaker, sometimes in a separate way, and sometimes intertwined.

When Deng Xiaoping initiated his reforms, the stumbling blocks were the old institutions under the centrally planned economy and the Stalinist bureaucracy. For example, the State Planning Commission from 1979 to 1993 was controlled by Chen Yun and his followers, including Yu Qiuli, Yao Yiling, Song Jian, and Zou Jiahua. These leaders did not oppose Deng's reforms entirely, but they did not like many of his bold policies nor did they like the speed with which they were implemented. So even if they did not directly oppose the reforms, they did procrastinate. Clearly, in the early years of Deng Xiaoping's reforms, he had to overcome resistance from the central bureaucracy, particularly from those ministries that were the backbones of the planned economy. Without directly attacking them himself, Deng followed two indirect strategies: First, he used the force of the NPC to discredit the conservative leaders, especially those in the ministries of heavy industry. Second, he "played to the provinces." For example, he supported Zhao Zhiyang's and Wan Li's bold reforms in Sichuan and Anhui, and later he promoted them to the State Council to take charge of the economy. Deng also accepted proposals from the local leaders in Guangdong and set up four SEZs along the Southern coast. With this legislative and local support, Deng's reforms could proceed.

Once the leaders agreed upon the policies for reforms, problems arose from other sources. As the Chinese economy started its rapid marketization and liberalization, two sets of problems were most serious.

(1) Because the Chinese transition was from a planned to a market economy, this transition created tremendous opportunities for governmental officials and state-owned enterprise managers to seek rent, to make state capital their own private property, and to give privileges to their own relatives.

Public choice economists have regarded China, both traditionally and under Communist rule, as a typical "rent-seeking society" (Buchanan,

94 The Dual Developmental State

Tollison, and Tullock 1980; Tullock 1987, 1989). A "rent-seeking society" is characterized by "the resource-wasting activities of individuals in seeking transfers of wealth through the aegis of the state" (Buchanan, Tollison and Tullock 1980, IX). "The term *rent-seeking* is designed to describe behavior in institutional settings where individual efforts to maximize value generate social waste rather than social surplus" (Buchanan, Tollison and Tullock 1980, 4). The institutional reason for rent-seeking activities lies in the interference of the economy by the state. The state intervention (including regulation, monopoly, etc.) creates monopoly profits, opening the door to rent-seeking behaviors. As the proportion of the state-controlled economy becomes greater, its rent-seeking activities are more likely to be widespread. But contrary to the expectation that the competitive forces of a mature market economy often decreased rent-seeking activities, rent-seeking activities flourished after China started its economic marketization. Actually, "the issues of CPC" (Corruption, Pollution, and Crime) are major problems in today's Chinese society.

There are several factors that explain this sudden surge of rent-seeking activity. Under the Maoist planned economy, the state had a monopoly over almost all important economic transactions. Although the state bureaucracy as a whole had unlimited access to collecting monopoly rent from state-controlled economic sectors, there was little opportunity for individual officials to transfer wealth into their own pockets. The tough political controls deterred officials from engaging in such behavior. As a result, a powerful rent-seeking state was characterized by the relative absence of rent-seeking officials.

However, marketization resulted in looser government control over the society as well as its own bureaucracy. As old norms of "serving the people" were replaced by new rules and norms of "to get rich is glorious," rules and laws were at best vague. Developing a market economy also offered more new opportunities to the government officials to seek rent. For example, when privatizing and transferring state ownership to the private sector, the questions of who should first get franchises, licenses, and special concessions from the government to establish businesses, who should import and export, and who should take over the state-owned enterprises, etc., were generated by marketization. The officials had less fear of punishment and more loopholes to exploit. Exploiting these new opportunities, more Chinese officials have engaged in such rent-seeking activities as taking bribes, accepting gifts, soliciting kickbacks, imposing

The Pillars of the Chinese Developmental State   95

arbitrary fees upon business-people, enterprises, and peasants, and transferring state property and capital to overseas accounts, registering them under the name of their children.

In the mid-1980s, the economic transition from a command economy to a commodity economy came to a crossroads. Two economic systems coexisted and engaged in a heated battle. The friction of the two systems produced severe problems, including two parallel price systems (state-controlled and market prices), and two sets of employment systems (life employment and contract employment). Taking advantage of the crises of these "dual track" systems, many officials in China used their power to seek private economic profits. As a result, corruption became rampant. The most notorious practice was that the state agencies established their own companies and engaged in commercial activities. Most of these companies were not involved in production, but rather in the processing of transactions. They were "bubble companies" or "brief-case companies." They were used as agencies for the state officials to solicit illegal economic profits. Political power, which controlled opportunities, licenses, franchises, and cheap materials under the state-controlled prices, immediately became a way for government officials to get rich overnight.

Rampant rent-seeking behaviors by the state officials could produce two serious consequences: First, the incentive of entrepreneurs to do business could be stifled. For example, in Fujian province, two businessmen bought 6,350 kilograms of bamboo shoots worth 1,524 yuan intending to transport them to Shanghai by truck. When just roughly half of the journey was finished in Zhejiang province, 13 fees and taxes, a total of 546.4 yuan, had been imposed on them. Uncertain how much more in fees they had to pay, they decided to sell the bamboo shoots there and then went home (Lyons and Nee 1994, 161). Second, people's discontent with the government could increase and a crisis of political legitimacy could break out. In the 1989 political crisis, the theme of anti-corruption and the cleaning up of "official profiteering" rather than the slogan in favor of democracy mobilized the Chinese masses nationwide. When two systems-economic planning and market regulation-coexisted, they both catalyzed rampant rent-seeking activities by government officials and threw Chinese market-oriented reforms into an unprecedented abyss of crisis and almost forfeited their future.

The collusion among those with power and money led to rampant corruption. Corruption has become a political cancer threatening the

96 The Dual Developmental State

legitimacy and efficiency of both the state and the market. How to control this corruption has become an overriding concern. The Chinese leadership has arrived at a consensus: The legislative branch, including the NPC and local people's congresses can play an effective part in this regard. Liu Zheng, Deputy General Secretary of NPC Standing Committee, related the supervisory role of people's congresses to the market economy and anti-corruption:

> In the process of developing a socialist market economy, the supervision, especially by the organs of state power, should be further strengthened. This is because the old system has not completely receded from the historical stage and the new system has not been fully completed. The government has not finished its transformation from a direct commanding economy to an indirect macro-management. Under such circumstances, the freedoms arising from the development of a market economy could be abused by some people in power enabling them to seek colossal profits under the aegis of power. If supervision is forceful, and law enforcement is rigorous, a variety of illegal behaviors, such as embezzlement and corruption, could be deterred. For these reasons, the work of supervision by the Standing Committees of the People's Congresses shall be further strengthened. We shall thoroughly comprehend and rigorously enforce the idea of Comrade Deng Xiaoping that clean government depends on the rule of law. In order to improve the mechanisms for supervision, we must use laws to promote honesty and to punish corruption. (*Quanguo Renda* 1994, 12).

(2) Because China is so huge, under a planned economy the ruling center was unable to give equal attention (such as investments, or other favorable policies) to all areas. As the Chinese central government has become developmental, it has required 31 developmental governments at the provincial level. But after the command economy was destroyed at the national level in the early 1990s, China faced a new economic phenomenon –"an economy of dukedom" as a result of economic decentralization during the economic reform. That means, 30 provincial units (later Chongqing was added) were "big dukedoms," 300 prefectures and cities were "middle dukedoms," and 2,000 counties were "small dukedoms." China's economy had become one "divided by dukes or princes under an emperor." China's economy had become a "ducal economy" (Zheng 1995, 30).

Even worse, the planned economy created a "small-sized command economy" centered on China's local bureaucracies and controlled by "local mandatory plans" (Jia and Lin 1994, 37). After it shifted to market economy in the early 1990s, the center further decentralized its control over enterprises, and gave localities more autonomy. During that period, some provincial and local governments captured power decentralized from the central government, and expanded their control over the enterprises. Appeared a phenomenon of "intermediate stasis" (*zhong genzu*), namely, "the two ends (the center and masses at the grassroots) are enthusiastic for reforms, while the intermediate (cadres at the intermediate level) is lukewarm." The marketization could be scuttled by this threat (Yuan and Han 1992, 170).

To reverse the power shift, as the center gave more autonomy to localities, it also kept some levers to maintain the public good. These included a unified national market, stable currency, reasonable inflation rate, etc. The central government also tightened its control over a few selected industries and macro-economic policies to keep a strategic coordination over the national economic transformation. The recent reforms of banking and the tax systems as well as the implementation of industrial policies for the four "pillar industries" were important steps toward this goal. In addition to measures at the national level, local developmentalism and entrepreneurship were needed. Thirty-one developmental, or entrepreneurial provinces, and thousands of developmental local governments were necessary for the elimination of the "ducal economy" and the maintenance of a developmental state. In the early half of reform era, the cautious strategy of the central government actually encouraged more experiments at the local level because when the central leadership was more uncertain about certain policies, it was more likely to allow localities to experiment. In other words, the gradual, cautious policy at the central level encouraged bold and innovative policies at local levels. Most governments at local levels became developmental. Thus local developmentalism has been one of the important reasons for explaining Chinese economic performances (Huang 1996; Zheng 1995, 44).

When Chinese leaders applied the developmental state model to China's modernization, the huge size of the country created a situation different from the one faced by the "Four Little dragons" wherein the developmental state model succeeded. It was more difficult for China to control its huge economy, given its scope, specialization, and complexity. As the organizer and conductor of both economic and political activities, the state had to balance its costs and benefits and had to make a trade-off between economic and political gains. When it decided to abandon the old Stalinist strategy and adopt the developmental state model owing to China's vast territory and

98 The Dual Developmental State

huge population, the transaction costs needed to maintain a developmental state were much higher. For one, it is difficult for the central authority to coordinate policy and supervise bureaucrats because it is costly to monitor enforcement and compliance. Resistance from different regions is more likely, and rent-seeking behavior and opportunism are difficult to control. Because of its state socialist experience, China had first to create markets in its transition. The task of "making markets" compounded the changing relationship between the state and economy.

Institutionalists remind us that the market is more than mere a price mechanism; it is a set of institutions embedded in a social, legal and cultural context. This structural transformation process imposes demands for assistance upon the state. Instead of "withering-away," the Chinese state, which under the Communist system was not well institutionalized, has had to institutionalize itself. The institutionalization of the market and the state occurred simultaneously and affected each other. To safeguard the integrity of the developmental state model, the Chinese system needed more mechanisms to enable it to economize on transaction costs. For example, the PPCs were expected to serve this purpose through the supervision of policy enforcement by the bureaucrats at the sub-national level and involved the compliance of policies by the people on the one hand, and the making of markets by legislative decrees on the other. As needed, a symbiotic interaction between the economic marketization and political institutionalization had to be achieved if the transition was to proceed. Ways had to be found to allow a developmental dictatorship and an active sub-national legislature to coexist.

The institutionalization of the PPCs therefore has become a part of China's transition process and they also have been market-facilitating by sustaining the developmental state model. As a result, in China, both decentralization and legislative expansion--local power and legislative power--have been the two conspicuous characteristics of political development during the reform era. This is why we have to turn to the legislative and local perspectives to have a full understanding of the Chinese developmental state.

Notes

1   It was indicated in the publication and then removal from the bookshelves in 1998 of the book *Political China* ed. by Dong and Shi 1998.

2   Larry Diamond observes that "democracy has been hollowed out in many countries" where the third wave of democracy swept over. For the same logic, can an authoritarian system be "hollowed out"? See: Larry Diamond, "Is the third wave over," *Journal of Democracy*, July, 1996, pp. 20-37.

3   In 1986, I attended and presented a paper to a national conference on the state function in Taiyuan, Shanxi. This consensus was formed among the participants (including Yan Jiaqi, a core member for drafting political report of the Thirteenth Party Congress): To reform the government, the first thing that should be done is to transform the state function. The collection of papers was first planned to be published by the Shangxi People's Publishing House, but unfortunately the change of political climate after the student protests in Shanghai and other cities discouraged the publisher from pursuing this project. Also discussion on the state function is reflected in the following books: Zhang Yunlun, ed., *Zhongguo Jigou de Yange* [*The Evolution of Institutions in China*] (Beijing: Zhongguo Jingji Chubanshe, 1988); Gui 1987.

4   In their studies on the central decision-making process, Kenneth Lieberthal and Michel Oksenberg quoted a Chinese official who described how *guanxi* is important to get anything done: "No unit or individual lets you have something strictly according to regulations. Rather, you must have *guanxi* or you come up with nothing. This is true everywhere but especially in the South. The *guanxi* is based on interest--strictly a "you scratch my back and I scratch yours" situation. The exchange of goods and favors seals the deal. This situation is pervasive because that is the way things are done at higher levels, and until they do things differently, nobody else will change." Lieberthal and Oksenberg 1988, 339.

5 The National People's Congress and China's Transition

Since the 1960s, political scientists have paid special attention to the question of "how legislatures relate to development" (Smith and Musolf 1979, 3; Kornberg and Musolf 1970). The focus of the first batch of publications was on the role of legislatures in modernization and nation building. Entering the 1990s, as "new parliaments abound" (Copeland and Patterson 1994, 1), the rekindled interest of political scientists has been directed more toward the role of legislatures in regime transition; namely how a single-party system with a controlled economy evolves into a democratic system with a market-oriented economy (Olsen and Mezey 1991; Remington 1994; Close 1995; Copeland and Patterson 1994; Olson and Norton 1996; Norton and Ahmed 1999). A common problem under study is how legislatures relate to economic change and democratization.

Within this theme, there are two different arguments, if here we leave out the "spontaneous order" and hands-off government arguments by the orthodox liberals. The first argument draws its inspiration from the Anglo-American experiences and states that an active legislature has a positive correlation with both economic growth and democratic construction. As Lloyd Musolf and Fred Riggs have argued, "Western countries that have successfully achieved industrialization and economic growth while safeguarding other democratic institutions also have had energetic and influential legislatures" (Kornberg and Musolf 1970, 501). They did not say explicitly that an energetic legislature is indispensable for economic growth, but they certainly believed that an active and energetic legislature is not a drag on economic growth. Actually, early in the 1940s, Karl Polanyi indicated the indispensable role of legislatures in the process of industrialization. He found that, England was governed exclusively through parliamentary legislation. It removed restrictions on the economy and enforced the laissez faire principle in the development of capitalism (Polanyi 1975, 139). Therefore, according to this argument, an active legislature, economic growth, and the development of democracy are compatible. It is possible to achieve "a benign dialectic--each contributing

100

The NPC and China's Transition 101

positively to the other" in which "all good things go together" (Almond and Powell 1978, 371).

In contrast, the so-called conservative legislature hypothesis argues that legislatures, because of their responsiveness to provincial and conservative constituency interests, "typically obstructed economic reforms" in the developing countries (Olson and Mezey 1991, 5). As Robert Packenham argued, "Strengthening legislatures in developing countries would, in most cases, probably impede the capacity for change that is often crucial for 'modernization' and economic development" (Kornberg and Musolf 1970). This conclusion is largely based on the observations of newly emerging nations in the process of modernization. Within a compressed temporal framework, it has become impossible for the latecomers to pursue all desirable goals simultaneously. They have had to prioritize--to pursue the chief goal at the expense of some less urgent issues. It can be noted that Bismarck believed that the "empty talks in the parliament" obstructed development, while the "iron and blood" way led to economic development. The Meiji Restoration restructured the Japanese politico-economic system in the image of the Bismarckian model. As a result, today's model of the Japanese developmental state is "under the rubric of the Meiji-Bismarckian pattern of development" (Johnson 1995, 12).

In Japan and those countries that followed the Japanese model, an assertive legislature was generally believed to undermine the state capacity and retard economic development. As a result, the legislatures were suppressed during the early stage of development (Haggard 1990; Johnson 1982; Wade 1990; Deyo 1987; *In Depth* 1993). Consequently, a widely accepted argument is that legislatures, especially sub-national ones, are often long on building democracy but short on expanding economic development. As many East Asian specialists have indicated, the developmental state theory does not see legislative development to be a part of the process of economic transition.

For a long time, in communist studies (which were dominated by Sovietology), the communist system was characterized as a party-state. A "partocracy" is "a hierarchical system of absolute political, economic, and ideological power, with the wielding of that power by one party.... In this one party legislature, controlling and administrative-proprietary functions are merged." "[T]he prerogatives of legislative power rest solely in the Party Central Committee" (Avtorkhanov 1966, 376, 231). Under this "totalitarian model," the legislatures in China as well as in other

102 *The Dual Developmental State*

Communist countries were described as a "transmission belt" and "rubber stamp" under the tight control of the Party (Nelson and White 1982, 1-2).

Clearly, against the big backdrop of either the East Asian developmental state or of Communist party-state, it is quite amazing to see the recent legislative development in China. In the past two decades, this phenomenon, unusual for most countries in transition, occurred in China: rapid economic change under the auspices of an authoritarian party-state has generated a hospitable environment for legislative development. The NPC and People's Congresses (PCs) at the local level have come out of the prior decay as a big winner in the twenty-year course of marketization and regime change. They have become better institutionalized and more assertive in using their power. As the first plenary meeting of the 9th NPC held in 1998 illustrated, the NPC has already become a center for power redistribution and policy debate; to get a position there can not be taken for granted and high-level leaders have had to fight for it. At the same time, an incremental process of institutionalization has evolved in the PCs at the local levels; most importantly, at the provincial level.

In this chapter, I will first relate the dynamics of the Chinese legislative development to the fundamental economic transition being undertaken in China. Second, I will discuss the scholarly evaluation of this relationship and the process of NPC's institutional development. Then I will explain the strategy the NPC employed to win the goodwill of other political institutions, especially of the Communist Party of China (CPC). I will examine how, given the constraints of the power structure and the developmental state, the NPC pursued the network strategy in its institutional development. Third, I will discuss how to assess the current state of NPC political status in Chinese political system vis-à-vis other power players. I will introduce an interdependence model to assess the power relationship between the NPC and other institutions. Based on a theoretical discussion of networks, I will argue, the NPC has become an integral part of the power grid in Chinese politics without forming a relationship either of domination or confrontation with the CPC.

Evolution of the System of the People's Congresses

The evolution of the PC system as a whole can be divided into three stages: First, the early development of ideas and the experimental practice of a system of PCs. Inspired by the Russian Soviet system, the Chinese

The NPC and China's Transition   103

Communists developed and implemented in "liberated regions" their own ideas for the people's conventions of delegates. The second stage was the establishment and suspension of the system of PCs. In January 1953, the central government decided first to hold elections for PCs at the village, county and provincial levels and then to hold their first NPC.

In September 1954, after the PCs at all sub-national levels were elected, the NPC was held in Beijing. In this conference, a new Constitution, *The Organic Law of the NPC of the PRC, The Organic Law of Local PCs and Local People's Governments of the PRC* were adopted. The PC system was established in China. At that time, the legislative authority of the NPC was more or less respected. A division of labor among the Party, State Council and the transitional legislature, the CPPCC (Chinese People's Political Consultative Conference), existed (Harmrin and Zhao 1995, 154). Later the Party Central Committee centralized power and put governmental affairs under its direct control.

In June 18, 1958, the CPC introduced another document, *Instruction on Establishing Groups for Financing and the Economy, Political and Legal Affairs, Foreign Affairs, Science and Technology, and Culture and Education,* in which the principle of "no distinction between the Party and the government" was endorsed for the first time. The Party directly dictated and commanded the government. The government also turned into an executive organ for the Party rather than the PC. This leadership system was copied at all levels, while the legislative branch was ignored (Wu and Liu 1991, 44).

Under the 1954 Constitution, the NPC was the sole legislative organ making laws in China, the only exception being that the autonomous regions of nationalities had the power to pass decrees for self-government. This legislative monopoly lasted for a quarter of a century. But even the NPC as the sole legislative organ did not pass many laws. For example, from 1957-1976 only one resolution on agricultural development and the 1975 Constitution were passed by the NPC. The autonomous regions of nationalities also passed few decrees. Meanwhile, the decrees from the State Council and ministries were less than during the first seven years after the founding of the PRC. In sum, China was ruled more by party policies and personal instructions than by laws and administrative degrees (*Zhongguo Falu* 1989, 93). At the subnational level, the PCs did not have Standing Committees (SCs) and their Plenary Sessions were rare (usually once a year) and very short (no longer than a week). The local governments took responsibility for conducting elections and preparing

104   *The Dual Developmental State*

meetings for the PCs. In practice, the government was both the executive organ and standing committee for the PCs.

Following the Cultural Revolution, the NPC did not meet from 1966 until 1975; the PPCs did not resume meetings until 1977. In September 1968, all 29 provincial units established "Revolutionary Committees," that merged all powers of the Party, government, army, enterprises, services, and mass organizations. The Party Committees and "Revolutionary Committees" at all levels kept two nameplates but shared the same personnel. It became standard in later years for "all important documents concerning government affairs at the national level to be issued to the country under the name of both the CPC Central Committee and the State Council, or sometimes under the name of just the center" (Wu and Liu 1991, 47). The 1975 Constitution clearly stated that "Revolutionary Committees" at all levels were both the executive organs and standing committees for the PCs.

The next stage in evolution of the PC system came after Mao's death and after the Cultural Revolution ended. In 1977, the NPC and the PPCs were re-institutionalized. On October 15, 1977, the CPC Central Committee decided to hold the Fifth NPC in the Spring of 1978 and asked all provinces first to hold their PPCs meetings in order to select deputies for the NPC. The "Revolutionary Committees" were abolished. In July 1, 1979, the Fifth NPC passed a resolution on revising the constitution. In accordance to this resolution, *Election Laws of NPC and Local PCs of the PRC, The Organic Law of Local PCs and Local People's Governments of the PRC* were passed and the PCs were established at all levels. In 1982, a new Constitution was made, which further institutionalized the powers of the PCs.

These landmark laws symbolized a new stage for the PCs. After more than one decade of development, the Chinese political system had become more differentiated. The legislative system in China had changed from a system of legislative monopoly by the NPC to a plural, multi-tiered system. Within it were these actors: the NPC and its SC that passed the most important laws for the whole nation; the State Council at the central level that was able to pass executive decrees and statutes; 31 PPCs and their Standing Committees; 27 PCs of provincial capital municipalities; 30 autonomous prefectures; 123 autonomous counties; more than a dozen of bigger cities and some SEZs. All of them are able to enact local statutes. Autonomous regions had to have their local statutes and specific regulations approved by the NPC before implementation. Provincial capital cities and some larger cities had only "semi-legislative power" because local statutes adopted by them had to be confirmed by the PPC Standing Committees (PPCSC). All local statutes were recorded with the NPC and the State Council. Up to the mid-Nineties, There were more than 3.5 million deputies of PCs at all levels (2,978 NPC deputies; 3,498,833 deputies at the sub-national level). There was one people's deputy for every 340 Chinese citizen (*PD* Feb. 13, 1995).

Dynamics for Legislative Activism in Chinese Development

Parliamentarianism was introduced to China during the late years of the Qing Dynasty and was tried by Nationalists in the Republican era. Because of its association with political chaos, corruption, and Western colonialism, it was stigmatized. Clearly Chinese history provides little in the way of a democratic legacy to inspire the institutionalization of legislatures in the 1980s.

There are three distinct explanations for the evolution of long-term legislative development during the past two decades. Firstly, some scholars attribute the development to the spontaneous democratic impulse in the Chinese political landscape. They viewed it as an integral part of China's process of legalization that has fostered people's democratic rights (*Quanguo Renda* 1994; Liu, et al., 1992, 286-300). Some scholars living outside of China acknowledge this democratic dimension.[1] The second group of scholars views the legislative development as a side-effect of a tactical maneuver by the Chinese leadership in a power struggle with its opponents. Some authors suspect that Deng Xiaoping actually used the system of PCs to build a coalition enabling him to win power from Hua Guofeng and later to ostracize his opponents (Solinger 1982; Shirk 1993, 149,150-151; Shirk in Lin and Robinson 1994, 23-57). Arthur Ding (1994) argues: "The CPC attitude toward the PCs, particularly the NPC, has been consistent since the implementation of the reform policy.... These powers (given to the deputies), however, can only be implemented through the system of hierarchic bureaucratic control." Although the congresses are expanding their activities in making economic laws, their other powers such as supervision and foreign affairs have become routine formalities (Ding 1994, 33).

However, if political power struggle is the only reason for establishing the PCs and expanding their roles, then the re-institutionalization process

106   *The Dual Developmental State*

after 1979 would have lost momentum as Deng ascended to dominance in Chinese politics. However, the development of the PCs has not followed the same pattern of their predecessors in 1960s. The important reason for this divergence is explained by the fact that Mao and Deng adopted two different economic development strategies with the market impulse having carried the institutionalization and power expansion of PCs further in the case of Deng. This then leads to the third explanation for the dynamics of legislative development in China.

The third explanation treats the legislative development as an integral part of market reform's package, namely as an accommodative institutional adjustment to serve the demands of marketization. As China's developmental strategy gradually shifted from a mobilization regime to the developmental state model, the growth of a market economy has required the institutionalization of the PCs. In the re-establishment and its later re-institutionalization, the economic impulse has become, if not the sole dynamic, the most important agent of change, or catalyst, to set the PCs onto a new path of development, different from the one under Mao.

In the late 1970s, three factors were immediately responsible for triggering the changes of the NPC and local PCs: First, the Cultural Revolution syndrome. There is no need to lay out once again its disastrous impact on every aspect of the Chinese body politic and society. The Constitution was trashed, the President and NPC Chairman Liu Shaoqi was physically attacked and left to die in prison. Deng Xiaoping was sent to the countryside for "reeducation through labor," 60 of 115 Third NPCSC members were accused of being "special agents," "traitors," "reactionaries," "revisionists," and "capitalist roaders," among them being NPC Chairman Zhu De and Vice-chairman Peng Zhen (Yuan 1994, 502). As victims of the Cultural Revolution, Deng Xiaoping and Peng Zhen were determined to prevent such an event from happening again. The ruling elite came to this consensus: The Cultural Revolution resulted from the destruction of democratic practices within the Party and state institutions. For the elite's own self-interest, democratic practices should be institutionalized and legalized (Wang et al, 1998). Second, the dismal Chinese economy was on the brink of collapse. To restore China's economy, Deng, after he returned to the central stage of politics, called for the creation of more laws. For the purpose of serving economic change, the NPC needed to be strengthened. Third, the political and economic crises depleted people's faith, trust and confidence in the Communist system and caused a crisis of legitimacy for the CPC. The CPC needed a democratic

The NPC and China's Transition 107

mechanism to provide support for the regime. As the CPC started to share responsibility, functions, and power with other state institutions, the old-style Stalinist system turned into a "consultative authoritarianism" or "fragmented authoritarianism" (Lieberthal 1995). As a result, the need by the CPC and the government for legitimation, as well as the social dynamics favoring economic marketization provided momentum for the early initiation of institutionalization. Certainly, a clear pattern has formed over the last twenty years: Every fundamental move in China's economy has prepared a new stage for legislative development. The pursuit of economic development has provided sustainable dynamics for the institutionalization of the PCs at various levels.

Deng and other Chinese top leaders, in the early years of legislative development--seeking to find remedies for China's political and economic problems--called on the PCs to make a contribution by playing two important roles: First, enact more laws for market creation and economic development. Second, supervise the government and the judicial system to keep the state competent and prevent it from degenerating into a predatory state. For Deng (1983, 322), "to improve the multi-level system of PCs" was regarded as a way to prevent the over-concentration of power. The power of the PCs to supervise the government, the court system, and the procuratorial system was a safeguard against irrational behavior and policies (e.g., the Cultural Revolution) in politics. An important speech by Deng in 1978 ushered in the policies of the Third Plenum of the 11th Congress and later became a guiding document for the development of legislatures and legislative work. In this speech, Deng (1983, 157-158) stated:

> To ensure a people's democracy, we must strengthen our legal system. Democracy has to be institutionalized and written into law, so as to make sure that institutions and laws do not change whenever the leadership changes, or whenever the leaders change their views or shift the focus of their attention. The trouble now is that our legal system is incomplete, with many laws yet to be enacted. Very often, what leaders say is taken as the law and anyone who disagrees is called a law-breaker. These kinds of laws change whenever a leader's view changes. So we must concentrate on enacting criminal and civil codes, procedural laws and other necessary laws concerning factories, people's communes, forests, grasslands and environmental protection, as well as labor laws and a law on investment by foreigners.

108 *The Dual Developmental State*

For meeting the challenges of the economy, Deng argued for more economic laws: "the relations between one enterprise and another, between enterprises and the state, between enterprises and individuals, and so on should also be defined by law, and many of the contradictions between them should be resolved by law." To make all these laws at the same time posed a formidable task for the state. Deng (1983, 157-158) suggested decentralization and local experiment as solutions:

> There is a lot of legislative work to do, and we do not have enough trained people. Therefore, legal provisions will have to be less than perfect to start with, then gradually improved upon. Some laws and statutes can be tried out in particular localities and later enacted nationally after the experience has been evaluated and improvements have been made. Individual legal provisions can be revised or supplemented one at a time, as necessary; there is no need to wait for a comprehensive revision of an entire body of law. In short, it is better to have some laws than none, and better to have them sooner than later. Moreover, we should intensify our study of international law.

The ensuing landmark Third Plenum of the 11th Party's Congress recognized that too much centralization and too little democracy were serious problems haunting the system. It called for improving the democracy within the party and guaranteeing people's rights to motivate people for socialist construction, to decentralize power to local governments and enterprises, to encourage and utilize their incentive for modernization, and to institutionalize and legalize a people's democracy in order to make this system and law stable, continuous, and authoritative. These important policy changes widened the possibilities for the development of the PCs.

In 1984, the CPC passed *The Resolution on Economic Reforms* in which "the planned commodity economy" became the blueprint for economic reforms. The start of urban reforms and a planned economy with market regulations prompted a new round of reforms for the PCs. The following Seventh Five-Year Plan called for more economic laws to construct a "relatively sound system of economic law" and urged the legislative bodies to change from a "retirement house for the old cadres" into a "working organ." Consequently, the PCs accelerated the making of laws, especially economic laws. More special committees were gradually established, the restrictions upon the municipal PCs of the provincial capitals and "larger cities" to make local statutes were further loosened, and a new generation of delegates replaced aging members within the congresses.

In 1987, as the economic reforms moved further toward establishing a "socialist commodity economy," Deng realized that "political reform and economic reform are reciprocal, and dependent on each other. They should be well coordinated. There surely will be a dead-end for the economic reform unless the political reform keeps up" (Hamrin and Zhao 1995, 139-140).

Given the green light by Deng, the 13th Party Congress adopted a resolution on political reforms. According to this resolution, the party, government, and legislature were to have different powers and functions under the principle of "separating the party from the government." The PCs as China's fundamental political system needed to be emphasized, and the legislative powers of the NPC and sub-national PCs respected. They were to have more capacity to supervise the government. The functions and roles of the SCs at all levels were perfected; their role as a rubber stamp was changed. To widen socialist democracy, elections became more democratic, and the decentralization of power was granted (Zhao 1987, 37). The report stated:

> The system of PCs is the fundamental system of government in China. In recent years the People's Congresses at various levels have made much progress in their work. In the years ahead, they and their SCs should continue to improve the way they function and to strengthen their work of legislation and supervision through law. They should maintain closer contact with the people to be better able to represent them and be supervised by them. (Zhao 1987, 42)

The Chinese leadership found the system of PCs to be the only available institution for resisting the Western-type democracy and therefore emphasized the urgency of improving the PCs upon which a "Chinese democracy" hinged. However, the word "democracy" in China is a code term and could not provide a clear vision for the development of the PPCs.

A new opportunity for the PCs to resume momentum came in 1992 when Deng had his Southern tour and the Party endorsed a market economy. In 1993, the CPC passed "The Decision of the CPC Central Committee on Some Issues Concerning the Establishment of a Socialist Market Economic Structure" and wrote the "socialist market economy" into the constitutions of the Party and the country. The PCs had an unprecedented opportunity for expanding their roles and autonomy, for

110　*The Dual Developmental State*

they were expected by the Party leadership to pass more laws that served to institute a market economy and to use their supervisory power more aggressively to control corruption. In the following years, their expanding role in building a market economy has been reflected in an explosion of supervisory and legislative activities.

As the Chinese economy changed further, the market impulse has been a sustained driving force for the expanding legislative power. Since 1992 the entire Party and the PCs have wholeheartedly endorsed the "socialist market economy" as its transformative role has gained new momentum. As Qiao Shi (1994, 3), Chairman of NPCSC, stated in 1994:

> To develop a socialist market economy sets a higher demand on the construction of laws. The establishment and improvement of socialist market economy require guidance, regulation and safeguard from a well-operated legal system....To achieve this goal, the first thing must be to speed up legislation, to speed up the making of laws concerning the market economy....The local PCs and their SCs that enjoy the authority to make local laws shall facilitate their local legislation in accordance to their own specific situations and demands arising from reform and construction in order to complement the legal system of a socialist market economy.

One top official of the NPC related legislation and supervision, the two major functions of the PCs, to the economic transformation in China: In terms of legislation, its focus was to help establish a legal framework for the market economy by speeding up legislation. The laws were used to "guide, facilitate, and safeguard" the smooth progress to a market economy. There was also a need to supervise the market economy. For example, there was a need to supervise the implementation of laws directly affecting economic development. Controlling corruption and maintaining an honest government are necessary conditions and important safeguards for a market economy (*Quanguo Renda* 1994, 3-4).

To capitalize on the new opportunity of the developing market economy, the PCs at both the national and provincial levels organized conferences to explore the best ways to become involved in the economic transition. For example, from August 16 to 19, 1993, the Hebei PPC organized a seminar concerning the relationship between a market economy and legislative work. There was an exploration of new strategies that the local legislatures could "adapt to, obey, and use to serve the market economy" (*Zhongguo Falu* 1994, 218). One month later, the NPC and Guangdong PPCSC also organized a five day conference with the central theme the relationship between a market economy and the work of the PCs. To a large extent, during the last 15 years, especially in the recent five years, the legislatures in China have taken as their central task the following of guidelines that would have them serve the economy by becoming involved in the economic transformation. In return, the legislatures' attention to market economy has provided opportunities for their organizational development and the expansion of their power.

The necessity for involving the PCs in the marketization process has been rooted in the Chinese leaders' perception of the weakness and negative impact of a market economy. While recognizing the merit of a market economy, the Chinese leaders and parliamentary scholars believe that it has several inherent weaknesses and negative consequences. They have embraced these beliefs: Markets cannot occur spontaneously; a market economy is an economy ruled by law and has to rely on a legal framework to survive. Therefore, if there are no legal statutes to guide, regulate, safeguard, and restrict the actors and their behaviors in the market and to maintain the normal order of the market, there will be no real market economy (*Quanguo Renda* 1994, 41).

As one official of the NPC argued, a market economy inevitably brings a series of negative consequences, such as "monopoly behaviors in the market, especially by a single company, local and regional protectionism, a decline of the production of public goods, counterfeit products and cheating in trade, the waste of public resources, environmental pollution and ecological deterioration, a widening income gap, etc." (*Quanguo Renda* 1994, 60, 46, 107). If these problems get out of control, they are going to harm the construction of a market economy and threaten the fundamental legitimacy of the CPC rule. Therefore, the state has to step in.

A market economy is an economy ruled by law. For China, to create markets means the creation of laws, norms, rules, and institutions. To a large extent, they fall within the jurisdiction of the legislatures. Besides, the failure of the command economy discredited the belief that a central planner is capable of solving problems in an economy. A market economy implies that there be a dispersion of decision-making centers. In other words, the marketization process is often simultaneously accompanied by decentralization, deconcentration, devolution, and delegation of powers. As decentralization happens, the local legislatures take on the responsibility to help develop markets and create a sound market society within its own

112   *The Dual Developmental State*

region. Furthermore, when the government has to give up some old functions and transform some others to serve the market economy, its optimal goal is to make itself smaller, more efficient, and less corrupt so that it can better steer the economic development. As an institution relatively closer to the common people than other state institutions and as an institution without influence over special economic interests and activities, local legislatures may be the best instruments within the current Communist political structure to facilitate an adjustment of the relationship between the government and the economy, to prevent the government from becoming predatory upon the economy, and to realize the political potential of a market economy as a means for popular control (Lindblom 1977, part 4)). Finally, local legislatures have the authority to supervise the courts and procurators in establishing a new legal order for the market economy. All these developments highlight the indispensable role played by the legislatures in transforming the Chinese economy into a market economy.

The NPC: Institution and Power

The 1st NPC convened in September of 1954, the new 9th NPC in March of 1998. During the golden years of the 1st NPC, the constitutional foundation for the Communist republic was laid down and some real work for the legalization, and institutionalization of the NPC was done. Unfortunately, soon the Great Leap Forward and the Cultural Revolution paralyzed the NPC, and it did not meet for almost eight years. The 4th NPC only met once in secret prior to 1975. At that time, the CPC relied more on its own control system fused with the government, the army and even the mass organizations for mobilization, legitimation, and governing. Even after entering the 1980s, it was reasonable to view the sporadic NPC meetings as a rubber stamp for the CPC. "The Party proposes, the NPC disposes" (Gasper 1982, 162). As another popular saying goes, "The Party waves a hand to order, the government uses a hand to work, and the NPC raises a hand to pass."[2] The NPC was only one of the insignificant junior partners infrequently being used to support the highly centralized Chinese party-state. Thus, the image of a rubber stamp had been in place for decades. The NPC carries this stigma to this day, partly owing to Western cold war propaganda.

Over the past two decades, parliamentary scholars and China specialists have observed fundamental changes within the NPC and its

The NPC and China's Transition   113

institutional environment. The development of the NPC began early in 1980 when Peng Zhen, Peng Chong, Xi Zhongxun and Yang Shangkun were elected NPC Vice Chairmen and became dynamos who jump-started the process of NPC's institutionalization. Peng Zhen took de facto control of the NPC long before he became the NPC Chairman. Despite being miscast by the Western media as an arch-conservative leader, Peng put his tremendous efforts to build the NPC under the banners of legalization and institutionalization made the biggest contribution to this institution. Under his leadership the NPC passed seven important laws in 1979 and a new constitution in 1982. These documents together laid down a solid foundation and secured an important role for the NPC. They guarantee it the status as the supreme power in China, while leave a great deal of room for the expansion of its power. It is not inappropriate to view Peng Zhen as the chief architect of the Chinese legislative and legal development, and "the major founder of [China's] socialist legal system" (*PD*, April 29, 1997).

Meanwhile, leaders and ordinary deputies started talking about democracy enthusiastically, using their democratic rights aggressively on the floor. Many of Deng's supporters, who were recently rehabilitated and put in the NPCSC, used the NPC as a forum to discredit the "whateverists" who stubbornly blocked Deng's fundamental reforms. As one Hong Kong deputy observed: "When the Whateverists were still in power, the pressure from the people's deputies was needed to push them back" (Wu 1990, 77). Li Ruihuan, then a deputy from Beijing, led deputies to file inquiries into the construction of Baoshan Steel and Iron Mill near Shanghai and held major leaders within the Ministry of Metallurgical Steel responsible. This huge project was criticized for being wasteful, polluting, and the result of a hasty, irrational decision. As a result, the NPC played an instrumental role in discrediting the pro-heavy industry faction within the government (The two best examples were the inquiries into the Baoshan Steel and Iron Mill and the Bohai incident) and ushered in reform-minded leaders with a pragmatic agenda (Wu 1990, 50; Solinger 1982, 1255). In 1981, deputies from Hong Kong and Macao rebelled by threatening not to vote (Wu 1990, 50, 56-57). Ordinary people used "campaigning" in large cities, particularly on university campuses, to influence and participate in politics.

As one scholar observed during this period of time: "[I]t would be an oversimplification to claim, as is sometimes done, that the NPC is merely a 'rubber-stamp' body" (Gasper 1982, 162). In her 1982 study, Dorothy Solinger (1982, 1241) observed that the NPC had started being used as the

114 *The Dual Developmental State*

center stage for policy debate and played a more active role in Chinese national politics from 1978 to 1982. The Chinese leaders used "the open forum of the NPC to address and sometimes mobilize supporters, and to make known their differences" (Solinger 1982).

In contrast to the transformative nature of Peng's tenure, the five years under Wan Li were more a period of continuation. He made his mark on the NPC by emphasizing "democratic, rational and scientific decision-making." Procedural rationalization instead of radical change was his major concern (*Guangming Ribao*, August 1, 1986). Wan Li's best opportunity to turn his tenure into a transformative one came in 1989 when the student demonstrations broke out all over China and some NPCSC members led by Hu Jiwei appealed to convene an emergency meeting to end martial law in Beijing and impeach Premier Li Peng. But he did not take the NPC as an institutional base to contest the CPC and the government. To the contrary, Hu was expelled from the NPCSC in 1990 (Hu 1993).

In his 1990 milestone study on the NPC, Kevin J. O'Brien examined the development of the NPC in the 1980s from a historical-comparative perspective (O'Brien 1990, 1994a, 1994b; O'Brien and Li 1993-94; O'Brien and Luehrmann 1998). He argued that the NPC then had "institutional reforms but no liberalization." With institutionalization, the NPC had become a helpmate but not a partner for the CPC. He concluded: "The position of the NPC on the eve of Zhao [Ziyang]'s fall [in 1989] suggested conditional steps toward rationalization and inclusion, combined with continuing rejection of liberalization. Despite notable efforts to reduce capriciousness and to broaden the base of the regime, the reforms of the 1980s did little to increase political competition or to institutionalize responsiveness" (O'Brien 1990, 6).

After O'Brien, significant insights pertaining to the NPC were made by Murray Scot Tanner who characterized the Chinese legislative process as a "multi-arena" politics (Tanner 1991, 1994a, 1994b, 1995). As party control over legislative politics eroded, he argued: "Power within the law-making system, just as in the rest of the Chinese policy-making system, is fragmented among numerous individuals and organizations. The result is a legislative system whose various parts are evolving and in which consensus decision making has become increasingly difficult" (Tanner 1994b, 87). According to Tanner, the NPC had become an autonomous political turf. The leaders, with their expertise and interests, regarded the

NPC their privileged domain and acted more autonomously. Other leaders in the Party and government for the most part respected their turf.

Qiao Shi, ranked No. 3 in the Standing Committee of the CPC Politburo, was elected the NPC Chairman in 1993. His entrance into the NPC and his advocacy for the rule of law were expected to strengthen the NPC's autonomy. At the same time, Tian Jiyun, ranked No. 10 and once a viable candidate for premiership, became the First Vice Chairman to supervise the everyday operation of the NPC. The choice of Qiao and Tian for its leadership greatly elevated the political standing of the NPC. Their high profile and the bold style of Tian aroused much speculation about its expanding role.

For a time, the "NPC faction" was taken as a major counterbalance to the Jiang (Zemin)-Li (Peng) axis. In fact, Qiao did not challenge Jiang, but he left the "rule of law" slogan as the most visible legacy from the 8th NPC. Starting from 1993, "rule of law" was introduced into the discussion on the establishment of a market economy in the PCs (*Quanguo Renda* 1994). This consensus was formed within the circle of the PCs: "A market economy demonstrates social rules through laws, leading and regulating social behavior by legal authority. In essence, a market economy is an economy under the rule of law" (*PD*, March 19, 1994). Qiao called on the lawmakers at different levels to work hard to write and pass laws for the emerging market economy.

Compared to old concepts of legalization and rule by law, which emphasize law as a tool for the ruler, the rule of law was a significant feature of the move to a more democratic China. Today, "rule of law" and "a state under the rule of law" are the major themes of the latest and 9th NPC meeting held in 1997. The working report of the NPCSC both began and ended with "working hard to push on the rule of law and building a state under the rule of law." Curiously, the newly elected NPC Chairman Li Peng entitled his inauguration speech with "Work Hard to Strengthen the Socialist Democracy and Legal System, and Push for the Rule of Law." If where you sit determines what you stand for, his change of tune also indicates the autonomous interest and institutional importance of the NPC.

In many ways, the passing of the baton from Qiao Shi to Li Peng was significant to the NPC as an institution. First, Qiao Shi's full retirement to a private citizen was taken as Qiao's last swan song, for it constituted a precedent that made it unthinkable that Jiang Zemin or Li Peng could stay on after their five year terms. Second, that the No. 2 leader Li Peng with three CPC Politburo members stayed in the NPC certainly enhanced its

116 *The Dual Developmental State*

political standing. Since the new premier Zhu Rongji was ranked No. 3 according to the party hierarchy, it solved the old problem the NPC had had in supervising the government.

Three important events caused unexpected repercussions pertaining to the institutional development of the NPC and local People's Congresses. First, in the late 1970s, a large number of old cadres who lost power during the Cultural Revolution were rehabilitated and returned to work. Among them were some of the most experienced leaders who once worked in the NPC even though many cadres who were no better than dead wood were also sent to the NPC and local PCs.

From 1982 to 1986, a "retirement policy" was gradually introduced and then strictly enforced. A two-term limitation upon most key positions was written into the Constitution. It caused the second wave of veteran leaders to leave for the legislative branch. For a time, the NPC and local PCs offered positions to those leaders who were kicked upstairs to the second front. The really powerful party chiefs often chose to stay in the CPC Advisory Committees at various levels before their full retirement. But after the 14th National Party's Congress abolished the system of advisory committees in 1992, the NPC and local PCs became the last institution within which elderly politicians were able to retain their formal power in Chinese politics. After the 1992-93 elections, the average quality of personnel was greatly improved. Thus, three policy changes outside of the legislatures kept sending the Standing Committees of PCs younger political entrepreneurs with a better education and a higher political standing in the Communist apparatus. Eventually, these leaders generated endogenous dynamics for the legislative development.

The new legislative leaders and members have a personal interest in building the system of PCs into a strong institution. They wish to add new institutions to it, maintain them, expand their power, and enhance their status in Chinese politics, because the institutional interest is tantamount to their personal power and political resources. Only the institutionalization of the legislatures and the expansion of their power will save them from falling into political irrelevancy and provide an institutional channel within which they can use their power. Since the Constitution has promised considerable power to the NPC and local PCs, it is worth an effort by the legislative leaders to grasp power through the legislative bodies. This constitutional possibility was made more realistic by one of the most important assets for expressing power that the veteran leaders possessed: the informal networks. Especially during the initial stages of institutionalization, the legislative leaders did not have a high political standing in the political system when compared to the party and government leaders. The informal networks associated with leaders such as Peng Zhen and Wan Li helped the PCs win respect from other institutions. Later, as more politburo members began to sit in the NPCSC and the NPC Chairman also became a member of the CPC Politburo Standing Committee, the NPC gradually shifted its reliance on informal power resources to institutional power resources. The same thing happened at the local level.

Institutionalization of the NPC

The empowerment of the NPC and its reinstitutionalization were embodied in the 1982 Constitution. This Constitution expanded the power of the NPC, especially the power of the NPCSC. Peng Zhen once said "The state power and the fate of one billion people are entrusted to the NPC, and often to the NPCSC (when the NPC is not in session)" (*Quanguo Renda* 1990, 589). In terms of the power of the NPCSC, the 1954 Constitution listed 19 items, the 1975 Constitution had only 7, the 1978 Constitution had 13, but the 1982 Constitution listed 21 (Yuan 1994, 519).

The NPCSC, with few restrictions, is allowed to share four important powers with the NPC: (1) The NPCSC has the power to make laws (except the basic laws, such as the Constitution, criminal law, civil law and organic laws pertaining to the state's structure) and to revise or add some articles to the basic laws; (2) The NPC and the NPCSC share the power to supervise the implementation of the constitution and other laws, and to interpret them (to some extent, this is judicial review as practiced in the United States.); (3) When the NPC is not in session, the NPCSC has the power to examine and approve the budget and any partial adjustments of the Plan for the National Economy and Social Development; (4) When the NPC is not in session, the NPCSC has power to approve the appointment or removal of minister-level officials submitted by the Premier.

The institutional change of the NPC did not follow the prescriptions of some Chinese leaders and parliamentary scholars in that it did not move towards bicameralism, become smaller, or institute political equality for all deputies (In Yan Jiaqi's words, "parliamentarization of the NPC") (O'Brien 1990: 137-139; Yan 1994, 85-89, 1995, 84-92). Instead, the NPC has become a hierarchy with concentric circles, or four chambers--the

118   *The Dual Developmental State*

Chairmen Group, the SC, Delegation Meetings, and Plenary Session. To some extent, the relationship among these four can be explained by this analogy: The Plenary Session is like a huge ship, the Delegation Meetings are numerous separate compartments, the SC its crew, the Chairmen Group the captain. Generally speaking, the Delegation Meetings generate information, lodge complaints, and represent societal demands. The Plenary Session mainly serves to legitimate the power and position of the NPCSC, the Chairmen Group and even the entire Chinese one-party regime. This happens mostly because the Chinese system does not allow for the politics of competitive parties and interest groups to exist. Outside of the system of PCs, there is no mechanism for articulating or representing the interests of Chinese society. In contrast, the NPCSC is the place where there is an aggregation of interests. As for decision-making, it usually takes place within the small circle of the Chairmen Group, particularly among the chairmen of Communist Party members, who form the ruling elite in Chinese political system along with the leaders in the CPC and the government.

The structure of the NPC, designed to meet the demands from society and the powerful players, is shaped by the choice-set arising from the developmental state model. Because the NPC is, in fact, differentiated into different institutions having different functions, there cannot be a general pattern of development for these institutions. In the past two decades, the institutions within the NPC have demonstrated an uneven pattern of gaining institutional maturity and expanding power.

The Plenary Session

When considering the expansion of the NPC power, the Plenary Session is a disappointment. Basically, the particular Plenary Sessions are expected by the Communist political elite to fulfill the function of representing diverse interests and creating political myths. For this reason, empowerment of ordinary deputies has never become a priority for legislative development. There are extensive limitations placed upon the power of deputies. For example, the size of the NPC decreased dramatically in the early 1980s, but stabilized at about 2,970 deputies. Thus, it has failed to decrease to a number that would be reasonable for an effective legislature. Because the NPC has not reduced to the optimum number of deputies, it is difficult to have frequent or long meetings. The power of inquiry was restricted in 1982 by increasing the minimum number of deputies. Speeches by the deputies to the Plenary Session, once allowed during the 1950s, have not been restored. Thus, the Plenary Session was named: "the dumb meeting."

Delegation meetings are organized according to regional criteria (except for the army), are scattered in different hotels throughout Beijing, and thus, separated from each other. Thirty-three delegations are further divided into more than 100 groups as cells. One Hong Kong commentator ridiculed the People's Congress as a "small group meeting" (*xiaohui*), not a "general meeting" (*dahui*). Yan Jiaqi (1994-95) calls this a "bee-hive structure." Deputies spend two-third of their time within the cells of the bee-hive, the only place where deputies have an opportunity to speak out. But more than 90% of the deputies are unable to hear what is being said. Moreover, no voting takes place or decisions are made within these cells.

Delegation meetings tend to be controlled by local party chiefs and government heads. The communication and information flow among different delegations are controlled by the Secretariat of the Plenary Session. Staff members are assigned to these delegations as clerks to record the speeches. A director of bulletins, who is often a cadre from the PPC, makes a summary. It is then signed by the leader of the delegation and sent back to the News Unit for circulation. The News Unit acts as a clearinghouse and gatekeeper to decide what is to be printed for circulation among other delegations. The oft-used standard is to suppress speeches deviating from the official policy guideline and to disseminate favorable ones. However, when the political climate is tolerant, such as in 1988, control is lessened. Consequently, the deputies have difficulty sharing their opinions with each other and difficulty forming a consensus on policy issues. Only the leaders who read special reports that are more frank can develop a broader view on national issues (Yan 1994-95).

Because of these structural limitations, the Plenary Session is a cumbersome place to use power. For example, legislative power is rarely used by the Plenary Session. Ninety percent of all laws were passed by the NPCSC (Li and Wang, 1998, 137; Zhang Sutang 1994, 26-29). But this does not mean that the Plenary Session has lost its political relevancy. Actually, its politically symbolic meaning has invited deputies, political dissidents, and ordinary people to use it to draw attention to their demands. As a result, the Plenary Session has turned more assertive inside and become more attractive to the outside. Starting in 1987, an increasing number of dissenting votes has shattered the "democracy with 3,000 yes votes vs. 0 nay" once endeared by former NPC Vice Chairman Zhou

120   *The Dual Developmental State*

Gucheng. That year, three deputies raised their hands to abstain from voting on a government work report, while on the budget vote, six deputies were against, 11 abstained. Widespread complaints against the Organic Regulation of the Villagers Committees forced the adjournment of the Plenary Session to be postponed (Hsiao 1993, 43).

In the 1988 Plenary Session, Huang Changxin, a NPCSC member and a former legislator in Taiwan, courageously raised his hand and made an impromptu speech against one pending bill awaiting final vote. He became the first deputy to "put up a rival show" in the Plenary Session (Xie 1989, 6-8). On his request, four booths were installed to protect the confidentiality of voting forms. He became the first person to use these booths for this purpose. Lively debates on important laws and policies have also become more frequent. In 1989, 274 deputies raised their hands against the legislative authorization to Shenzhen, and 805 abstained. One third of the deputies (more than 800 voted against or abstained) did not support the Three Gorges Project in 1992 (Hsiao 1993, 41).

Traditionally, deputies deferred to the personnel appointments from the Party. In 1987, this trend continued with three nominees for the cabinet receiving negative votes. In 1988, all the top leaders (including Deng Xiaoping and Wan Li) received negative votes (O'Brien 1990, 143). In 1993, Li Peng received 330 negative votes (plus 220 abstains) in his reelection as Premier. It was rumored that he was so upset, he had a heart attack and disappeared from public view for more than a month. Another nominee for State Councilor, Li Tieying, received 859 negative votes which was record high (Hsiao 1993, 41, 44; Editorial 1993, 7). In addition, the deputies also have cast negative votes against their own NPC leadership. In 1988 Zhou Gucheng's continued nomination as Vice-Chairman and Chairman for a special committee was boycotted by a large number of deputies because of his age (he was then 90). In the 1998 election, Li Peng had a lower approval rate (88.5%--2,616 yea, 200 nay, 126 abstain) from the deputies than all his predecessors. (The approval rate was 97.4% for Wan Li, and 97.6% for Qiao Shi), and also lagged far behind Tian Jiyun (who had 2,941 yea, 41 nay, 0 abstain, an approval rate of 98.6%) (Tanner 1994b, 79; O'Brien 1990, 130; *South China Morning Post*, March 17, 1998; *Mingpao*, March 18, 19, 1998).

There are several reasons for the assertiveness of the deputies in the Plenary Session including the increased quality of the deputies, the enhanced sense of democracy, and improved political environment. One major reason for the new assertiveness involves the manner in which votes are tabulated. There has been a change from voting by raising hands, to writing ballots, to finally today's electronic voting system. Since 1987 and 1989, the NPCSC and the NPC, respectively, have had electronic voting systems installed. In 1998, the whole system was upgraded. The deputies now press buttons to cast their votes, with the voting results automatically appearing on several big screens. Their confidentiality is now really protected (Hsiao 1993, 41-42; *Lianhe Zaobao*, March 5, 1998). This new technology has become an important agent for democratization.

The increased unpredictability on the NPC floor draws more news coverage and has led to an increase in the number of petitions from the public to the deputies and the Plenary Session. For example, Beijing college students volunteered to polish shoes for the deputies in 1987 to protest Premier Li's educational policy. The 1989 demonstrations at Tiananmen Square and the Signature Campaign organized by Hu Jiwei also drew international attention to the NPC. It has become a ritual for political dissidents at home or overseas to use the NPC meeting as a forum to state their demands (such as, reevaluating and reversing the verdict on the June 4th, 1989 crackdown at Tiananmen Square). In the latest 1998 Plenary Session, dramatic changes of personnel, individual appeals from wronged peasants and laid-off workers further demonstrate that the NPC has become an arena for the expression of conflicts of interest and political struggle.

The Standing Committee and the Chairmen Group

The Chairmen Group is the brain and the NPCSC is the heart of the NPC. The former controls the agenda of the NPC in that it controls what, when, and where (in the NPCSC or the Plenary Session) matters should be discussed. Even with the small Chairmen Group, not everyone has equal right. Usually the Communist Chairman and Vice-Chairmen form a Party Core Group and provide guidelines to the Communist members within the NPC.

The keystone of the NPC institution and its power is the "golden partnership" between the NPCSC Chairman and the First Vice Chairman. The strength of this partnership is often based on the political standing of the former and parliamentary skill of the latter, as well as their relationship of trust. Ye Jianying and Peng Zhen, Peng Zhen and Chen Pixian, Wan Li and Peng Chong, and Qiao Shi and Tian Jiyun are clear cases. For Li Peng, the first challenge to his role reversal was to build a partnership with his

122   *The Dual Developmental State*

First Vice-Chairman, Tian Jiyun, who once was a major competitor for Li Peng's NPC chairmanship.

In this partnership, the NPC Chairman always acts like a foreign secretary on behalf of the NPC, spending more time on maintaining relationship with other power players, particularly the Party center and the government, in order to secure an hospitable environment for its own institutional maintenance and to fight for its own turf. In contrast, the Home Secretary is the First Vice Chairman. He is the workhorse who supervises the routine operation of the NPCSC, its special committees and support staff; develops vertical relationship with the PCs at the sub-national levels, and often reads the work report on behalf of the NPCSC. To distinguish himself from other Vice Chairmen, he is often a Politburo member, the Deputy Secretary of the NPC Party Group, the former Secretary of Political and Legal Affairs for the Party, or occupies the position of either NPC General Secretary or Chairman of the Law Committee or the Legislation Work Committee.

The NPCSC benefited most from the restructuring of the power relationship in the 1980s. This can be illustrated by the following four important changes: (1) Expansion of power. As previously mentioned, the new Constitution expanded the power of the NPCSC. (2) Institution building. In 1978, the paralyzed General Bureau of the NPC was resuscitated. Starting from 1979, the Legislation Work Committee and the Nationalities Committee were established, along with five other special committees. Under the 9th NPC, a total of nine special committees exists. (3) Improvement of procedures. The drafting of procedural law for the NPCSC started in 1981. Obviously, it was treated as a priority. In 1987, this law was passed. Two years later, the procedural law for the NPC also was passed. The Rules for the NPCSC Members and Laws for the Deputies of the NPC and Local PCs were adopted in 1992 and 1993. They played a significant role in making the decision-making within the NPCSC more efficient and democratic. (4) A change in the composition of the NPCSC membership.

Because an institution is designed by and made of men, the fundamental characteristics of the NPCSC are determined by the individuals who staff it. NPCSC members have experienced several important changes that have proved beneficial to its institutionalization: (1) More members are full-timers and reside in Beijing. The 1982 Constitution bars the NPCSC members from taking positions in the executive and judicial branches. In 1987, Peng Chong required the NPC to increase its full-time positions to 70% of the membership. For the Standing Committee the requirements were for an even higher percentage (*Quanguo Renda* 1990, 612). According to Kevin J. O'Brien (1990, 149), in 1989, "each NPCSC Vice Chairman maintained a residence in the capital, most of them had no other job, and at least several reported to the Great Hall everyday. Furthermore, 60% to 80% of ordinary NPCSC members lived in Beijing and were available for SC work." In 1987, the NPCSC enlarged the size of its special committees by 60%, with 63% of its members being assigned to them. In 1988, this percentage increased to 74%, and then later to 80% (Zhang, 1993, 158-237; Liu and Chen 1992, 260). (2) They have become younger, more energetic and better educated. For example, the 1993 NPCSC election followed this principle: members older than 71 cannot stay, while new nominees, except for some non-Communist dignitaries, cannot be older than 68 (Quan 1993, 25). Because of the large number of intellectuals, the 9th NPCSC was praised by the Hong Kong media as "an intellectual-type standing committee"(*Ta Kung Pao*, March 17, 1998). (3) Their last positions before entering the NPCSC were more prestigious. More NPCSC members were former ministers, party secretaries and governors.

The various stages of the NPC evolution can be summarized with the use of an evolving metaphor: For a long time, the NPC was an inconsequential rubber-stamping mill run for and manipulated by the Party. Later, it became a theater that provided a stage for policy-debate. Gradually, as the NPC institutionalized itself, the theater's stage came to be furnished with its own props. When more political entrepreneurs committed themselves to the NPC as full-time members and more staff members were recruited, this theater turned into a temple with its own masters and monks. This temple has been presented to the people as a holy one. On the one hand, these masters and monks tend to expand their turf and assert their power; while on the other hand, the party-state needs them for some important policy changes (e.g., rapid legislation, legalization and democratization, rule of law, etc.) and regime support. As the NPC is described as the "supreme power organ," it has become a grand house in the Chinese political landscape.

Some scholars see true democratic activities taking place in this grand house. In discussing parliamentary elections and People's Congresses in China, Suzanne Ogden (1993, 238) has found that these institutions, which were designed to look democratic but were not, have changed considerably in the way they function and have shown that there is "an increasingly

124   *The Dual Developmental State*

democratic content attaching to their democratic form." Hu Shikai (1993, 3-34) also argued, because of the significant progress the NPC made in the past decade on improving representation, a "silent revolution" has taken place within the NPC, moving it to the center of the political scene and enabling it to play a key role the in decision-making process.

"Mohe" (Co-petition): Strategy for Legislative Development

The development of the NPC and local PCs was encouraged by Deng Xiaoping and other important leaders. Deng Xiaoping once said, "We on the Chinese mainland do not practice multiparty election contests, a separation of the three powers, or bicameralism. We have a single Congress, namely, the NPC. This best suits China's reality. If the policy is correct and the orientation is correct, this system has great benefits, is very conducive to the country's prosperity, and avoids many difficulties" (Cited from Zhou 1995). But catch-words were emphasized. To encourage innovation and to reduce bureaucratism, the relationships among the PCs at different levels should not copy the vertical control system of the Party and the government. To avoid "difficulties" and to support the developmental state strategy, the separation of powers and "putting a rival show" by the PCs vis-à-vis the party and the executive should not be tolerated.

The adoption of the developmental state model, or the so called soft-authoritarian system, imposed constraints upon the course of NPC institutionalization and its expansion of power. Under Deng Xiaoping's formula, which was strongly influenced by the successful experiences in other East Asian countries, the market is free, but the people are not. He regarded the state capacity as a key to his success in transforming China to a wealthy and strong nation. Thus, anything that is good for the state capacity (or his catchword, "stability") is allowed; otherwise, it is suppressed. For this reason, Deng Xiaoping insisted that China needed 50 years to transit to a national popular election (*Shierda yilai* 1988, 1365-1366, 1448-1449). The sophisticated leadership within the NPC has tried to blaze a path for its development, tailoring it according to Deng's formula.

In the terminology of institutional economics, social, political and economic activities are basically organized through two modalities: there is the bureaucracy (or hierarchy, because of its emphasis on hierarchical control to distribute resources), and there is the market (which emphasizes the autonomy and equality of actors, and the distribution of resources through contractual relationships, such as bargaining, and the exchange of resources and services). Viewing the legislative development, Deng Xiaoping tried to do away with the Stalinist bureaucratic system in China by strengthening the NPC. On the other hand, he and other leaders did not want to embrace completely a market mode of governance, because they did not like the haggling and bargaining associated with the market mode. Barred from both the bureaucratic and market mode of governance, the NPC and local PCs had to navigate through difficult political waters by means of a hybrid mode, both to satisfy the expectations from the top leadership and to achieve their own goal of institutionalization.

The expansion of the NPC's power means that there has been a re-adjustment of the power relationships in Chinese politics. In a pluralist political system, power conflicts and friction are unavoidable. In Chinese politics, there is competition and contestation, but there is not American-style power clashing and confrontation. The more important aspects of Chinese politics are the ability to minimize friction and affinity for conformity. The NPC expanded its power by supporting the regime, gathering information, facilitating market creation, and integrating the nation. The breakout of a power struggle and a final showdown often indicate the decay or crisis of a regime; it is not its normal state.

Unlike legislative development in present day Eastern Europe and many other Third World countries, China has remained successfully immune from what might be called the dilemma of legislature, a disease that paralyzes many countries. The transition of democratization and marketization often generate two conflicting impulses for legislatures: Democratization requires the empowerment of legislatures and the participation and representation of people through it, while marketization often requires that tough decisions be made by a strong and effective government that can resist societal demands, particularly those from the conservative sectors of the society (e.g., landowners, state-owned enterprises and bureaucrats). In China, the legislatures are detached from the society and are well-grounded in the ruling establishment. They have never been a parliament in the Western sense of being a representative organ on behalf of society to challenge the state. They do not even provide a forum for interest groups to work to safeguard their interests vis-à-vis the state. Instead, they have been an integral part of the state in assisting the economic transition in China. The functional peculiarity of the NPC can be

126   *The Dual Developmental State*

explained by looking at its institutional designs and its strategy for the institution building.

Notorious for its emphasis on "connections" (*guanxi*), Chinese political culture also provides a conducive environment for the network approach. Because network approach gives special importance to linkages among actors, it provides efficient, complex channels for communication, consultation, and problem solving without generating many open confrontations among the major political actors.

In the early years of its development, the NPC and the local PCs relied more on the informal network of their leaders for gathering information and expanding power. Later, the NPC leaders deliberately capitalized on their increasing importance in the political structure and turned the informal network into a formal network by weaving a set of complex linkages with the PCs at the local level as well as linking with other political actors.

The impact of the network approach on both the institution and behavior of the NPC has been tremendous. First, the NPC has a very peculiar structure when compared with other parliaments in the world. Because of the concern for internal control and efficiency, the NPC has a hierarchical structure that is divided into two levels: the Plenary Session and the SC led by the Chairmen Group and assisted by the special committees. Their relationship is guided by a democratic centralism: the Plenary Session elects the SC, but the latter controls the former. In terms of the relationship of the NPC with the local PCs, both are encouraged to be autonomous, as a looser relationship exists. Thus, the NPC does not provide leadership to the local PCs. Second, as a result of the network approach, particularism, instead of universalism, is featured in the way that the NPC uses its power and deals with other political actors. Although "the rule of law" is a slogan that provides a normative justification for the strengthening role of the NPC in political life, it would pose a potential challenge to the network approach if the NPC were to treat all political actors in a universal way. Particularism continues to impede the universal application of the Constitution and other laws. The NPC has been selective in the use of its power. It does not alienate the most powerful actors (most often the party) too much while it often targets the vulnerable ones. As is the case with other political institutions, the NPC means to use power with self-restraint. Open confrontations have been minimized. But when conflict becomes unavoidable, the NPC has always tried not to become too belligerent.

The power of the NPC does not derive from its autonomy from or its contesting with other power players. Rather, it derives more from its ability to affect what can be done, to define the themes for national debate, to decide the focus of public attention, and from its central position within the political structure, especially to provide legitimacy to the regime and a mandate to individual officials.

There are many aspects to the expansion of the function and power of the NPC: (1) Legislative effectiveness: It is difficult to argue that the NPC is still "a rubber-stamp," because the NPC and its SC have passed more than 332 laws from 1978 to March 1998 and have led China into an unprecedented "time of legislation" (A Ji 1997, 1-4; Li and Wang 1998, 131-137; *PD*, March 23, 1998). (2)Economic decision-making: The NPC is more interested in expanding its functions in economic matters than to contest and confront the core leadership. The 8th NPCSC, for example, "took speeding up economic legislation as its first task," as almost half of the 72 laws passed belong to the economic category (A Ji 1997; *Quanguo Renda* 1996; Seidman et al, 1997). Under the name of helping develop economy, the NPC always can turn a wide range of issues into development-related issues (e.g., fighting corruption) as a way to exert its influence. (3) Expanding power in the periphery: It is not completely correct to argue that there is no liberalization within the NPC system. The NPC has demonstrated a great degree of self-restraint in its own behavior of using and expanding power at the national level; for instance, the way Wan Li handled the 1989 democracy movement and the NPC dealt with Hu Jiwei Signature Incident. But the NPC had developed a very liberal attitude toward the expansion of power by the PCs at the sub-national level, and had given crucial support to these congresses when they were fighting to establish their power. The NPC had provided crucial support to the liberalization of village elections, for instance, to the PPCs in Hunan and Sichuan in their efforts to oust their governors. In 1989, a Vice Governor in Hunan was removed by the deputies. When the local leaders were reluctant to proceed with a vote of no confidence, the NPCSC sent an urgent note to the Hunan PPCSC stating that by law the people's deputies have the right to remove any leader they elected even though this official was not involved in any obvious wrong-doing nor violated any law. If the deputies lost their trust in this official, they can remove him (Zhang 1993, 796; *Hunan Nianjian 1989* 1990, 89). The political ramification of this constitutional interpretation has not been fully recognized by Chinese legal scholars. If someday a spillover process starts, it will cause a real

128   *The Dual Developmental State*

democratic revolution in China. (4) A phenomenon of mutual support between the NPC and the sub-national PCs: Facing the same political environment, they have learned strategy and institution building from each other. For example, the local PCs started the practice of reviewing officials and their work reports. The NPC has supported this practice and indicated its willingness to apply it to officials in the central government. (5) Judicial Review: The power to interpret the laws and determine the constitutionality of local laws and administrative decrees resides in the NPC and NPCSC. (6) Informational power: The NPC has changed from a non-cohesive to a cohesive institution by occupying a central position in the Chinese political system. This can been seen from its complex linkages with other political organizations. (7) Veto power: Potential resistance from the NPC and its NPCSC has imposed constraints on the power of the CPC and turned the Chinese authoritarian regime into a "semi-anticipatory democracy." In 1983, the NPCSC for the first time postponed a vote on a bill. In 1989, it first voted down a bill (Zhang Sutang 1994, 26-27). Now it takes months to pass a bill. The practice of "three readings" introduced by Li Peng is required for every important bill.

To avoid inviting too many conflicts, the Party first has changed its way of ruling and now only focuses on crucial issues, pursuing a strategy of selectivity. The Party has lessened its intervention into the everyday life of its citizens, and in many areas has receded altogether into the background of power structure. The NPC does not take this as an invitation to expand power at the cost of the Party. It simply uses power with caution and self-restraint. The Party is still always consulted and kept informed of the important activities within the NPC. Constructive suggestions and critical comments are often passed to the Party through private channels. In legislation, the NPC sends its NPCSC members and staff members to the initial discussions of the drafting stage and invites the government officials to be involved. It uses its influence during this earlier stage instead of waiting until later to reject or revise finished bills. Differences are smoothed over in this way.

In personnel appointments, the CPC always sends a list of candidates to the NPC Chairmen Group for comments. This list is then sent to the NPCSC if the Chairmen Group does not express strong reservations. If some candidate creates a major controversy among the NPCSC, the Chairmen Group will suggest that the CPC withhold the controversial candidate for a time until there is further discussion, or withdraw this candidate. The CPC usually complies to avoid the embarrassment of losing the vote. When the Premier and other heads of the judicial branch prepare their work reports for the annual NPC Plenary Session, they always send their drafts to the members of the NPC, scholars, and even ordinary citizens for the purpose of soliciting comments and criticisms. Before the work reports are formally read to the NPC, they may have been revised several times, with hundreds of changes being implemented according to the feedback they have received. For this reason, the work reports have little difficulty being accepted. The NPC also has increased its inspection of law enforcement. If problems are found, it does not publicize them through the mass media. Instead, the NPC usually writes a letter expressing its views and passes it on to the relevant ministry, urging that improvements be made. The NPC also pays great attention to its contact with the local PCs, exchanging information with them and relying on the complex network of PCs at different levels to gather information and mobilize support. To some extent, both the Party and the NPC have engaged in a win-win case: Power absent is power strengthened; power with restraint is power with weight.

Several 7th NPC members provided their insights on the "Chinese-style democracy of consultation plus voting." When asked why yes votes were always very high, a worker deputy said: "Because we have already been fully consulted. Consultation first, voting second. We vote after the consultation is completed. Certainly our support votes mean much more than the previous negative votes." Another professional deputy said: "I could not understand this conformity before. Since I was elected to the 6th and 7th NPC and have been a deputy for nine years, I also have joined in the army voting yes. Why? Because the bills, proposals, and list of candidates pending a vote have long been circulated among the deputies for discussion and comments. Good suggestions have been adopted, something needing change is changed, bills causing a great controversy are postponed, and controversial candidates are replaced. After a consensus is achieved among the diverse views, voting proceeds. The uniformity of the vote is certainly high. In my opinion, this 'democracy of consultation plus vote' is Chinese-style democracy, a real democracy" (Zhang 1992b, 228-231).

In my research trip to China in the summer of 1998, many Chinese scholars mentioned a concept to describe the interactive pattern of power: "*mohe*". Its English equivalent is "burning in" or "grinding." But according to the context in which this term is used, it indicates a continuing process of cooperation through friction and mutual adjustment.

130   *The Dual Developmental State*

Like driving a new car or running a new machine, all parts need a period of "burning in" or "grinding" in order to accommodate each other. Different parts are at variance, friction happens. But it is a process of mutual adjustment. Every part loses its inharmonious qualities and becomes smooth and flexible. Friction consequently produces cooperation rather than conflict. This concept of "*mohe*" is better translated as "co-petition," a combination of cooperation and competition.

Many important examples illustrate the pattern of "*mohe*": Peng Zhen worked arduously to help to establish the power of the NPC, but he also advised his colleagues not to run "a rival show" with the Party and the government. Wan Li indicated his willingness to use the NPC as an arena to solve the 1989 crisis, but he eventually backed down once he saw the danger of a final showdown with the Party leadership. Qiao Shi resisted the nomination of Li Peng as the NPC Chairman. He had Tian Jiyun as his preferred candidate. After difficult bargaining, Li Peng moved to the NPC, and Tian Jiyun sided with Li and formed a new alliance with him. Qiao retired in honor. Another recent example involves Jiang Zemin, who intended to bring two more Shanghai leaders (the current Party Secretary and Mayor) into the Cabinet. Anticipating strong resistance from the NPC, he relented. The NPC vote gave an unusually low approval rating to the two cabinet members Jiang transferred from Shanghai (the Minister of Education and General Procuratorate).

Several Chinese scholars I met in my trip angrily criticized the Americans for imposing a pluralist model upon the Chinese, to "use a pair of colored glasses, that is pluralism, to interpret and judge Chinese politics." One of them writing to me said: "When we handle internal politics, we emphasis harmony and compatibility, and on external relationship, we avoid hegemonism."[3] Without paying attention to democratic consultation and supervision, one cannot understand the relationship between the NPC and other political institutions. I believe they have a point. The phenomenon of "*mohe*" cannot be satisfactorily explained by either a market mode of governance (its classic example is pluralism, checks and balances) or the hierarchical mode (Stalinism is its classic example). It is related to the hybrid mode; namely, the network strategy in Chinese economic and political development. The peculiar institutional design and the conflict-averse behavior of the NPC can only be explained by this network strategy.

Although scholars engage in arguments on the NPC that arise from conflicting interpretations of its recent changes, many scholars (including

The NPC and China's Transition   131

some discussed above) tend to make this basic assumption for their research: They tend to define power as an asymmetrical relationship in which one social actor exerts greater control over other's behavior. As a result, they put the NPC in a dyadic relationship with the CPC (either domination or contestation) and use competition and contestation as a litmus test to evaluate its political power and effectiveness.

When the NPC clashes with other political institutions, the latter believe that the NPC has power; when they cannot see clashes, they believe the NPC is controlled. For this reason, some believe that the NPC's power lies in its "martyr spirit" (Yu 1995, 3). However, this frame of reference has at least two flaws: First, from Ye Jianying to Qiao Shi, the relationship between the NPC and other power players has always been stressed as being a "division of labor," not a separation of power, not "putting on a rival show." It can be noted that both Wan Li and Qiao Shi did not use the NPC as a power base to have a final showdown with the party state. Second, unlike the above-mentioned authors, Ann and Robert B. Seidman (1997) have found that a competitive election does not necessarily guarantee the elected representatives real power to make laws. Many studies show that competitive elections must produce neither liberal, developmental nor effective legislatures. Therefore, a case may be made that a more powerful and effective NPC can be built beyond the pluralistic prescription of competition and contestation.

Institutional changes within the Chinese political structure and high economic growth rate differentiate Chinese development from East European liberal strategy. By 1994, it became clear that the different strategies pursued by China and Russia for their political and economic reforms produced contrasting consequences in legislative development.

The Russian soviets were activated from "rubber stamps" into assertive political actors by the 1988 election reforms sponsored by Mr. Gorbachev. Over the next two years, competitive elections were implemented, first at the national level, and then carried out by the regional and local soviets. When Boris Yeltsin was elected Chairman, and the Parliament members owed their positions to popular mandate instead of the party, the Russian Parliament turned into the "dominant institution of the Russian political system" (Hahn 1996, 15). Some parliamentary scholars optimistically predicted that "In the former Soviet Union, parliaments have taken on much greater importance and show signs of evolving into more democratic bodies" (Copeland and Paterson 1994, 1). But soon the Russian Parliament turned against President Yeltsin and became a stronghold used by

132   *The Dual Developmental State*

the conservatives to resist his more radical market reforms. The legislatures at various levels were accused of not only being economically obstructive, but also politically conservative (Hahn 1995, 228). Yeltsin claimed, "Soviets are incompatible with democracy" (Hahn 1995, 107). The legislative-executive conflicts ended with the killing of Parliamentary members, the burning of the Parliamentary building, Yeltsin's order to abolish all national and local soviets, and the hollowing out of Russia's electoral democracy and its replacement by a psudo-democracy. Another long-term consequence was the 1993 Constitution which gave the president unprecedented power to dissolve both the parliament and the government, but restricted parliament's ability to remove the president. As Jeffrey Hahn (1995, 252, 257, 259) has observed: "Perhaps the main trend in Russian politics since 1990, nationally and locally, has been the steady tendency toward unlimited executive rule." "Conversely, the new local legislatures came increasingly to resemble the old soviets." The legitimacy and authority of these Parliaments were eroded and endangered by the backlash from the executive branches (Pei 1994, 30-31). Meantime, the Chinese legislative development lacked theatrics and has never achieved liberalization comparable to their Russian counterparts; but neither have they suffered Russian-style setbacks.

Generally speaking, the NPC in the past two decades, by following a low-profile strategy, has incrementally brought about substantial achievements: a higher institutional maturity, stronger legitimacy and efficiency, and more so than its predecessors, a greater importance placed on developing the Chinese political economy. The PCs have been recognized as the fundamental political system and have become an important part of the governing process. It is difficult to imagine that the Chinese central Party and its executives could now abolish the PCs nationwide without destroying their own legitimacy and rule. In sum, although the NPC is still distant from a parliamentary democracy, its achievements are considerable. Even though it has not attracted attention from Western observers as have the Russian soviets, it has secured a stronger mooring in the Chinese political system and society, and has positioned itself well for further organizational development.

Stimulated by different strategies, the fates of legislative development in China and Russia have differed. Russian legislatures, with more resources (especially the people's mandate by direct elections), have alienated both the executive branch and ordinary voters, and have not realized their full potential. The Chinese legislatures, with less favorable conditions, have reversed their initial structural disadvantages, secured a solid mooring in the regime and society, and achieved a greater degree of institutionalization than was the case previously. Some parliamentary scholars have suggested that a role subordinate to the executive by the new legislatures may contribute more to the legislative development and the long-term democratization (O'Brien 1994b; Hahn 1995, 237). However, the Chinese experience has gone beyond the choice between a subordinate and an unruly role. Relying on networks, the legislatures are able to align with some political actors to challenge others. With political sophistication and tactics, political entrepreneurs within the legislatures, even the local ones, are able to be assertive in using and expanding their power. The Chinese legislative branch has helped maintain the state capacity, avoiding a chronic economic crisis in the aftermath of the East European and Soviet Communist collapse that is often blamed on the dissipation of state capacity, and which is rooted in legislative activism and political opposition at all levels.

Constructive Strategy, Positive Results

This chapter moves beyond the frame of reference that views power relationships as either confrontation or domination, and views the power relationship between the NPC and other power players as a power grid, or network. This perspective has changed the nature of power relationships among the major players (the NPC, the CPC, and the government) from a relationship of dependency (or antagonistic tension when liberalization occurs) to one of interdependence. Power is defined as a combination of domination and influence. Without domination, a political actor still has room to accumulate power (Knoke 1990, 3-7). To explain why this has happened, I have examined the political environment and internal dynamics for the NPC's development.

By reviewing the milestone studies on the NPC and the tenures of different chairmen, I have discussed various images of the NPC in its various stages of evolution. I have found, despite the disagreements among these studies, a common assumption links them together: They have applied the pluralist approach to evaluate the NPC's power by focusing on competition and contestation. My study has traced the historical background to identify the salient factors for the NPC's development. Deng Xiaoping's guideline for China's reform course and his choice of the developmental state model cast a choice-set upon the Chinese legislative

134 *The Dual Developmental State*

development, and set it on the track of a hybrid mode of governance, distinguishable from both the market and hierarchical modes of governance as a way for organizing politico-economic transactions. Defined by the parameters of the hybrid mode, the institutional design of the NPC has inherited legacies from the hierarchical mode of Stalinism and has also included some qualities associated with the market mode. As a result, the NPC is characterized by a hierarchical structure internally with loose linkages to local PCs and other political institutions. The loose linkages are characterized by a mixture of competition and cooperation, autonomy and interdependence.

The institutional design of the NPC and its political environment imposed tremendous constraints upon the behavior of the NPC in its interactions with other political institutions, especially the Party and the government. Subsequently, three waves of veteran leaders moving to the NPC brought political influence and connections to this institution. The hybrid mode (the network strategy) for Chinese development, a traditional political culture of *"guanxi,"* produced a phenomenon of *"mohe"* in Chinese political life. It has presented a way of interpreting the political life of China.

My study shows why the NPC has played a unique role when compared to that generally played by legislatures in a political and economic transition. Parliaments in transitional societies easily become either a docile prey of the executive power or a bellicose challenger to it. In the former case, under a hierarchy of bureaucratic control, the hegemonic executive often hampers legislative development. Parliaments are often marginal and become either irrelevant to the economic transition or, at best, merely a junior helpmate for the executive or party-dominated state. In the latter case, under the competitive mode of pluralism, liberalized parliaments often intensify their confrontation and hostility to other power players. Political bickering and paralysis turn parliaments into bodies that obstruct economic development. The soviets under the former Soviet Union and today's Russia illustrate these two situations. China's NPC has demonstrated that, by skillfully using a network strategy, a legislature can develop connections with other power players, create a friendly environment for the expansion of its functions and power, and facilitate its institutionalization. The NPC has illustrated a very rare case in which legislative development and economic development have formed a mutually beneficial relationship, achieving major goals at the same time.

Notes

1   For example, Suzanne Ogden (1993) has argued that the existing institutions including the local PC have become increasingly democratic. Even "the spread of democratic procedures in the 1980s was not a response to popular demands but the result of the reform leadership's conclusion that greater democratization would serve well its own purposes of political reform and economic modernization." Real democratization reflected in local elections and PC institutions is an on going process. Sen Lin (1993, 37) argues, "Since the people's congress consisted of elected deputies and is deemed as the institution that embodies popular sovereignty, the increasing of its authority and power indicates the enhancement of democracy in democratic centralism."

2   Ordinary Chinese people mocked the NPC as the "forum for idle debate," "the two-hands conference" (to raise and clap hands), and the "eras of the deaf man" in the late 1970s and early 1980s. I heard these remarks in 1985 at a national conference on the function of the state in Taiyuan, Shanxi. Even in the speeches of Chinese leaders, these folklore style political comments were made.

3   From May 30 to July 23, I toured six provinces and municipalities (including Beijing, Shanghai, Sichuan, Gansu, Shenzhen, Jiangsu) and interviewed more than thirty leaders or deputies who work for the People's Congresses and more than twenty parliamentary scholars. A parliamentary scholar at Fudan University in Shanghai first drew my attention to the concept of "*mohe*". Later, two scholars working in the Shanghai Academy of Social Sciences and China Academy of Social Sciences respectively used this concept to analyze the operation of the People's Congresses, especially their external relations with the party and government. For this reason, I asked several parliamentarians about this concept and they gave me examples to support this analysis.

6 Developmentalism and the Provincial People's Congresses

Since Chinese provinces are larger than most countries and have their own regional property, their influence on the national economy is significant. Granted legislative power and located in the middle of both the hierarchical and horizontal relationships, the Provincial People's Congresses (PPCs[1]) provide a good opportunity to explore the legislative-executive and central-local relationships which may increase or decrease the state capacity and national integration, and to learn about the impact of the economic development upon political institutions. It is also important to determine whether the developments of PPCs assist the process of economic transformation, and to assess how the institutional arrangements and functions of PPCs have served the East Asian developmental state model.

In this chapter, I will first show that the institutionalization process of the PPCs has proceeded under the constraint of an economic marketization process within the context of the developmental state model. Marketization provides the dynamic for the institutional changes occurring within PPCs, and the developmental state model provides a context, shaping and structuring this process. Accordingly, the political entrepreneurs who drove the institutional development of the PPCs carefully adopted a network strategy to seek expansion of their power. Related to this, the structural design of the PPCs has been like neither the Western-type parliaments (market mode) nor Soviet-style legislatures (hierarchical mode), but instead has been a two-tier structure with a loose linkage between the two tiers. Thanks to this peculiar institutional design, the institutionalized PPCs have been actively able to apply consensual politics to facilitate market creation and maintain the developmental state strategy.

The Institutionalization of the PPCs

The PPCs, produced by indirect elections, are unicameral and very huge. Of the 30 PPCs in 1991, 25 had more members than the two houses of the

136

US Congress combined. Immediately after their re-establishment in 1979, PPCs became even larger: for example, Sichuan had 1,990 deputies. The total number of people's deputies at all levels has exceeded six million (Wu and Liu 1991, 85). Therefore, they only meet once a year, and a typical Plenary Session lasts one week. Once the central leadership realized that it was critical to improve the effectiveness of the PCs, a fundamental change in the structure and personnel of PPCs was instituted in 1984: their organizational structures were streamlined, their personnel replaced, and the plenary conference cut in size. Within their first ten years (1977-87), the total number of PPC people's deputies decreased by 36.4%, from 32,142 to 20,438. The mean size of the PPCs' changed from 1,108 people's deputies to 704.[2] Although a decrease in the number of deputies usually would lead to increased efficiency and effectiveness, the size of the PPCs basically has remained stable and has failed to return to the level of the first term. This is so because some leaders feared that further downsizing might sacrifice their representative mandate. Besides, the large size of PPCs makes it difficult for the deputies to affect the decision-making process but easier for the leaders to impose their control.

To balance representation and efficiency, Standing Committees (SCs) were set up from 1979 to 1980, followed by the Chairmen Group, and Special Committees. The sizes of the PPC Standing Committees (PPCSCs) range from 35 to 65. Their average number was 59 in 1988. Considering the vast diversity of the population and the geographic size of the different provinces, it is interesting to note that PPCs tend to be about the same size. This is even more the case for the PPCSCs. The PPCSCs are small enough to allow frequent (at least one every two months) and effective meetings, each one usually lasting from one day to a week. In one year, a PPCSC typically meets for a total of about five to seven weeks. To make it easier for the PPCSC to convene a special and urgent meeting, the number of full-time members, as well as members who live in the provincial capital city, had increased gradually from 50% to 70% of the entire body. Meanwhile, more and more SC members and Vice Chairmen are living in the provincial capital. The PPCSCs have increasingly become the most important forum for discussions and other important activities.

The core of a SC is the Chairmen Group, which consists of the Chairman, all other Vice Chairmen, and the General Secretary who supervises the routine operation of the SC and deals with important issues. The Chairmen Groups conduct regular meetings at least once a month,

138   *The Dual Developmental State*

sometimes once every two weeks. As their most important action is to set the agenda for the PPCSCs and Plenary Sessions, the Chairmen Groups are to some extent steering committees for the PPCs. The Chairmen Groups meet more frequently than the SCs but for a shorter period of time. In December 1986, Special Committees were established within the PPCs. These include political, legal affairs, financial, economic, educational, scientific, and cultural committees, among others. These committees are an integral part of state power. They have the authority to initiate, evaluate, draft, and review bills, to report their work and explain the making of laws to the SC and Plenary Session, and to process the proposals and legislative initiations from the Presidium and SC.

During the past decade, the lack of a competent staff has been a serious challenge to the PPCs' institutionalization. The PPCs also have fought hard to get new members in the face of the streamlining through downsizing of the government. In 1980, Peng Zhen requested that the PPC staff be built into a "coolie team." Those who were young, energetic, efficient, and hard-working should be recruited. Later in 1987, NPC leaders expected the PPC staff to be both a "coolie team" and an "intellectual team." As age and education were emphasized, the staff system developed rapidly and the quality of staff members improved (*Sichuansheng Renda* 1991, 31; *Quanguo Renda* 1990, 470-473). From 1979 to 1983, the staff members in 29 PPCs increased to 2,054. In five PPCs, the staff size exceeded 100, and one PPC had 120 staff members. From 1983 to 1987, the overall authorized size of the PPC staffs increased by another 1,600. All PPCs had more than 100 authorized staff members, while 11 PPCs exceeded 120, and one had 206. After 1988, the staff size of all PPCs exceeded 4,700, more than double that in 1983(Cai 1992, 411). When considered in light of their low initial size, the increase of staff members has been encouraging. Even when compared to many developing countries, the staff support in China is substantial (Cai 1992, 414-415). The major responsibility of the staff is to assist and serve three meetings: the Plenary Session, the SC meeting, and the Chairmen Group meeting. Since the Plenary Session lasts only about a week and most deputies and many SC members do not live in the provincial capital, the core leadership of the Chairmen Group and some SC members who reside in the provincial capitals have, in reality, been those who for the most part have taken advantage of the staff support.

While rules provide stability, regularity, and predictability to the operation of PPCs, their improvement has been another indication of the institutional maturity of the PPCs. In almost every aspect of their work, PPCs have their self-imposed rules and processes to follow. In 1990, there were 360 local statutes concerning the self-construction of local PCs and their SCs, accounting for 20% of the local statutes passed (*Quanguo Renda* 1992, 276-277). Again from 1992 to 1994, 115 local laws concerning the operation of the PCs were adopted, accounting for 8% of all laws passed in this period (*Zhonghua Renmin* 1995).

Unlike almost all legislatures in Western democracies, the Chinese PPC system comprises three organizations that differ in size, in the length of their meetings, in their prestige, in their ability to access resources and support staff, and in their distance from the decision-making center. In theory, the Plenary Session is the most important organization within the PPC and the highest political body within that Province. But lack of direct elections and a constituency of their own has deprived the PPC deputies of a mandate to represent various interests. If elections are indirect, mass media tightly controlled, and competitive parties and interest groups nonexistent, then there are few legal mechanisms that serve as a means of political representation and interest articulation. By default, PPCs are used for interest articulation in the Chinese political system because they attract diverse ideas current within the society and provide a forum that enables the leaders to feel the pulse of the community. They also gather information for the interest aggregation and decision-making that is accomplished elsewhere. As a result, PPCs have gradually become a hierarchical structure: The Plenary Session is for the purpose of legitimating the regime and representing various demands of the masses, and serving as a safety valve, among others. PCCs function efficiently when they accurately reflect the mood of the entire community. The SC serves as liaison between the Plenary Session and the Chairmen Group and is the most efficient part of the PPC. It is particularly responsible for interest aggregation and acts as a funnel and filter to bring together and then extract political inputs for the decision-makers, such as the Chairmen Group meeting. As for the decision-making function, it is often reserved to the Chairman and the Chairmen Group. Because the Chairman always is a member of, or sits in the Provincial Party Standing Committee meeting when he is not a member, the decision-making core is connected with the Party decision-making mechanism. The expansion of power actually has occurred more within the core of the PPCs rather than within the Plenary

140   *The Dual Developmental State*

Sessions. The "iron law of oligarchy" has not spared these so-called "people's organizations for representation."

The Change of PPC Personnel

Institutionalization and the quality of an institution are dependent on the people who staff and run the institution. The PPCs, especially their leadership and the members of the SCs, have experienced significant personnel changes since early 1980s. The Chairmen and Vice Chairmen deserve special attention, since they have occupied a crucial place in the development of PPCs.

There were 33 PPC chairmen in the 5th Congress (from 1979 to 1983) in 29 provinces. Among them, all except one (Li Jianzheng of Guangdong) were male. Only seven had a college level education (including education in the Chinese People's Anti-Japanese Military and Political College in Yanan). All the others only had a high school or middle school education. Many had only a primary school education. All of them except one had worked in more than one province. Half of them had worked in the departments or ministries at the Central government level. Almost all of them (except the chairmen in Tibet and Xinjiang) joined the CPC during 1930s or earlier. Some of them joined the army, took part in the Long March, or worked as underground Party workers. Because the Party and the government were fused in the late 1970s in most provinces, the Party Secretaries held the chairman positions in the PPCs. In some provinces, the Party Secretaries held positions in the government and the PPC at the same time.

As the Party Secretaries gave up their positions in the PPCs, many retired government and Party officials, and most of their second level officials, exited to PPCs. The 1983 elections did not extend the generational shift of personnel. The average age of the chairmen rose and the political stature of PPC leaders degenerated. In many cases this caused a leadership change even before the terms were completed. Despite the mid-term changes, there was still only one woman (Li Guiying of Yunnan) among the 46 chairmen, only seven had a college education, and more leaders than the previous group of chairmen had experience in only one province (10 out of 46), or no experience in the agencies at the central government level (37 out of 46). The collective profile of PPC chairmen during this term tended to be that of older CPC veterans who were less

Developmentalism and the PPCs 141

educated, less experienced in Beijing and central ministries, more parochial, rich in local and party politics, more generalist, and lower in political stature. The image of "the house of old men" was formed during this period of time. PPCs all over the country had a severe crisis in leadership and personnel. Senile leaders and deputies were a fixture of the PPCs. Announcement of eulogies became one of their major activities. They were paralyzed by "a senile atrophy."

The rejuvenation of the PPC leadership started in 1985: sixteen PPC Chairmen among 29 were replaced, and a large number of Vice Chairmen and SC members stepped down. In 1986, the candidates for positions in the PCs were expected to be able to stay on for at least one term before meeting the retirement age. To retain the continuity of personnel, some leaders were allowed to complete two terms (*Sichuansheng Renda* 1991, 319). As a result, the 7th PPC Congresses that were constituted in 1988 maintained continuity with the 1985-86 Congresses that were depleted by their large turnovers. Of the 30 Chairmen, 14 were re-elected, 6 were promoted from the position of Vice Chairman, and 10 were newly elected, including those in Hainan, a new province established in 1988. It is important to note that among these ten new elected Chairmen, five were re-elected the following term. Almost all of them were still active and were able to fulfil their terms.

The 1993 elections of the PPCs brought dramatic changes to the PPC chairmanship. Of 30 Chairmen, 8 were re-elected, one was promoted from the Vice Chairman position, and 21 were newly elected. The only woman holding that office dropped out, and no other female was promoted to that position. Among these 21 new leaders, 10 had a college education, 4 once were senior engineers or university professors, 15 had experiences in the positions of Party Secretary and/or Governor, 4 as Deputy Secretary, one as Deputy Mayor, and 8 were also Party Secretaries and 4 were Deputy Secretaries at the same time. In comparison to previous groups, this group was better educated and had a higher status in the political system. They were also younger. Almost all of them were born in the 1930s and joined the Party after 1949. They lacked experience in the army, but moved up through administrative and party bureaucracies. As in the government, the PPCs leadership had shifted from revolutionary cadre to party technocrats (Lee 1991; Li and White 1988; Zang 1991).

Like the Chairmen, the Vice Chairmen as a whole have undergone important changes over the past twenty years. In the early 1980s, some

142   *The Dual Developmental State*

Vice Chairmen were former Vice Governors but most held an equivalent rank in the bureaucracy and were concurrently the members of the Standing Committee of the Provincial Party Committee who were kicked upstairs. Since most of the Chairmen were former Vice Governors who came to the PPCs as their last stop before full retirement, the Vice Chairman position did not have much appeal to aging Vice Governors who were near retirement. After 1986, the situation changed. The central Party and NPC leadership assigned to the PPCs many younger, more physically energetic and intellectually competent leaders who were at the height of their political importance. Of the Vice Chairmen 114 or 46.9% were re-elected in 1988. This high retention rate was a consequence of the 1984-86 changes. In addition, before becoming Vice Chairmen in the PPCs, 58 of them were Vice Governors, 7 Deputy Party Secretaries, and 11 were Party Secretaries for Political and Legal Affairs. After the 1993 elections, this trend of occupying two position concurrently continued. From the 1993 class of 241 Vice Chairmen, 47 were former Vice Governors, 9 Deputy Party Secretaries, and 12 Party Secretaries for Political and Legal Affairs. Many of them became the First Vice Chairmen of the PPCSCs and took responsibility for running the PPC system. The "golden partnerships" at the national level could also be found at the provincial level. For example, Vice Chairmen Bai Shangwu of Sichuan, Zhang Zhigang of Hebei, Xie Yong of Heilongjiang, and Yuan Qitong of Fujian were such crucial figures. Because of the large influx of ambitious political leaders into the PPCs in the late 1980s and early 1990s, PPCs have been driven by their political activism, evolving from "retirement homes" into "power houses" of sub-national politics.

From the 1988 class to the 1993 class of Vice Chairmen, there were several clear trends: First, the class of 1993 was younger than all previous classes. Its average age was 62.15, more than three years younger than that of the previous PPCs (which was 65.49). Since the deadline for their retirement was often 65, it meant that all of them could fulfill at least one term before meeting the retirement age. Second, more well-educated people had been recruited into the leadership of the PPCs. More than half of the Vice Chairmen in the class of 1993 had a college level education. Of these, many had a post-graduate education. Some even studied abroad, got their doctoral degrees there, and held senior professional titles. Third, a fair number of Vice Chairmen had been promoted through the internal system of PCs and, as a result, an independent system for promotion has emerged. Fourth, the percentage of Communist Vice Chairmen increased while the non-communist vice-chairmen decreased, dropping from 80 (32.92%) in 1988 to 62 (25.73%) in 1993.

The official propaganda declares that the development of the PCs symbolizes the achievement of the Chinese socialist democracy. However when analyzing the makeup of the PPC deputies and leaders, the decline in the participation of women sticks out as problem. According to the guidelines from the central leadership for local elections, the number of women should not fall below 20%. Actually, among the people's deputies of the PCs at all levels, this percentage had been met. However, in the elections between 1970 to 1988, the number of women had declined. The total number of female Vice Chairpersons and Standing Committee members, as well as their percentage among the Vice Chairpersons and SC members also declined in the 1980s. This was much lower than the number and percentage of woman who are Congressional deputies. And as we move closer to the real places of power, the participation and influence of women lessens.

Contrary to Xiaowei Zang (1991)'s study on Chinese provincial elite that excluded the leaders of PPCs and treated them as "non-elite" provincial leaders, since the 1988 elections, the leaders in the PPCs have been gradually incorporated into the provincial elite. This is illustrated by the increasing two-way exchange of cadres between the PPCs and party-government organizations. A survey conducted by the General Office of the NPCSC showed that from 1988 to 1994, 439 cadres were transferred from the party and government organizations to the SCs of 30 PPCs, and 188 cadres were transferred from the latter to the former. Although this is an uneven exchange, there are cases such as that of a Vice Chairwoman in Shanghai who was transferred to the position of Deputy Secretary in the Party Committee.

The improvement of PPCs has been reflected in their ability to make more and better laws. When the *Local Organic Law* was promulgated in 1979, the PPCs and their SCs started to generate some laws. But in the first four years (from 1979 to 1983), which were regarded as a period of exploration and experiment, the quantity and quality of local laws were low. Comparing and contrasting laws passed before and after 1984, we can find a change in the number of laws passed each year (in 1979 there were 5 items; in 1980, 104; in 1981, 152; in 1982, 147; in 1983, 95; in 1984, 117; in 1985, 83; in 1986, 142; in 1987, 193; in 1988, 239; in 1989, 308; in 1990, 363; in 1991, 277; in 1992, 355; in 1993, 425; and in 1994, 770) as

144　*The Dual Developmental State*

well as an improvement in the quality of the laws. Of the 616 laws passed before 1984, 215 (35%) were promulgated in the form of "temporary regulations" and "experimental rules" (Xu 1991, 170-171). Because these laws were very roughly drafted, they were revised or annulled later. Of the laws passed before 1984 (including 1984), half were revised or invalidated (*Difangxin Fagui* 1991). However, from 1979 through 1989, about 1,585 local laws were enacted and only about one quarter of them had to be either revised or invalidated by 1991.

Moreover, when people were asked to evaluate the performances of major political institutions in Chinese politics in a 1987 survey, the PCs received higher scores than the CPC, the government and the administrative institutions.[3] When asked in a 1988 survey what was the most effective way to influence the government, 14% of Chinese citizens chose contacting the people's deputies. This was the third most frequently used channel. When compared with the findings of Gabriel Almond and Sidney Verba during the 1960s, this 14% figure is lower than the percentages in the US and England, but higher than those of Germany, Italy and Mexico (Zhang Mingsu 1994, 100-101).

The Strategies for Legislative Development

Judged by their institutional complexity, quality of leadership, staff support, legislative effectiveness, and legitimacy, PPCs have obviously been moving in a positive direction. This institutionalization can be attributed to the changes in the political environment, the determination and ambition of the political entrepreneurs within the PPCs, and the strategies they used.

(1) Weaving Institutional Linkages

Western legislatures are more pluralist than hierarchically controlled institutions. The old socialist legislatures employed a hegemonic system of hierarchical control characterized by the dependency of the legislative on the executive branch, and of the various sub-national groups on the national legislatures (Bihari 1970, 152; Zhang 1988, 297-298). When the Chinese leaders started addressing the problems of the legislative system they did not want to establish another hierarchical bureaucracy in addition to the existing Party apparatus and government bureaucracy because this would merely further centralize political power. Many local leaders were eager to strengthen their attachment to the NPC through a hierarchical relationship so that they might benefit from associating with and being subordinate to the powerful ruling organs (Kevin J. O'Brien's calls this tendency of "bureaucratic attachment"). However, such a relationship of "leading and being led" between the NPC and local PCs was ruled out. And yet, the Chinese leadership did not intend to go too far in adopting a market strategy with the requisite emphasis on democratization and liberalization, as had been the case in Russia. The leadership worried that liberalization could dramatically challenge the fundamental nature of Chinese Communist authoritarianism, possibly increase the friction among the state organizations, and weaken the state capacity in steering the political-economic transition. They made it clear from the outset that strengthening the role of the PCs is not "to put on a rival show." The legislative-executive relationship is only a "division of labor," not "a separation of powers" (*Quanguo Renda* 1990, 592-603). They envisioned a relationship of "work contact" and "work communication," a kind of "contractual relationship" between itself and the sub-national PCs, as was repeatedly emphasized by Peng Zhen (*Quanguo Renda* 1990, 392, 580).

This denial of either pluralism or hierarchical control as models of political development posed an immediate structural problem for the early development of the PPCs, because they had neither political roots, a popular mandate created by elections, nor a clear line of command or political patronage from the NPC. They were left as "political orphans." As latecomers to an already crowded political arena, PPCs were extremely vulnerable to resistance and attack from other established institutions of power. In order to survive and develop, PPCs had to form a network strategy by constructing a complex of institutional linkages to maximize informational efficiency and to expand their political base. By weaving institutional linkages among themselves, with other major political actors, and with the major social forces, PPCs have built up a complex network for their institutional development and expansion of power.

As Milton J. Esman argued, "Every organization is engaged in a network of interactions with other institutions, at a minimum to exchange goods and services. Aside from these business-like transactions, an innovative organization is concerned with gaining support and overcoming resistance, and in bringing about changes in other organizations with which it interacts. This network of inter-organizational relationships is

146　*The Dual Developmental State*

designated as linkages" (Eaton 1972, 32). The institutional linkages of PPCs can be divided into four categories: First, there are the enabling linkages, which provide the authority and protect the PPCs from attack. For example, the relationships with the Party and the NPC, the two organizations superior to the PPCs, belong to this category. Second, there are functional linkages, which provide inputs and take outputs, such as the relationships with their deputies, voters, lower level PCs, and social forces. Third, there are the normative linkages, which provide moral support and create a favorable image. Such linkages include the matter of how PPCs influence the mass media, and public opinion, or how PPCs coordinate their policies among themselves. Fourth, there are diffuse linkages, which indirectly help PPCs innovate policies and create new resources, such as the contacts with foreign parliaments, communication with outside scholars and professionals, etc. (Eaton 1972, 21-39).

Under the "work contact system" (*gongzuo lianxi zhidu*) along with the leaders and deputies of the NPC, the PPCs, and other local PCs, the leaders and deputies of PCs at the lower level have been invited to attend the SC meetings of PC at the higher level, where specialized work conferences were sponsored by the SCs and Special Committees of both the NPC and PPCs. Presently, they provide legal and work guidance and training for the PCs at the lower levels. They also exchange their official documents among themselves. "The exchange of work experience and information system" (*gongzuo jinyan he xinxi jiaoliu zhidu*) enables PPCs to observe and emulate one other closely to improve the efficiency of their information and the rationality of their policy. The PPCs at the regional level coordinate and cooperate with one other. In addition to the exchange of documents, provinces with similar characteristics try to learn from one other. Since the provinces located in the same area share many of the same problems, it is easy for them to establish various linkages. The information-poor provinces always pay close attention to the policies in the information-rich provinces and send "investigation and study delegations" to the latter. For example, in the 1980s, Guangdong and Fujian led the nation in making new economic laws. After the Fujian PPCSC passed the "Regulation for Protecting the Legal Rights and Interests of Consumers" in 1987, 24 provinces sent delegations to learn from its experience.

Under the "request and report system" (*qinshi huibao zhidu*), which structures their relationship with the Party Committees, the PPCs normally request instructions before and submitting reports to the Party after

Developmentalism and the PPCs 147

engaging with any important issue. The Chairmen of the PPCSCs report to the provincial Party Committees on the work of the PPCs once or twice a year. Before discussing and passing important bills and resolutions or convening important meetings, they always request instructions from the Party. After the meetings, they report the results and developments to the Party Committees. They also report the important findings of their investigations to the Party, and sometimes give constructive suggestions concerning personnel appointment. In this way, PPCs are able to keep themselves well-informed about the intent and possible changes of important policies, conduct their own work by focusing on the issues of most concern to the top decision-makers, and make indispensable contributions to the entire regime. Once the Party is kept informed about PPC activities, it becomes less suspicious and defensive, and more relaxed and supportive.

As with the Party, the PPCs follow a cautious strategy when dealing with the governments and judicial branch. To minimize misunderstandings and to smooth away potential conflicts, the PPCs have since the mid-1980s created "joint conference systems" (*lianxi huiyi zhidu*) with governmental and judicial organizations. In what has become routine in many provinces, PPCSC Chairmen hold conferences with the Governors, the Chief Judges, and the Provincial Procuratorates General twice a year. This system serves at least three functions: First, because PPCs have the power to supervise the governments and judicial organizations, they are able to find a forum to manage their conflicts. Second, the governments and judicial organizations are able to report their work to the PPCs. And third, PPCs are able to learn the legislative plans of the governments and judicial organizations in advance; as a result, they are able to involve themselves in the bill-drafting stage. This stands in contrast to the old pattern of waiting for bills to be brought before them for routine passage.

After the two waves of student demonstrations, the CPC leadership adopted a series of policies to strengthen the systems of political consultation and social dialogue. PPCs gradually created a situation through which they were able to intensify their efforts to contact the people's deputies. The PPCSCs came to realize that people and their deputies were their power base and had a stronger incentive to organize deputies into a "liaison networks of deputies" (*daibiao lianxi wangluo zhidu*). The people's deputies have been organized into "deputy groups," based on geography or profession. These groups conduct inspection and

148   *The Dual Developmental State*

investigative activities, and two to three times a year study recent important documents.

The SCs have established the specific organizations responsible for organizing deputies and have opened special reception rooms in which deputies may submit their suggestions or complaints. Some have fixed dates for the SC Chairmen and Vice Chairmen to meet with the visiting deputies. During their trips of inspection or investigation, they also have made it a habit of meeting with some deputies to hear their opinions.

The Prefecture Work Committees for Liaison as agencies of the PPCSC have been widely established to take chief responsibility for communicating between the PPCSCs and the PCs at the county and township levels. The PPCSCs have maintained a correspondence with their deputies. They keep deputies informed about important events and decisions in the SCs by means of circulars and documents, and sometimes by convening a face-to-face conference for circulating information. They also encourage deputies to write letters by providing them with stationery and paid envelopes. The PPCs have issued "deputy ID cards" and given financial compensation to the deputies for conducting their visits.

"The letter and visit system" (*renmin xinfang zhidu*) was designed for the general public. Anyone can walk into the Office of Letter and Visit to present an oral or a written appeal and ask for assistance, even if they lack backdoor connections to powerful officials. During the past decade, the number of such letters and visits has rapidly increased. Judged by public cases, this system has become a common way for the ordinary people to approach the state. It has become a weapon of the weak and powerless (*PD*, December 5, 1996).

As PPCs have received more feedback from the community, their legitimacy has been strengthened, and their authority has come to be taken seriously by the citizens (*PD*, January 11, 1996). Since 1987, Wan Li, the NPC Chairman, had been an advocate for democratic and scientific decision-making, for complementing inadequate staff support, and for adding "an aura of rationality" to their decisions. PPCs have also reached out to the experts (Pfeffer 1981, 142). Under the "consultation with expert system" (*zhuanjia zixun zhidu*), some PPCs (for example, Beijing and Shanghai) have hired and exploited the talents of legal advisors. Many PPCs have organized professional associations to study the work of PCs. In one such case, the Center for Taiwanese Law Studies is affiliated with the Fujian PPC to help it assimilate the economic laws of Taiwan. Finally, PPCs conduct their own foreign affairs by receiving legislative delegations

Developmentalism and the PPCs 149

from other countries or sending their leaders to visit foreign legislatures to study their legislative development.

(2) Consensual Politics of Local Legislation

Drafting laws is an integral part of the political decision-making process. The legislative process at the provincial level presents, as a pattern of interaction, a consensual model for Chinese legislative politics. This makes it easier for the political elites to overcome their resistance, build a consensus, and manage conflicts (Lijphart 1969, 1984, 1996).

Legislation first starts with planning that can involve a one-year, two- to three-year, or five-year plan. Legislative plans are needed because the PPCSCs want to control their own agenda and be involved in the process of initiating and drafting bills in advance when faced with a heavier legislative load. Usually, before making its legislative plan, the SCs, or their Special Committees and Research Offices, contact the Party, the Government, the Court, and the Procuratorate first and ask if they have any initiatives that they would like to introduce. Now, according to the laws for the legislative process, all institutions that initiate laws are required to send their legislative plans to the PPCSCs in advance. In composing the legislative plan, the PPCSCs pay special attention to the Party's guideline for recent work, the national and provincial Five-Year-plans, the NPC legislative plan, and the provincial government's plan. Because most bills derive from the government (for example, 95% during the 1979 to 1986 period), the two legislative plans of the government and PPC are always coordinated.

Upon receiving these various suggestions, the SCs conduct their preliminary review and evaluation. A draft for a legislative plan is then sent to the relevant government departments, the Party, judicial organizations, experts in universities and research institutes to solicit comments and suggestions. Several conferences may be conducted for this purpose. Based on the feedback, the PPC staff finishes a final draft and submits it to the Chairmen Group meeting for approval. Once approved, the plan is sent to relevant organizations and government departments for their record and reference (Tang 1992, 73; *Quanguo Renda* 1996, 9). For example, the Five Year Legislation Plan of the Jiangsu PPC (1993-97) went through three stages with more than 10 forums with 203 officials from 87 provincial governmental organizations, and 389 officials from 170

150   *The Dual Developmental State*

departments in 11 cities. It collected 342 items for potential legislation. Two delegations were organized by the PPC, consisting of government and PPC officials, and deputies from the municipal PCs. One delegation then was sent to Guangdong Province to learn from its experience, while another was dispatched to Beijing to learn the guidelines and listen to the comments from the leaders in the NPCSC and the Legislation Bureau of the State Council.

Based on the information collected, the Chairmen Group and the SC discussed and finally approved the Legislative Plan. Through this complicated and protracted process, the haggling over jurisdiction among different government departments as well as between the center and the localities was preempted or reduced as was the direct confrontation between the PPC and the government, especially its Legislation Bureau. Misunderstanding and conflict were kept to a minimum and solved quickly through compromise.

Based on a legislative plan, each specific item is assigned to one organization. A draft group either was associated with one government agency, or an independent, inter-governmental temporary organization was established. In both cases, members from more than one government agency and social organization were included. For example, in 1985, in Shanghai, a draft group under the aegis of the Municipal PC for the "Regulations for the Protection of Minors" included members from its own Legislation Work Committee, the Municipal Committee of Communist Youth League, the Propaganda Department of Municipal CPC Committee, the Office for Education and Health of the Municipal Government, the Public Security Bureau, the Municipal Higher People's Court, the Municipal Higher People's Procuratorate, the Bureau of Justice, the Reform through Labor Bureau, the East China College of Politics and Law, the Law Department of Fudan University, and certain mass organizations (*Quanguo Renda* 1992, 37; Chen Pengsheng 1993, 83-84).

The first task for the draft group is to formalize a guideline and then send it to the PPCSC, and occasionally to the Party, for approval in principle. They then start collecting data and conduct an investigation. Based on reports about the issue they want to solve, the problems they face, and what they can learn from the experiences of other provinces and countries, they write their first draft. During this process, the draft group may send an investigative group to other provinces where similar laws have been passed. For the "Regulations for the Protection of Minors" in Shanghai, 70 reports were generated, seven problem areas and 103 problems were identified as needing to be addressed through regulation (Chen Pengsheng 1993, 37). In the case of Gansu's Nationality Autonomy Regulation, the draft group conducted investigative visits to Yunnan, Guizhou, Sichuan, and Qinghai where the nationality issues are similar to their own. After Fujian became the first province in China to pass regulations protecting consumer rights, 24 provinces and municipalities sent investigative groups to Fujian to learn from its experience.

After a first draft is prepared, instead of being sent to the SC for approval, it is channeled into a consultation process for comments and suggestions. To improve the first draft several different organizations are consulted: the Party, the central government, the NPC, the experts, and the public. After a draft has gone through the described process, it will be sent finally to the PPC or its SC for deliberation and approval. The PPC leaders almost exclusively use the SCs for passing laws and always bypass the Plenary Session because the annual Plenary Session usually lasts only one week and has a large number of deputies.

The review process of a bill in the SC has changed from a "rubber-stamping" formality into a process involving two hearings. After a draft bill is sent to the SC, the Chairmen Group will first review and discuss it before deciding whether to submit it to the SC for review. When SC receives a draft bill, it will not vote on it immediately. After the first hearing, the SC, with its Special Committees (which one depends on the nature of the bill), Work Committees (especially the Legislation Work Committee or Legislation Work Office), and staff will conduct their own research and feedback conferences. During this period, suggestions for revision and change may be sent to the draft group. Based on the feedback from the SC, the Chairmen Group will decide whether to submit the bill to the SC for a vote. Sometimes, the Chairmen Group will postpone the vote until they think it is appropriate. After the Chairmen Group decides to submit a bill for a vote, the SC will have the second hearing on the bill and vote on it. At this time, although it happens rarely, a bill may be rejected and returned to the draft group for further improvement. Now, in practice, the "two hearings in four months" process is applied to most bills. Sometimes, "three hearings in half a year," and even "three hearings in one year" have become regular in the reviewing and passing of a bill in the SC (Lin 1993, 213, 216).

Some Chinese scholars have summed up this legislative process as follows: the PPCSCs, or their Special Committees and staff, involve

152   *The Dual Developmental State*

themselves in the earlier stage of the drafting of a bill. Bills are then drafted jointly by the government and the PPC. Democratic consultation and discussion are conducted for the purpose of soliciting opinions. The law-making process follows a scientific methodology (for example, evidence from scholars and scientists). The most conspicuous characteristic of this process is the close collaboration between the PPCSC, Special Committees, and the government with its departments at all stages of law-making from bill-drafting, to review, revision, deliberation, and approval. The Chinese call this process "a democracy of consultation and voting" (Zhang 1992a, 228-231).

The legislative process has become protracted, and the number of actors involved has proliferated. In this development, the PPC, especially its SC and special committees, has expanded its power in drafting laws through its early involvement in the preparatory investigations and the drafting of bills, through the coordination of different institutions and actors, through participation in revision, and through the extensive scrutiny and review preceding and leading up to the vote on bills. Some Chinese leaders and scholars once were concerned that PPCs might use their legislative power to invalidate the laws from the NPC, resulting in "legal decentralism" (*falu fenshan zuyi*). If laws come through numerous doors (*fachu duomeng*), confusion and chaos could destroy the integrity of law. Or, the legislative branch might grab more power from the government and sacrifice government efficiency and the state capacity. Worst of all, PPCs might rely on the people's mandate to challenge the legitimacy of the CPC. In reality, all these concerns did not materialize. The expansion of power by the PPCs has neither posed a serious challenge to nor created conflict with other actors, because it has pursued a style of self-denial.

Self-restraint has been reflected in their relationship with the NPC. The NPC has never used its power of legal review to overturn a single local law over the past twenty years, even though some local laws were in conflict with some provisions of the national laws. However, many PPCSCs prefer the integrity of a national policy to a policy grounded in the interests of constituents. Conflicts between national and local laws have been solved mainly through self-annulment and self-revision by the PPCs. A case in Sichuan in 1987 illustrates this point. The SC voluntarily aborted a bill on price controls, then popular among the people and deputies, to avoid a potential clash with the recently initiated economic reforms (Lin 1993, 178-180, 215). Clearly in the current Chinese legislative politics, the interest of local constituencies has not become the predominant concern of the PPC leaders.

The legislative process is like a "shuttle," in which a bill or a proposal for a bill travels back and forth among the Party, the government, and the PPC and its SC. At each stop, we can identify almost the same group of actors: The Party, the PPC, or its SC and Special Committee, and the related Government department are always involved. In this "shuttle" process, bargains, conflicts, and struggles have frequently occurred, but the dominant pattern has been active consultation, voluntary cooperation, and the intentional preempting of conflict. Furthermore, this consensual behavior is not a continuation of the coerced obedience that was the norm under old Communist command system, but rather reflects new institutional arrangements and norms, and rules of interaction. With regard to institutional arrangements, a large number of new mechanisms and rules have been developed by the political leaders to institutionalize consensual behaviors. Linkages have been established to reduce friction in the operation of the system that comes from the misunderstandings, struggles, and conflicts among the various actors and institutions. The development of institutional arrangements for the cooperation among the various institutions and actors was not a spontaneous process. Instead it was a deliberate development involving two simultaneous processes: Fragmentation produced differentiation, autonomy, and contention while linkages produced reciprocal coordination, mutual embeddedness, and the localization of conflict. Many scholars have neglected the development of conflict-reducing mechanisms and exaggerated the threat posed by the legislative development to either the CPC or the NPC.

(3) Keeping Relevancy in Marketization

PPCs were actively involved in market creation and played a significant transformative role in economic development during the reform era in China. PPCs now have two major functions. First, they compensate for market failures. PPCs have taken responsibility for creating markets, controlling externalities, and maintaining public goods. Second, they have taken responsibility for preventing the failure of the state. PPCs have taken responsibility to prod the executive and judicial branches to develop property rights and enforce contracts; to keep the government and legal system efficient and free of corruption through supervision; to prevent

154　*The Dual Developmental State*

over-centralization of power and to minimize transaction costs; and to improve the efficiency of information dissemination throughout the system. They have exceeded the conventional domain of activities and have become involved in a constructive way in the political and economic transition, especially in the process of creating a market economy.

We cannot say that their active involvement in preventing both market and state failures has eliminated the transaction costs in the process of creating a market economy, but, at least, these costs have been effectively controlled in most cases to such an extent that the rewards for economic actors have been much greater than the costs they have had to pay because of state or market failures. The successful and sustained economic performance in China and the widespread local developmentalism serve to support this argument. It is imaginable that if the PPCs had not been involved in the process of transforming the economy and the regime, the market economy might have stagnated, and the Chinese state might have by now degenerated into a predatory state.

a. Countervailing the "Market Failure"

PPCs have a number of ways of counteracting market failures: First, they can exercise their primary function and make laws. Second, because they do not have direct control over any specific sector of the economy, they are able to be a guardian for the general interest, safeguarding the integrity of the market economy. Third, market failures undermine the public good. As representative organs, they are best able to show concern for and maintain the public good. Fourth, because they have a large number of deputies and a complex system of communication, which can be easily turned into a monitoring network, they are best equipped to provide access to ordinary consumers and to shadow the illegal activities in market economy.

　●*Market Creation*

Because the Chinese leadership was uncertain about how to proceed, localities played a pioneering role in marketization. A large number of laws regarding marketization were first introduced at the provincial level. By 1995, there were more than 1,000 local economic laws passed, accounting for 40% of all local laws, and 70% of the economic laws passed by the NPC and local PCs (Sun and Zhang 1996, 22). They are classified into four categories: those regulating actors (producers and consumers, etc.) in the market, those regulating the market as such, those for macro-regulation over the market economy, and those protecting labor.

Laws Regulating Actors: These laws are intended to define the nature and status of economic actors in a market economy. The provinces were pioneers in laying down a legal framework for economic actors and introduced some important adjustments to the Chinese economic system. Three famous examples are the "Regulations for Corporations in the Special Economic Zones," "The Shenzhen Special Economic Zone Land Administration Act" of Guangdong Province, and "The Regulation for Protecting the Legal Rights of Consumers" in Fujian Province in 1987 (*Quanguo Renda* 1992, 8). The positive results invited the emulation of these laws by other provinces: 24 provinces and cities sent investigative delegations to Fujian to study its experience. Within two years, by 1989, 21 PPCs and Municipal PCs drafted identical laws. After two more years, by 1991, 24 PPCs and 4 Municipal PCs also drafted such laws. In each case, these laws greatly improved the protection of consumer rights (Zhang 1993, 998). More importantly, local law also affected the drafting of a similar law at the national level. In 1993, after summing up local practices and experiences, the NPC finally passed a consumer protection law for the entire nation.

Laws Regulating the Market Economic Order: When an economic system is in transition, old rules fall into disuse, and new rules may not be in place or respected even if established. Thus, anomies are often produced. Examples include unfair competition, cheating, adulteration, inadequate sanitation, etc. In the Chinese economic transition, PPCs have played a role in alleviating these problems. With respect to some issues, they have been one step ahead of the national legislation. At the same time, they have also demonstrated flexibility by adapting to more mature and comprehensive laws once they have been enacted at the national level.

In the early development of the market economy, one of the biggest problems is adulteration, because business people have not realized the importance of reputation and trust. Inevitably, fake, defective, or adulterated products flow into the market, and some merchants use gimmicks to cheat customers. In Beijing, legislation was used to target these unfair practices and achieved results. "The Act of Commercial Instruments of Weights and Measures in Beijing" of 1983 and "The Temporary Regulation on the Quality of Seeds for Farm Plants" of 1987 were two good examples (Zhang 1993, 984-985).

Laws for Macro-Regulation over Market Economy: PPCs have involved themselves in macro-economic regulation by drafting laws in the

156   *The Dual Developmental State*

areas of price, budget, and special policies for one geographic area or industrial sector. In the 1980s, many PPCs were enthusiastic about drafting laws to control runaway prices. These acts alleviated the concerns of and resistance from ordinary consumers against the marketization reforms. As the reforms continued, people became used to price changes, and some PPCs suspended their acts or improved them in accordance with the economic changes. Some PPCs, concerned with inflation, blamed the provincial governments for spending more than their budgets permitted. They decided to intensify their control over budget and extra-budget spending. Shandong, Liaoning and other provinces enacted laws supervising the making and implementation of the budget. After the corruption scandal in Beijing (implicating Chen Xitong, the former Mayor, Party Secretary and Politburo member, and Wang Baosen, the Deputy Mayor, who committed suicide) was exposed, the outraged people's deputies of the Beijing Municipal PC drafted in 1996 a law to supervise extra-budgetary spending (*PD*, December 26, 1996). Some PPCs have shared power with the government in pursuing economic policy. The Shanghai Municipal PC enacted "The Temporary Act for Developing New Technologies and Industries" on August 14, 1987. This act created a local industrial policy to encourage investment and development in some targeted industries. Industrial policies are an important feature of a developmental state, and selective industrial policies were first introduced in China by the local governing bodies.

To develop the local economy, PPCs have actively passed laws to establish "development zones" or "new technology development zones" where tax breaks, favorable investment policies, and special land prices were established to attract foreign investment. In 1993 the Chairmen Group of the Tianjin Municipal PC decided to draft five laws for its duty-free zone. From the initiative of these proposals to the drafting and adoption by the SC, it took only three months (*Quanguo Renda* 1996, 5-6). At the same time, inland provinces started to catch up, producing a "fever of development zones." For example, the PPC Standing Committee in Neimenggu (Inner Mongolia) believed that the Mongolian traditional fair, Nadam Fair, provided a good opportunity to attract tourists and investors. To capitalize on this opportunity, the Standing Committee worked very hard to pass "The Act for Encouraging Foreign Investment" on June 29, 1991, just before the Fair started (Zhang 1993, 1009).

Laws for Protecting Labor: The gradualism of the Chinese economic transition is reflected in the fact that labor laws have kept abreast of the marketization. The drafting of laws regarding labor protection has changed its focus over the past twenty years: At first, more laws addressed the problem of the safety and health of workers. As more and more joint ventures were established, the issue of the union of workers with these joint ventures became urgent. Entering the 1990s, with the Chinese economy continuing to liberalize itself and with the "iron-bowl" employment system being abandoned, laws were needed to deal with issues like medical insurance, minimum wage, unemployment aid, retirement pensions, etc. More laws were introduced to establish a social welfare system.

In the realm of social security, the Hainan PPC once again led the nation. Early in 1991, the government enacted three temporary statutes concerning old-age pension, unemployment insurance and on-duty injury insurance. But their enforcement met with strong resistance. Up until 1993, 42% of all enterprises (and 67.3% of all foreign-invested enterprises) that were required to join these plans refused to do so. To enhance the authority of the social security statutes, in late 1993, the Hainan PPCSC drafted three laws to protect old-age pensions, unemployment insurance and on-duty injury insurance. Thanks to these three laws, the government has a legal instrument to force enterprises to comply with the social security system, and after one year, 77% of all enterprises joined these insurance programs. To further increase this percentage, in 1995, in accordance with these laws the Hainan Higher Court established a tribunal for social security and made it more difficult for employers to evade their responsibility for their employees' social security (*PD*, May 30, 1995).

•*Externalities Control*

In economics, "externality" refers to the consequences of an economic transaction upon a non-participant third party. Since the market mechanism usually cannot solve these problems efficiently, the state has to take actions to curb the externalities. For the state, there are several ways to deal with this problem. It can impose fees and fines, impose regulations, or file lawsuits against the producer of the externalities. The Chinese PPCs have actively passed laws to legitimate the authority of governments to impose fees and fines, and to regulate polluters. This is reflected in the number of laws enacted by PPCs regarding these issues in the 1980s. Local laws concerning externalities and public goods from November 1979 to July 1990 totaled 237 (*Difangxin Fagui* 1991). By 1995, 17 PPCs had passed comprehensive local environmental protection laws, and thirteen

158   *The Dual Developmental State*

PPCSCs had established "Special or Work Committees for Environmental and Resources Protection" (*PD*, June 2, 1995; September 14, 1994).

Hainan province provides a good example of what has been done in this area. In the first Plenary Session of the Hainan PPC a guideline was provided for construction in Hainan: "Developmental construction must proceed simultaneously with environmental protection." In its first seven years, the Hainan PPC drafted eight local laws concerning environmental protection. At the same time, the provincial government also drafted more than twenty statutes that dealt with environmental issues (*PD*, July 22, 1996; June 10, 1995).

Reviewing the practices of the last twenty years, PPCs and their SCs have been relevant to the problem of externalities by playing a number of roles: First, the PPCs have provided a forum for the deputies to complain about the problems. It is not unusual for the members of the SCs and ordinary deputies to act like "muckrakers" to identify problems on their inspection visits and report them to the Plenary Sessions, the SC meetings, or the mass media (Zhang 1993, 1068; *Quanguo Renda* 1992, 157-158; *PD*, January 4, 1995; June 2, 1995).

Secondly, to highlight the urgency and importance of some problems, PPCs and their SCs often have drafted resolutions on individual issues drawing the attention of the Party, the government, and the public, resulting in these issues getting placed on the government agenda. PPCs and their SCs have acted as "pressure groups," prodding the government to take action on these issues (*Quanguo Renda* 1992, 69-70). For example, as a base for China's energy (coal), heavy and chemical industries, Shanxi province has had a serious problem of pollution. So the Shanxi PPCSC has paid special attention to this problem. Its first local law was a regulation imposing fees and fines on work units that released pollution above a certain level. To identify more problems, in 1984, it organized an investigative committee on environmental protection and conducted a nine-month inspection of 77 work units in four cities and numerous counties. Its determination to protect the environment was reflected in an encounter with the central government: One large mine had not taken the appropriate measures for environmental protection. The SC did not allow it to start production, even though the central government required the mining operation to meet a deadline and supply coal to the Baoshan Steel and Iron Mill in Shanghai, since the ribbon-cutting ceremony had already been scheduled, and important leaders had been invited (Zhang 1993, 1023-1024, 1028; *Jilingsheng* 1989, 191-192).

Thirdly, the PPCs and their SCs also have been policy initiators and have provided policy options to the government. At the same time, they have been moderators and facilitators coordinating various agencies of the governments at different levels to achieve various policy goals. In 1985, some people's deputies in Guangdong submitted a motion to the Plenary Session concerning the problem of soil erosion in the upstream areas of Bei River and Han River. In response, the provincial government submitted a project plan to the SC and promised to spend eight million yuans each year on the prevention of soil erosion in these two areas (Zhang 1993, 1154). In 1987, in a case in Shandong, the PPCSC prioritized the issue of heavy pollution in the Xiaoqing River and a lake, passed a specific resolution, ordered the provincial government to control the pollution and to solve the problem of drinking water for local residents, and also suggested ways to solve the problem. The provincial government followed the resolution and pledged a series of projects to control the pollution. In the following two years, the SC continued their oversight and at the same time helped solve problems (for example, finding sponsorship for foreign loan, coordinating conflicts between the government agencies, etc.) (*Quanguo Renda* 1992, 66-68).

Finally, the PPCs and their SCs have played a "watch-dog" role, keeping watching over problems until they have been solved. The long-term follow-up is made possible by the institutionalization of staff and the accumulation of institutional memory. For instance, because the drinking water of more than ten million Shanghai residents is from the Huangpu River, in the past ten years, the pollution along the Huangpu River has been a constant and major concern for the SC of the Shanghai Municipal PC (*Quanguo Renda* 1992, 158-160). Through legislation, regular inspection, pressure put on the government, and exposure through mass media, the pollution was, if not completely put under control, prevented from becoming worse.

●*Maintenance of Public Goods*

In contrast to the externalities, economists believe that public goods are always under-produced, if there is not the concerted effort of collective action. Projects such as roads, dams, irrigation systems, etc., once completed, benefit all residents. But it is extremely difficult to exclude those people who did not pay their share from getting access. The combining characteristics of the commonality of the supply and the impossibility of exclusion invite "free-riders" and justify state intervention

160   *The Dual Developmental State*

(Olsen 1971). In China, for centuries the risk of floods has posed an extreme challenge to the society when it has come to maintaining public projects. However, the abject poverty of the Chinese people has made it very difficult for them to participate in the maintenance of those public projects. The state has long taken the primary responsibility for these public goods. Karl Wittfogel (1957) described it as "hydraulic oriental despotism." This tradition that has the state maintain the public goods with little involvement of the general public persists to this day. However, this has started to change during the reform era. As the old mobilization regime collapsed, the state's traditional capacity of maintaining public goods has been weakened by the reforms. To compensate for this loss, the state gradually has shifted its role from that of mobilization to the use of legal instruments. With this change, the PPCs have found a way to expand their role in the realm of public goods.

As with the control of externalities, the PPCs have used the same instruments of power to make their voices heard: Certainly they have drafted many laws dealing with the public good over the past twenty years. But most importantly, they have been able to conduct their flexible, frequent inspections for the enforcement of laws, making sure that the laws are respected and strictly enforced. Many local laws regarding the public goods were initiated and passed by the PPCs when there was no corresponding national legislation, and they have proven effective in improving the provision of public goods. Jiangxi's "Act of Ferry Management," Liaoning's "The River Course Administration Regulation," and Beijing's "Act of Irrigation Works Protection" are some examples (*Quanguo Renda* 1992, 20, 22-23; Zhang 1993, 984).

Despite the increased activism of the PPCs in controlling externalities and maintaining the public goods, the deterioration of the environment and public projects still is a serious problem. This problem is created partly by the fact that the new system has not been able to fill completely the void left by the old mobilization regime. There are three reasons for this: First, the PPCs have been short of members with legal expertise. Thus, the expectation for more laws has exceeded the capacity of PPCs. As a result, many enacted laws are ambiguous, contradictory, and without clear penalties. Second, the explosion of local legislation in the past decade has gone far beyond the capacity of law enforcement agencies to enforce them. Third, many law enforcement officials and common citizens have been unaware of most of the newly enacted laws. Their legal ignorance has retarded the effective enforcement of valid laws. The old problem of

Developmentalism and the PPCs 161

having no laws to follow has been replaced by two new problems: the low quality of some laws and the lax enforcement of laws, which together fall into the category of "state failure." To address these two problems, PPCs have made efforts to recruit more well-educated members and staff, heighten their supervision over the executive branch and inspection of law enforcement, and popularize the education about existing laws.

b. Countervailing the "State Failure"

Non-market institutions are not free of their own failings, which include "state failure," "bureaucratic failure," or "organizational failure" (Wolf 1988; Williamson, 1996). To counteract these failings, decision-makers often resort to the market mechanism. This has been the case in China. Over the past 20 years, Chinese reformers have relied on increasing competition among organizations to solve the problems of bureaucratic incompetence, rent-seeking behavior of officials, and the structural deficiency of over-centralization and communication failure. As a result, the PPCs as well as the PCs at other levels have been given a larger role in the political economy

•*Assisting the Enforcement of Property Rights*

The clarification of property rights is the first step in establishing a market economy (Pitelis 1993, 188-216). Not only does it enable legal entities to enter into markets and negotiate contracts, making exchanges possible, it also provides incentives for these entities to pursue profits within a legal framework, ultimately helping the economy as well as themselves. However, the transition process from a state ownership to a diverse ownership, from a hierarchical social relationship to a contractual one marks a fundamental social, economic and political revolution, and proves difficult to implement. Throughout Chinese history, property rights and contracts defining property rights have not been respected. Beginning in the 1980s, the Chinese state confronted the overwhelming issue of the violation of property rights and the breach of contracts (Lyons and Nee 1994, 141-168). To eliminate these obstacles to the market economy, the governments at various levels needed to institutionalize markets and played a chief role as "transaction cost minimizers" (Pitelis 1993, 189). But because of the limitations of the governments and the extent of the violations of property rights, the PCs at various levels also involved themselves in this process.

162 *The Dual Developmental State*

Marketization is an educational process directed towards accepting the idea of property rights. As it goes on, people become more willing to assert their property rights. In the case of China, disputes over property rights between individuals, and between the state and individuals have multiplied. Government agencies and courts at various levels have been the first to deal with these disputes, but since so many of these cases could not be solved by these organizations they were sent to the PPCs. For example, disputes between the owner and a government agency over a house was finally resolved under the auspices of the Tianjin Municipal PC. The PCs in Tianjin and Hebei have also actively provided assistance to the establishment of property rights in the countryside, by helping to solve conflicts over the use of land surrounding a house (Zhang 1992a, 78-80; 81-92).

Entering the 1990s, as the wind of the market economy swept over some inland provinces, some entrepreneurs and intellectuals made money by selling their services. But many of them were sent to jail by the courts for the earnings from these services. In several cases in Qinghai, Tibet and Yunnan, the PPCs had to intervene and order the courts to review their decisions. Under the supervision of the PPCs, several publicized cases were overturned and the entrepreneurs were set free (*Quanguo Renda* 1992, 190-191, 196-198). These cases seemed to be disputes over trivialities. But taken together, they actually reflect one of the most exciting transitional processes going on in China today. The PPCs have realized the importance of this transition regarding property rights and, therefore, have tried to highlight some cases to arouse the people's awareness of property rights.

●*Assisting the Enforcement of Contracts*

To protect property rights, contracts must be respected. But this has been a daunting challenge to Chinese society. Because of a lack of traditions that might support a respect for contracts, defecting, cheating, and shirking from contractual responsibilities have occurred quite often. Because of local protectionism, some local governments and courts have been unwilling or unable to help to enforce contracts. The enforcement of contracts naturally has attracted the attention of the PPCs. For example, in 1988, PPCs nationwide conducted inspections on the enforcement of The Law of Economic Contracts and The Law of Foreign Economic Contracts. The Guangdong PPCSC dispatched nine groups, respectively, headed by the Chairman, seven Vice Chairmen, and one Vice Governor. These groups included 580 sub-groups consisting of 1,000 municipal and county

Developmentalism and the PPCs 163

officials, 785 cadres, and 2,891 people's deputies at various levels. They went to 1500 departments and units, 3300 enterprises, inspected more than 140,000 economic contracts, corrected some law-breaking activities, recovered some economic losses, and popularized the idea of an economic contract. In Zhejiang Province, the inspections organized by the PPCSC helped to recover 270 millions yuans of overdue payments and 12.66 million yuans of overdue foreign loans (Zhang 1993, 1080-1081; 1154-1155).

Because of the lack of any systematic information, it is difficult to gauge exactly the extent to which PPCs have assisted with the enforcement of contracts. But according to statistics from the Guangzhou Municipality, the impact of the Municipal PC there was enormous.[4] The Guangzhou Municipal PC is different from the PPCs and Guangzhou has also moved ahead of many other provinces, so we cannot generalize that other provinces have had the same success as Guangzhou. Nonetheless, it is safe to say that during the 1980s the use of contracts to guide economic activities had been assisted by the activities of PCs at all levels.

•*Supervision over the Government*

Because the current Communist regime in China has based its legitimacy upon the performance of the economic development, the need to effectively minimize rent-seeking behavior is not only required to reduce the transaction costs for business-people, it is also a political imperative if the risk of governing is to be reduced. Therefore, the PPCs with support and encouragement from the Party have asserted their powers actively in the supervision of government. From November 1979 to July 1990, the PPCs enacted 49 local laws for the purpose of correcting state behavior. These laws dealt with supervising the government, the judiciary and the procuratorate, regulations imposing fines and fees, lessening the peasants' burden, and protecting people's complaints and written accusations against government officials (*Difangxin Fagui* 1991).

To clean up the official corruption and to calm down popular resentment, the PPCs nationwide started their drives against rent-seeking companies with the campaigns for "the rectification of companies" in the 1980s. The PPCs imposed great pressure upon the governments, fiercely targeted the phenomena of "official profiteering", and put a brake on the fever of setting up too many companies. For example, in 1985, the Zhejiang PPCSC devoted one whole year to this task. It prodded the provincial government to adopt tough policies to discipline the government

164   *The Dual Developmental State*

agencies and eliminate illegal companies involved in economic transactions. As a result, of the 21,272 companies in the whole province, only 7,604 survived the rectification, accounting for 36% of the total. However, after two years, the "fever of companies" came back, and another 4,737 companies were established. The PPCSC again had to pass two resolutions, ordering the provincial government first to rectify the companies owned by the provincial government and then to continue punishing the illegal activities in the economy. Consequently, 3,518 companies were merged or eliminated, accounting for 30% of the total (Zhang 1993, 1078-1079). Same tough measures were also imposed by the PPCs in Guangdong, Xinjiang, and Hunan. Significant tangible results were achieved (Zhang 1993, 796, 1157; *Quanguo Renda* 1992, 184-185; Zhang 1992b, 227-228).

As the Chinese economy has gradually moved to a market economy, the control of "the three arbitrarys" ("*sanluan*" including "arbitrary fines, arbitrary fees, and arbitrary apportionment.") and "the four excessives" ("*siduo*" including "excessive fund-raising and apportionment, excessive fees in exchange for exemption from labor, excessive extra fees, and excessive village management fees") has become another tenacious issue and one of the long standing priorities for the PPCs' agenda. Although the central government has reiterated for a long time that all kinds of fees imposed on peasants should not exceed 5% of the last year's per capita net income, and the burden placed on enterprises should be controlled, the problem of excessive fees upon peasants, entrepreneurs, and enterprises has never been effectively controlled. According to the statistics in Jiangxi province, from 1983 to 1989, the increased rate of collective deduction allowed by the contracts was 338.1%, far exceeding the 126.7% increase in the peasants' per capita net income. In one village, from 1988 to 1990, the average per capita net income increased 20% (1988: 746.9 yuans; 1989: 871 yuans; 1990: 895 yuans), but the burdens increased more than seven times (total fees were 79,757 in 1988, 179,778 in 1990, 577,051 in 1991). It created a weird situation for the peasants: "After one year's backbreaking work and sale of grain, you still have a money-losing deal." In Hunan, another big agricultural province in China, the situation was even worse and the old tragedy that "exorbitant taxes and levies are fiercer than a tiger" was repeated. There were several incidents of suicide, and peasant riots have occurred there since the early 1990s.

There can be no more tragic case than what happened in China's countryside to illustrate how the local states have become so predatory and

Developmentalism and the PPCs 165

local state officials have become bandits who rob powerless peasants. The state-sponsored banditry at the local level is an example of localized state failure. If it is not effectively controlled, a market economy and contractual society will not be established. Even worse, because not all peasants are passive, many peasants, when the opportunity has arisen, have rebelled. In Renshou County, Sichuan Province in the early 1990s, the peasants rebelled against excessive taxes and levies, looting and burning official buildings. These types of threats posed a severe challenge to the maintenance and operation of a developmental state. For these reasons, both the central state and provincial authorities have been concerned with the behavior of local state officials.

To prevent the abuse of power at the local level, PPCs have actively involved themselves in the issue of peasants' and enterprises' burdens and played the role of a remonstrator on behalf of peasants and entrepreneurs. As the Chairman of Fujian PPCSC Chen Xu argued, the problem of inspection stations and arbitrarily fines is obstructing the development of a market economy. To solve this problem, Chen believed that "we should increase the transparency of the law and strengthen public oversight. If the relevant laws and regulations are the monopoly of a few people, it does not make for the observance of the law by the public and it permits the abuse of the law for the private benefit of the few" (Lyons and Nee 1994, 163).

The PPCSC in Jiangxi adopted a local law in 1990 to regulate the fees peasants should pay. Several tragic cases prompted the Hunan PPCSC to take more aggressive measures, and a special meeting was devoted to a discussion of this problem. The SC also dispatched its members to conduct investigations and tightened its supervision over the enforcement of central and provincial laws, regulations, and policies at the local level. In Shandong, the PPCSC further passed "The Act of Lessening the Burden of Peasants in Shandong." In Heilongjiang, in the late 1980s, the PPCSC passed "Regulations Concerning the Burden on Peasants," "Regulations Concerning Imposing Fees and Raising Funds," and "Regulations of Urban and Rural Trade Management." To keep pressure on the government, the PPCSCs conducted follow-up inspections and the provincial governments abolished many programs and fees imposed upon enterprises and peasants. After one year's work in 1991, the Shandong provincial government suspended 117 cases of arbitrary fees, fines and apportionment, and did the same in 456 cases involving other local governments. A total burden of six hundred million yuans was lifted from enterprises and individuals. In the

166   *The Dual Developmental State*

1980s, Heilongjiang Province saved at least 123 million yuans for the enterprises and 153 million yuans for peasants (Zhang 1993, 1120-1121, 1062). In Guangdong Province, 3,081 inappropriate fees were abolished, and 2,301 fees were lowered during the late Eighties (Zhang 1993, 1154).

Despite these efforts, it is difficult to say that the phenomenon of the predatory state at local levels has been totally controlled. PPCs have limited human and financial resources to monitor every village and activity. But the actions and legislation from the PPCs at least have had two important results: First, they have demonstrated to the local PCs at all levels how to supervise the government agencies and control their predatory behavior and rent-seeking activities; Second, they have provided support and justification to the popular resistance to the excessive fees and taxes from the governments.

•*Supervision over Judicial Organizations*

To overcome obstacles to a market economy, the assistance of state intervention, especially from the legal system, is needed. However, the traditional Chinese legal system has always been quick to pursue criminal cases and to protect the interests of the state and officials, but lax in civil and economic cases concerning the economic interests and property rights of common people. It has been a relatively efficient "sitting-tiger" for the state office (*yamen*), but a bad "watch-dog" for people's rights and liberties. This tradition still remains and is reflected in the following cases in which the legal system failed badly to respond to conflicts arising from the new situations arising from the creation of a market economy. To a large degree, PPCs have had to develop new legal responsibilities and to educate the officials in the legal system about the new requirements.

In the process of marketization, the Chinese legal system was inadequate in the following three areas: First, the judicial organizations in the legal system were ill-equipped to deal with economic crimes and contractual conflicts. They were unwilling to take these cases and tried to pass them on to each other. As a result, it was difficult to file a lawsuit. For example, the Tianjin PPCSC helped a farmer from Hebei use the legal system. The Higher Court ordered a District Court to take the case after the farmer was abused for years (Zhang 1992a, 117-123). If such evasion of responsibility and bureaucratism are allow to continue, the development of a market economy could be bogged down. The leaders of the PPCs have realized this danger. Because their legitimacy is associated with the public's support, they have been more responsive to popular demands and have considered the general efficiency of the system instead of parochial

Developmentalism and the PPCs 167

departmentalism. Therefore, they were able to prod the judicial organizations to change in accordance with new economic developments. Judged on this point, PPCs have helped the whole system find remedies for its failings.

Second, even when a lawsuit is accepted and heard, conflict between the court, the Procuratorate, and the Public Security Bureau often produces delays. It is difficult to make a decision and many cases have been delayed for many years. For example, in Tianjian, a case in 1980 was delayed for more than three years without judicial decision. The Political and Legal Committee of the PPC organized its own investigations, held hearings on the evidence, and listened to reports from the Court and the Procuratorate. Under the judicial supervision of the Legal and Political Committee, the court at last made its decision and announced its verdicts sentencing seven cadres and businessmen involved in bribing and embezzlement to jail, with terms ranging from 2 to 15 years (Zhang 1992b, 67-77).

Third, after a judicial decision is made, the executive branch often refuses to enforce it or enforces it in a sloppy way. Justice is still difficult to achieve. Sometimes the courts cannot enforce their decisions and have had to resort to help from PPCs. One case in Shanxi Province illustrates that even the Higher Court sometimes lacks power to enforce its court order.

PPCs have actively involved themselves in the area of corruption control. Compared with the government and party branches, PPCs are less corrupt simply because they are not in control of concrete economic transactions and resources. Moreover, there is no lobbying activity by interest groups to influence lawmakers. But it does not mean that PPCs are immune from the "CPC syndrome." In the 1980s, Hu Lijiao, the Chairman of the Shanghai Municipal PC was implicated in a scandal after the mass media reported that his son raped several women (including some famous actresses). In the 1990s, the Guizhou PPC Chairman, Liu Zhenwei, was forced to step down from the position and was transferred to Beijing after his wife was arrested and executed for embezzlement. Meanwhile, another six Vice Chairpersons (Respectively Han Fuchai of Qinghai, Ouyang De and Yu Fei of Guangdong, Tie Ying of Beijing, Jiang Dianwu of Hebei and Wei Zefang of Hainan) were removed and ousted from the Party for accepting bribes and embezzlement. All were sentenced to long jail terms (*PD*, Feb. 6, 1996; Feb. 9; April 20,; Jan. 7, 1997; Jan. 14, 1999). However, all these corruption cases share one characteristic in common:

168 *The Dual Developmental State*

the crimes were often committed when the perpetrators were Party or government officials (Han was a Vice Governor, Ouyang a Municipal Party Secretary, Yu a Vice Governor, Tie the General Secretary of the Municipal Government and Deputy Mayor, Jiang a Vice Governor, and Wei the Party Secretary for Political and Legal affairs).

(4) Building Alliance for Legislative Contestation

It is important to note that the PPCs have become more independent-minded and rebellious, challenging the Party, the government, and other powerful institutions. However, it is more important to understand how the PPCs have accomplished this.

Under the current system, the PC has several legal instruments to change its power relationship with the government. These include supervision, inquiry and questioning, special investigations, and impeachment. For a long time, only the power to supervise the government was used, and then only in a perfunctory manner. The Party nominated provincial governors. Hence the PPCs were wary of challenging the government. In the early 1980s, they stuck to the principle of "embedding supervision within support." As a result, supervision became impossible, and the other three more confrontational instruments fell into disuse. However, beginning in the biennium of 1987-88, more deputies newly elected into the PPCs were willing to intensify their scrutiny of the government and started to use more confrontational methods.

One surprising case in Hunan involved all three procedures of inquiry, impeachment and special investigation and became the first impeachment case against a vice-governor in PRC history. On May 12, 1989, when the Hunan PPC was in Plenary Session, 31 deputies filed an inquiry on the "rectification campaign against bubble companies" under the aegis of the Leading Group for Rectification of Companies headed by Vice Governor Yang Huiquan. The deputies were not satisfied with the lack of progress. His corruption and inability to answer questions during the inquiry angered many deputies and led to an impeachment initiative against him. The PPC asked for legal direction from the Legislation Work Committee of the NPCSC. The latter stated that one-tenth of the deputies of a PPC was sufficient to initiate impeachment proceedings, and that the Plenary Session has the authority to decide by vote whether to go directly to impeachment proceedings or first to establish an investigation commission to look into the matter. Ultimately, the Plenary Session voted on the

Developmentalism and the PPCs 169

impeachment question and dismissed this Vice Governor (Zhang 1993, 796; Zhang 1992b, 227-228; *Quanguo Renda* 1992, 223-224).

Two cases in Sichuan reveal that political contestation continued after 1989. In 1989, the Sichuan PPCSC and its Political and Legal Committee decided to take action to facilitate an investigation into two powerful individuals. One had connections with important leaders in the provincial and central governments, and another was the son of a Vice Governor. To overcome the strong resistance from the government and to get political support from Beijing, the PPC sent a letter to the Procuratorate General in Beijing, who was eventually transferred to Jiang Zemin and Qiao Shi. The Standing Committee summoned the Sichuan Party Secretary, criticizing the work of the Sichuan leaders and prodded him to solve the problem. Under all this pressure, the judicial branch acted immediately, arresting and later sentencing these two to death with a two year reprieve, and eight years in jail, respectively. At the same time, the PPCSC members tried to establish a special committee to investigate the stonewalling by the Vice Governor. This caused the sudden break down of the Vice Governor in a meeting, leading to his sudden death (Interviews, 1996, 1998).

Only three years later, another shocking case of economic crime broke out: A state-owned company in the Municipality of Chongqing had engaged in the speculation of foreign exchange, stock, gold, and silver in Hong Kong, incurring a loss of US$18 million to the state. Because it implicated the governor of Sichuan, Xiao Yang, who used to be the Party Secretary and Mayor of Chongqing, the Sichuan PPCSC submitted a motion requiring the Provincial Procuratorate to investigate the case. The head of the company was arrested, but the case could not be decided. The delay caused popular resentment and stimulated the deputies of the new PPC to initiate an inquiry. After one year without any substantive progress, some PPC members started to target the cover-up by Governor Xiao Yang and attempted to impeach him. In 1997, even though the case was still being blocked, it took a major victim. Governor Xiao Yang was forced to resign and was assigned to the post of the Fifth Deputy Director of the Sanxia (Three Gorges) Project Commission. But before he took office, he was hospitalized for lung cancer and died later in Beijing.

The relationship between the PPCs and the CPC is defined as "political leadership" and "the provision of general guidelines" through the Party Groups within PPCs. The Party is not supposed to interfere with the work of PPCs and has no right to give direct administrative orders to the

170   The Dual Developmental State

legislative bodies. Because the Party controls the nomenclatura system in China, including the nominations of most PPC leaders, and also subjects party members within the PPCs to party discipline, it is still the crucial factor in the institutional environment in which the PC operates. It is very important for the PC to maintain a favorable relationship with the Party in order to get institutional support. This also fosters a friendly environment for the PC's institutional development.

In 1986, Zhang Youyu, an instrumental jurist for the Chinese 1982 Constitution and Local Organic Law and a Vice Chairman of the Legislation Work Committee of the NPCSC, told leaders in the PPCs how they should handle the relationship with the Party:

> As for incorrect policies and guidelines from the Party, should we accept them? Here are two solutions: one is to report your opinion to the Party Committee. If you are a member of the Party Committee, you may debate and contest in its meeting. If the Party Committee still insists, what should we do? If the issues involved are not urgent, you may report to the Party Committee of the higher level and let the superior consider it. If they are urgent, you should implement them but keep your opinions to yourself, and then raise them for debate and contestation. This is allowed. Another solution is to be a "hard-bone" (dauntless and unyielding). If the Party Committee hurts the interest of the Party and revolution, you can say: "I shall not obey. I do not fear a contest in front of the superior Party Committee and an expulsion from the Party." In this case, you can have a confrontation with the Party Committee. If the disagreement is too important, and the execution of a policy will damage the interest of the Party and the people, you should be a hard-bone. Didn't Comrade Mao Zedong once say, "Don't fear an expulsion from the Party, don't fear a divorce!" But, this is an extreme measure and should not be used casually (Zhang 1988, 7).

Since 1986, especially after the 13th Party Congress, there has been a more tolerant environment for contestation with the Party. To some extent, the PPCs have been even encouraged by the leadership to contest some policies of the Party Committee at the same level. The Party's monopoly over personnel began to undergo change in the 1988 elections as a consequence of the Local Organic Law and Elections Law which laid down two important principles in 1986: "more than one candidate for each position" and "the right of voters and deputies (requiring a minimum number of ten) to nominate candidates." Among 28 provincial units (provinces, autonomous regions as Tibet and Xinjiang, and municipalities

Developmentalism and the PPCs 171

under the central government such as Beijing, Shanghai and Tianjin) in the 1988 elections, 12 candidates nominated by deputies were elected to important positions: 4 PPC Chairmen, 2 Vice Chairmen, 5 Vice Governors and Deputy Mayors, and 1 Chief Judge of the Provincial Higher Court (*Quanguo Renda* 1992, 289).

In the 1993 nationwide elections, the Party's monopoly control over gubernatorial elections continued to weaken. In Guizhou province, the Party center recommended incumbent governor Wang Chaowen for reelection. The deputies considered him old and incompetent and nominated another candidate, Chen Shineng, a 55-year-old Qinghua-trained engineer and Vice Governor. As a result, two candidates were voted upon. Chen was elected governor. This was the first time in the PRC history that more than one candidate was listed as a candidate for the governorship; it was also the first time that a candidate nominated by deputies was elected governor. Ironically, later the Guizhou PPC accepted Wang Chaowen as the Chairman of the SC. It reflected the PPC's own ambivalent perception of its identity: On the one hand, the PPC is eager to assert its power; on the other hand, it degraded its political standing by electing a "loser" to its top position. But in a long run, Wang Chaowen's exit to the PPC strengthened its power position vis-à-vis other power rivals, because Wang, as former Party Secretary and Governor, was well connected and powerful.

Several days later following the Guizhou event, a similar event occurred in the PPC of Zhejiang province (*Cheng Ming*, January, 1991, 22). Ge Hongsheng, the acting governor for one year, was designated the only official candidate for governor. However, many deputies supported a new face, Wan Xueyuan, a former Secretary General of the Shanghai Municipal Government and recently transferred to Zhejiang to be Vice Governor. Ultimately, Wan was elected Governor instead of the Party-designated candidate and acting Governor (Chen Hongyi 1993; Fewsmith 1994, 250). Meanwhile, two other Party-designated candidates for governor in Sichuan and Anhui Provinces encountered almost the same difficulties (*Cheng Ming*, March 1993, 53-56).

Although successful nominations by ordinary deputies and voters (at the county and township levels) have accounted for only a tiny number of all elected officials, and the deputy-supported candidates largely have been from the Party rank, the psychological impact of these nominations upon the office-holders and the Party bosses at all levels is enormous. The party

172   *The Dual Developmental State*

has certainly paid more attention to screening candidates. The elected officials have to worry about losing an election, and have become more attentive to public opinion and more accountable to the deputies. Another important Chinese political tradition has been reshaped. The safe old days are over when the office-holders were solely dependent upon their superiors. Now they are held more accountable to the people. The cases involving the Vice Governor and Governor in Sichuan and Hunan are examples that today's Chinese officials sometimes have to pay highly for their misconduct. The challenges and scrutiny from the PPC deputies could be fatal to their political as well as physical lives, as was the case with the two Sichuan leaders who suffered tragically. In sum, although not all PPCs have used their power aggressively to promote and widen local interests, it is clear that a pattern of using power more aggressively by the PCs has begun to emerge. Significantly, this pattern has come to be seen by more and more officials and ordinary people as evidence of political life in transition.

Politics of Smoothness

Institutionalization has happened to PPCs in China. Their institutional complexity, the regularization of rules and work procedures, the improvement of leadership qualities, their level of institutional maturity, the increase of staff size, their effectiveness in terms of legislative outputs, and their relevancy in market-facilitating functions illustrate this. We can safely argue that the legislative branch has become an important bureaucracy in the Chinese political system. However, we should also note that there are at least three distinctive parts with different status, powers and functions within the PPCs. As we move from the Plenary Session, to the SC, and then to the Chairmen Group and Chairman, we move to more institutionalized and powerful bodies. This uneven development of political power has turned the PPCs into hierarchical structures in which few core leaders are involved in the inner circle of decision-making.

The SC shares some decision-making power, but its major function is to aggregate interest for the Chairmen Group. The Plenary Session and the ordinary deputies are chosen as a sample group to circulate diverse interests in the rapidly changing Chinese society. Because of this hierarchical nature, the PPC system is still a good system for political control. The large-scale penetration of the Communist leaders into the

Developmentalism and the PPCs 173

PPCs and the deteriorating positions and influence of women and the various Democratic Parties in the top ruling apparatus of PPCs indicate that the CPC has turned the PPC system into a new supporting system for controlling the society and maintaining its one-party rule. If power dispersion has occurred, it is restricted to the top political elites and does not involve the sharing of power with various social forces. PPCs have not yet become a place where social forces and ruling elite interact. It is not yet a bridge connecting civil society with the state. No viable independent political forces are emerging in society to articulate the demands of the populace, and it is difficult to expect well-organized political organizations to pose any substantial challenge to the ruling CPC.

As the structure of PPCs changes, their legitimacy within the system also has been consolidated. In the eyes of other powerful actors, they are now indispensable. In the eyes of the people, they have become more important. Since the Chinese leaders wanted to reduce bureaucratism and increase incentives, especially local incentives, while at the same time maintaining central state capacity (or "general efficiency" in Deng Xiaoping's terms), legislative decentralization was used as a kind of sub-contracting. PPCs have been given more autonomy in order to experiment and find new institutions and policies for the national level, and to supervise bureaucracies in order to control bureaucratism. These two measures serve to reduce the transaction costs of the system. The first can avoid reckless policies at the national level, and the later can reduce corruption and rent-seeking behavior from the government officials, which are new types of transaction costs exploded in the marketization process. With regard to autonomy, another often used criterion for institutionalization, PPCs have become more mature and independent-minded and more disposed to assert their power vis-à-vis the government, court, the Procuratorate, and even the Party, all of which are traditionally more powerful than the PPCs in Chinese politics.

The explanation for the institutionalization and the expansion of power by the PPCs can be attributed to three important factors: the change of Chinese political and economic environment which has been discussed in the previous chapters, the entrance of a large number of influential political entrepreneurs, and most importantly their skilled use of a peculiar strategy for the building of institutions.

Constrained by the developmental state strategy and its stress on the state capacity, the institutionalization of the PPCs has been undertaken in

174   *The Dual Developmental State*

such a way that it will not weaken the state capacity for political control, or will not be accompanied by obvious democratization. The Chinese legislatures were staved off from the market and hierarchical modes used to guide their development, and had to develop a network strategy for institutional maintenance and development. The PPCs deliberately took advantage of the changes in the political environment to weave their own information network for their institutional survival and development. Its chief rationale is to economize on transaction costs. A network for acquiring, processing, assessing, and disseminating information is so complex that it is embedded into the NPCSC and reaches down to the deputies and ordinary citizens. By building up networks, PPCs have connected themselves with the power center in Beijing, become embedded into society, and created a favorable environment for their institutionalization and the expansion of their power. More importantly, institutional linkages developed by PPCs have provided channels of communication and mechanisms of policy emulation within the system of PPCs.

In the process of expanding their political power, PPCs have benefited from the tactics they used to build enabling linkages or support coalitions for their activities. First, in dealing with the government and the judicial branch, they have paid special attention to winning support from the Party and the NPCSC. Their support has always helped the PPCs triumph over their rivals for power. The NPC support of the PCCs is more reliable than the support of the Party, for the NPC also can strengthen its own position in assisting in the institutionalization of the lower-level PPCs. Second, in order to strengthen their positions vis-à-vis the Party, PPCs have carefully selected their targets based upon the state of public opinion. Many high profile, "hotspot" issues have been exploited by PPCs. Popular attention and pressure make these cases difficult for the Party to cover up or evade. At the same time, PPCs can demonstrate their potential utility by solving problems and preventing them from exploding and causing further damage to the whole system. Third, to avoid a "trouble-maker" image, PPCs have established a system of institutional linkages with the Party, Government, Courts, and Procuratorate to facilitate mutual understanding and preempt as much as possible a final showdown. PPCs and their SCs have actually achieved their goals principally by institutionalized consultations with other institutions with power.

Necessitated by concerns for transaction costs and the need to stabilize a new elite and build a consensus of the elite, many new institutions and practices have been deliberately and systematically developed by the Chinese political elite for increasing the cooperation and reducing the friction. The legislative process reveals the pattern of interactions among major political institutions. Self-denial, self-restraint, preemptive consultation and coordination, and voluntary power sharing have become conspicuous characteristics of Chinese provincial legislative politics under reform. The self-imposed restraints revealed from the behavior of all major actors for reducing conflicts have highlighted the consensual characteristics of Chinese politics. In his studies, Arend Lijphart has identified "consociational democracy" as a pattern of democratic government distinct from pluralist democracy. Although China is not in any sense a democracy, nonetheless, China's elite politics has been close to the "politics of smoothness" found in a consociational model. China has evolved into a government by an elite cartel (although not a democratic elite) designed to turn political friction into consensus. The political elites in China have been able to accommodate newcomers to the political power game and build up a consensus in the process of the dramatic political and economic transformation. They have also been able to provide substantial political stability and cohesion to the society, especially to the economic development. They have a strong awareness of the importance of political stability for the society, state, and their own political fortune. They also realize that broad popular movements rise up when there is dissonance among the elite (Lijphart 1969).

In Lijphart's study, consociational politics is used by democratic political elites to organize democratic politics based upon people's participation and competitive elections. In China, consensual politics can be viewed as a kind of consensual politics without democratic substance, and it is more or less restricted to the interactions among undemocratic elites, being a means for them to regulate their conflicts. For Lijphart's consociational democracy, social cleavages make such a pattern of government necessary. For the Chinese elites, two dilemmas have led them to follow the politics of smoothness: First, the pursuit of modernization in China has generated and will continue to generate more and more cleavages and conflicts; and at the same time, the success of modernization depends on the maintenance of political stability and cohesion. Second, the pursuit of a market economy has dismantled and will continue to dismantle the Stalinist system (and its inherent bureaucratism and low incentives); at the same time, the transformation that results from steering a command

176   *The Dual Developmental State*

economy into a market economy requires a capable and effective state. Smooth legislative politics is a part of a larger design for building consensus and economizing on transaction costs in the whole political governance.

A mixture of consultation and confrontation in the interactions among major political institutions indicates a change of the mode of political governance in China. For many scholars, authoritarianism is usually regarded as a "mechanistic solidarity," to borrow from Emile Durkheim (1964), and the fragmentation of a "mechanistic solidarity" often leads to dissolution and disintegration. But in the Chinese political system, some institutions, such as the PPCs, are emerging that are providing new processes of integration. In other words, some institutions for "organic solidarity" have emerged in the process of division of labor among the major political institutions. Therefore, structural fragmentation and functional differentiation do not necessarily mean a loss of coherence and solidarity. This is what the "fragmented authoritarianism" model has often overlooked when it is used to try to predict China's future course.

The "politics of smoothness" partially arose from the needs of the transition of the entire Chinese political economy, but it was made possible by the political skill of new political entrepreneurs recruited into the PPCs after several rounds of personnel changes. The personnel of the PPCs still have less education and are older than the leaders in the party and government organizations. However, as a whole, they have been getting younger, better educated. Moreover, they are becoming more important having attained a higher political stature. Fortunately, PPCs have attracted many former leaders in the Party, government, and legal branch, and thus, have enhanced their political standing. These seasoned politicians were able to take advantage of their good connections and long experience within the Party, government or legal branch, and were skilled in balancing the use of consultation and confrontation, to strengthen instead of weaken each other. This mutually embedded relationship between the Party-government organizations and the PPCs has strengthened the coherence of the provincial ruling elite and served the needs for a state with a strong capacity. China has successfully developed a peculiar pattern that shows that an activism of the legislative branch at sub-national level is compatible with an economic transformation and marketization.

Notes

1   The PPCs include the legislatures in twenty-two provinces, five autonomous regions, and four municipalities under the direct control of the central government. Even Taiwan is claimed by China as a province; Hong Kong and Macao after 1997 and 1999, respectively, became special administrative regions. They are not covered in this study. To simplify my account, these 31 provincial unites are treated as "provinces." The "PPCs" are used even in the context of autonomous regions and municipalities that are under the direct control of the central government.

2   The Hainan PPC was established in 1988 and is not included here. Hainan PPC has 291 deputies and is the smallest. It makes the mean size even smaller.

3   This survey revealed: 15.39% of more than two thousand respondents believed that the local PCs had played a "very important role"; 45.52% believed a "fair average role"; 22.59% thought they played "no role at all". 38.67% respondents expected local people's congresses to play a large role in the process of democratization; 38.73% had reservations; and, 13.55% did not expect them to play a role in democratization. See: Ming 1989, 64-67; 85-94.

4   Two years after "The Contract Law" was implemented in December 1981, a survey was conducted in one district of Guangzhou on 2,400 contracts. Only six among them met the criteria of "The Contract Law." That year, 4,200 disputes broke out over illegitimate contracts and led to more than 46 million Yuans in economic losses. In 1986, the SC of the Guangzhou Municipal PC drafted the first local law for economic contracts and the Guangdong PPC Standing Committee passed it. This local contract law has provided needed guidance. After several years of contract law propagation, in 1989, Guangzhou had another survey. Among 4,200 contracts selected for examination, there was only one invalid contract. See: Zhou 1991, 101-103.

7 The Shenzhen Revolution and Central-Local Synergism

The territorial perspective of the central-local interaction has been absent in the classic developmental state model. The reason could be that small countries (or areas) like Singapore and Hong Kong did not leave room for local governments to play a part in economic development. However, Muramatsu Michio, a Japanese scholar, has pointed out that Japan may be different, and the assumption of a vertical control model by the administration in Japanese politics is false. He has argued that: "The economic development of postwar Japan began at the local level in the form of local development policy." Therefore, "the horizontal political competition" should be addressed, since "an interdependent relationship model of the Japanese central-local relationship" is more appropriate (Muramatsu 1997, 35). Since systematic studies on the central-local relationship in other East Asian Newly Industrialized Economies (NIEs) are not easy to get, it is difficult to judge to what extent this conclusion also applies to them. But we can safely say that the neglect of the central-local interaction by the original developmental state model has been challenged and probably will become increasingly problematic if more studies are undertaken that focus upon the central-local dimension.

The debate on the role of local governments in the economic development in China has been reflected in three distinct interpretive approaches. The first group thinks that China had "a revolution from above." According to this approach the economic transformation is "a specific political project" designed and controlled by the top leadership. The central government has been and should be the primary motor for economic development. In the literature on authoritarian development, neo-authoritarianism, developmental state theory, state capacity, and stability, this approach is evident (Castells 1998, 287-307; Shirk 1993; Huang 1996; Wang and Hu 1993). Undoubtedly, the central state, especially under the core leadership of Deng Xiaoping, has played a great part in transforming China from state socialism to capitalism. But the chaotic political economy in the aftermath of the Great Leap Forward and the Cultural Revolution indicated the total failure of the state and the non-existence of a market. This approach often fails to answer this question: How does one use a failed state to create markets?

Secondly, some studies, although increasingly getting more currency, identified the main dynamics for transition as emanating from the grassroots, i.e., a revolution from bottom (Zhou 1996; White 1998). Discussions on the "Wenzhou model," the "Sunan (Southern Jiangsu) Model," the township and village-owned enterprises (TVEs), and the responsibility system in the countryside tend to view market development as a spontaneous and bottom-up process (McKinnon 1992; Foster 1990-1991; Nolan and Dong 1990b). According to this approach, China's development either has been at the cost of the central authority or the state capacity, or has been made possible by the failure of the center to intervene. Actually, almost all these developments aforementioned have received clear or tacit support from the top leadership. This approach fails to pay enough attention to the developmental role of the central government.

The third approach focuses on the provincial governments and regions. This approach places a special emphasis on how the development of regional and provincial property rights has been a strong incentive for local developmentalism (Granick 1990; Cheung, et al., 1998). Recently, a Chinese scholar has presented China's strategy as a trilogy. Initially, top-down innovations sponsored by the central state kicked off the Chinese transition. But then the local actors acquired resources for bottom-up initiatives as decentralization happened. Currently, intermediate agents, such as provincial governments, have seen their efforts permeating up to the center and filtering down to the localities. If the current trend continues, the guiding hand from the center or the provincial governments will become less important and necessary, and China's transition will ultimately turn into a demand-induced system of change (Yang Ruilong 1998). The biggest problem with this analysis is its inability to explain the resistance from bureaucrats at the intermediate level, or the phenomenon of "intermediate stasis" (zhonggenzhu) in the Chinese development that is reflected in local protectionism and bureaucratic inertia from officials within ministries at the intermediate level. This analysis is also unable to explain how this resistance was overcome (Winiechi in Alston 1996). In fact, the central state's developmental role often constitutes a constraint upon localism and an enforcement of a market economy.

180   *The Dual Developmental State*

Obviously, it is not new anymore to credit the local governments for initiating and sustaining the Chinese economic development. Numerous studies on local developmentalism and provincial entrepreneurial efforts have revealed that local governments have been strong dynamos for economic development in China (Vogel 1989; Goodman and Segal 1994; Blecher and Shue 1995; Zheng 1995; Huang 1996; Cheun, et al, 1998; White 1998). However, scholars differ over how to interpret the ramifications of localism for a developmental state. Considering the recent findings of local dynamism, can the argument that China's reforms have been a top-down process be refuted? What can be said about an analysis that sees the reforms as a "revolution from above" or a shift from the "bottom-up?" To what extent is the dichotomy of "stately wisdom" and "unstately power" (White 1998) any use for accounting for the causes of Chinese reforms, or for helping us to understand their dynamics?

Some scholars have accepted the fallacious view that local governments often benefit from the failure of the central government to control or intervene in their economic development. What is a bane for the central state is a boon for the local states. It seems that a zero-sum game exists between the center and the localities. But think this: if we take the perspective of stately wisdom, Susan Shirk has argued that one of Deng Xiaoping's wise and frequently used strategies was "playing to the provinces." She argues that Chinese leaders have chosen "the strategy of achieving market reform by devolving authority and resources to local officials (and thereby allowing them to build up local political machines)" (Shirk 1993, 1994, 23-57). Even in Wenzhou, where marketization has often been regarded as a "spontaneous order" with the city benefiting from the "benign neglect" of the central and provincial governments, there was still the long shadow of the central government (Parris 1993).

Actually there has been a cooperative relationship between the central government and localities from the beginning right up to the present. As Alston, et al, has argued, "In most instances, the decentralization of power cannot be modeled in terms of a maximization calculus of a single rule bent on maximizing the national base. Rather, it is more appropriate to analyze such developments within the framework of game theory and picture them as strategic behavior by various players in a repeated game" (Alston, et al, 1996, 132). Following this view, the sources for change in China have come from the interactions between the central and local states.

Actually in China, the central state, and local governments have both constrained and supported each other's developmentalism. They have formed a symbiotic partnership, giving rise to a complex equilibrium of interdependence between the central and local states. Without this essential, complementary relationship, developmentalism, neither at the central level nor at the local level, could be sustained. The Municipality of Shenzhen, where the first Special Economic Zone (SEZ) was established (Crane 1990; Douw and Post 1996; Kleinberg 1990; Lyons and Nee 1994; Park 1997; Shenzhen Visiting Scholars 1997; Wank 1998; Wong and Chu 1985; Yeung and Hu 1992; Yeung and Chu 1998), is used as a case study to illustrate the interactive pattern and the dyadic dynamics between the center and localities in the Chinese development process. It further helps us understand the limitations of the Chinese developmental state as well as its strengths.

Deng Xiaoping as a Midwife of the Reform

Two stories have been told and retold, and ultimately they have become myths about how the Chinese reforms started. One is about the initiation and implementation of the rural household responsibility system (*baocan daohu*) in the village of Xiaogang, Fengyang County, Anhui Province, while the other is about how the SEZ was established in Shenzhen. Here, by taking a second look at these two cases, we can provide further evidence to support the argument that the Chinese reforms were not put forth single-handedly by the central leadership, nor were they started with only local initiatives in defiance of the leadership at the center or the provincial level. They were born in the interaction between the initiatives of the central leadership (especially the reform-minded leaders led by Deng) and the initiatives from the localities.

The Chinese reform first started in the countryside. On the night of December 1978, 20 peasants representing 20 households in Xiaogang signed a contract to divide the land for each household and, as a result, started the household responsibility system. This was a blow against the commune system anointed by Mao Zedong and vigorously maintained by his successor, Hua Guofeng. Only twenty years ago, many high ranking officials lost power, and many local leaders were sent to prison simply for advocating this policy. But this time, the actions of these peasants were not challenged and, were instead even encouraged by some leaders.

182　*The Dual Developmental State*

Before this contract was signed, the then First Party Secretary Wan Li suggested to Chairman Hua that the responsibility system would be an effective policy with which to combat the agricultural crisis. Hua strongly opposed this suggestion in arguments with Wan. Deng Xiaoping was present and gave his support to Wan and his policy that eventually challenged and toppled the system of people's communes. Upon returning to Anhui, Wan introduced a series of reform policies and carried them out across the province. Another reformer, Zhao Ziyang, the First Party Secretary of Sichuan, carried out the same policies in Sichuan. When Chen Yonggui, then Vice Premier and former leader of Dazai Brigade, admonished Wan for cutting down the red flag of Dazai, Wan replied, "You go your way, I will go mine." ("You take the open road, I will cross the log bridge.") Thus, the responsibility system continued even as some important leaders (including the top leader Hua) resisted. Not until 1980, after this policy had been in effect for two years, and Deng finally had consolidated his power in the Third Plenary Session of the Eleventh Party Congress, did Deng Xiaoping gave his open support to this policy. Soon it was popularized nationwide (Ma and Ling 1997, 125-142; Guo 1997, 218-246).

Shenzhen, a fishing township twenty years ago in Guangdong Province, covers an area of 2,020 square kilometers, almost twice as large as its adjacent city, Hong Kong. In 1979, it was no better known than Xiaogang Village. If some Chinese happened to know of this place, most likely it was because thousands of Chinese escaped from here to Hong Kong. As one Shenzhen official told me, the barbed-wire barrier there was "China's Berlin Wall." However, when Deng Xiaoping was searching for a strategy to lead the Chinese out of its shattered economy and catastrophic politics, the proposal made by local leaders from Guangdong to several top leaders touched the right chord in him and catapulted this city into international fame. These Guangdong officials (Xi Zhongxun and Yang Shangkuan) asked for the right to implement special policies so that they might experiment with the economy of capitalist management in some selected localities (Shenzhen was the first on the list) in their province.

Hua Guofeng was strongly against it, but Deng was very enthusiastic about this idea. He thought that just as Yanan had been a special zone, Shenzhen could be one as well. According to him, Yanan was a special red district under the nationalist government. From there Mao and other leaders followed the bloody path to win control over all of China. Why cannot Shenzhen be a base for fighting a new battle for China's modernization? Therefore, he encouraged the officials in Guangdong and Shenzhen "to conduct bold experiments, to innovate creatively, and to break through a bloody path (for China)." With his support, Shenzhen set apart a piece of land, named it "the special zone," and started bold experiments.

Rural and urban reforms were started, setting China on a path of no return. In the rural case, it is hard to say that the top leadership was against the responsibility policy. Actually Deng Xiaoping developed his "theory of cats" from the experiences of the responsibility system. It had never been a secret that he and Liu Shaoqi were advocates for it. In terms of the SEZ initiative, Deng was less certain of what kinds of results he would see. But he thought that it was worth a try within a small, limited geographic area. As he said in the Third Plenary Session of the Eleventh Party Congress in December 1978: "Before a uniform national project is produced, we can start with a restricted area, in a region or an industry, then, gradually popularize. The departments of the center must allow the localities to conduct these types of experiments" (Guo 1997, 237).

Judging from these two events, it is problematic to argue that local initiative shook the Chinese system and introduced reforms. The fact is that the leadership was not a conservative monolith; the localities were not an avant-garde for reforms as a whole. In fact, the disunity among the leadership and the disparity of resources among the localities allowed complex interactions and political alliances to happen between them. In this process, the reformers at the central government and at the local levels relied on each other's support and secured their power position through reforms.

No single leader, no one level of government, and no single group from among the citizens have had a monopoly over the initiation and sustaining of the Chinese reforms. This is confirmed by the modesty of the "chief architect." Although Deng Xiaoping was the paramount leader in China for 15 years (1979-93), he had refused many flattering titles. But he comfortably accepted this title: "the chief architect of the Chinese reforms." Did this title really fit him? Was he really a general designer with a complex master plan, elaborate blueprint, and comprehensive strategy in mind? I think this is a questionable proposition when considering "the development strategy," "institutional design," and "institutional arrangements" in China. As James Scott (1998, 4) warns in his study: "So many well-intended schemes to improve the human

184 *The Dual Developmental State*

condition have gone tragically awry." The Chinese know this very well from the sufferings of the "Great Leap Forward" and the "Great Cultural Revolution." Many of these great projects of social engineering often were motivated by great utopian ideals that assumed the possibility of transforming nature and the social order, prescribed comprehensive panaceas, and relied upon authoritarian methods. Their common cognitive flaw was "an imperial or hegemonic planning mentality that excludes the necessary role of local knowledge and know-how" (Scott 1998, 6).

Returning to Deng Xiaoping, although he thought that he was a chief architect for China's reforms, fortunately, he did not act like an omnipotent general designer and never "commanded" the Chinese to follow one specific blueprint. In contrast to Mao Zedong during the Great Leap Forward and the Great Cultural Revolution, Deng emphasized "seeking truth from facts instead of books." He was driven by instinct, respecting the national wealth instead of the doctrines of communism. He allowed improvisation instead of seeking legibility and neatness. He used experiments instead of mass mobilization and large-scale campaigns. He respected local conditions instead of applying a top-down universal standard, and to win support, he used effective demonstrations more than crass coercion. He certainly did not pretend to be a "great leader and wise teacher" as did Mao. If Deng had wisdom that an overoptimistic, overconfident Mao did not, that would have been his agnostic attitude toward one person's infallibility.

His swan song, formulated as the last article of his three volumes of selected works, and therefore, to be taken more seriously as his political testament, were his speeches during his 1992 Southern Inspection Tour. Gong Yuzhi, Vice Chancellor of the Central Party School, once said, "If Deng Xiaoping's speech, 'Liberate Our Minds, Seek Truth from Facts, and Unite to Look Forward,' was the keynote for the Third Plenary Session of the Eleventh Party Congress and a manifesto of liberating minds for the beginning of a new era; then, his speech during the Southern Tour was a new manifesto of liberating minds, indicating a new stage of the new era" (Ma and Lin 1997, 198). On this journey, this "Chief Architect" emphasized how he embraced the initiatives from the grassroots, and said: "The success of our reforms did not rely on books, but on practices, on seeking truth from practice. The inventor's patent right for household responsibility in rural areas shall belong to the peasants. Many good practices in rural reforms were first initiated at the grassroots, and then we took them for further elaboration and synthesis, and popularized them nationwide" (Deng 1993, 370-383).

After household responsibility system was first introduced by the Anhui farmers, the then Party Secretary Wan Li faced strong pressure from both the center and the grassroots. Wan once described his difficult situation in a conference speech in 1980: "'Household responsibility' was not our policy. The issue is, that the child was born, his mother was very happy with it, exclaiming, aha, what a good result! The baby is lovely. Please register his residence card. Many people also went there to take a look and became excited. But once they arrived home, their warm hearts cooled down. Why? Because it was illegal and should be criticized. In fact, household responsibility was not horrible. Our principle is not to hurt people's enthusiasm. If the masses have practiced and are begging us: Let us try two years, OK? Comrades, please agree. Why not? Why do we criticize so much? I disagree with these critical opinions." (Guo 1997, 243).

In this controversy, Deng Xiaoping spoke out to give his support to Wang Li, and to the experiments in other areas. His conversation with some responsible leaders on May 31, 1980, cleared obstacles to a later important party document on Sept. 27, 1980, that gave a green light to the household responsibility system. As one Chinese writer puts it: "Deng insisted that the invention patent of the rural household responsibility system belonged to peasants. What he did was give this almost aborted infant a birth certificate and make him a legitimate citizen on the soil of the PRC" (Xiao 1996, 186). Therefore, after he read the political resolution of the 14th Party Congress, he instructed the authors not to exaggerate his role. He said the contributions credited to him should be credited to the collective leadership of the party. New ideas cannot just come from one person. They came from the collective wisdom of the masses. Many good practices and policies came out of the experience of the people. His major achievement was to synthesize these new ideas and to advocate and popularize them all over the country (Tang 1997, 371-372).

By considering his talks on the "Chinese characteristics," his view that "to each locality according to its own characteristics," his respect for the peasants' practical knowledge on how to catch a mouse (his cats theory), his praise for his grandson's wisdom,[1] and his policy to "bring the initiative of both the center and localities into full play," we can tease out the most important features of Deng's ideas that have contributed to

186   *The Dual Developmental State*

China's recent success. He subjected his strategy to improvisation, innovation, and adjustment by the people based on their practical knowledge, specific environment, and commonsensical judgment. Also, he let his national strategy open to revision by the regional and local forces.

Based on Deng's own account, a new title, "the midwife of the Chinese reforms" for Deng Xiaoping is more appropriate. In one of Plato's dialogues, Socrates, as an "intellectual midwife," cannot give birth to wisdom, but he assists people to see the problem clearly and to state it distinctly. The art of midwifery includes three important functions: First, the midwife helps men to recollect their ideas and wisdom; second, the midwife has the power to prove whether someone's thought is a "false phantom or instinct with life and truth;" and finally, if the idea is a bad one, the midwife has to act in a ruthless way to destroy it (Crombie 1964, 16-17, 37-39; Hamilton and Cairns 1961, 854-855).

Relating the concept of the midwife to Deng Xiaoping, he actually played two important roles in the Chinese reform: As Chief Architect, he designed a smooth transition from state socialism to capitalism; as midwife, he helped the Chinese people and decision-makers clarify ideas for reform and assisted the birth of many reform policies; at the same time, he was not hesitant to destroy any ideas he deemed dangerous and not good for China. For instance, he stopped the tendency of "bourgeois liberalization" and brutally clamped down on the student demonstrations in Tiananmen. Therefore, a combination of these two titles more accurately describes the much more complex role Deng Xiaoping had played in the process of the Chinese reforms. It also makes evident the role that local leaders and people played in initiating many policies. The establishment of the SEZ in Shenzhen is another case to illustrate how Deng Xiaoping delivered the new baby of Chinese reforms.

Shenzhen: The First Special Economic Zone

In a 1980 speech, Deng Xiaoping said that for a huge country like China, there was no shortcut for development. Experiences from the small countries in East Asia, namely, the Four Little Dragons, would not be applicable. He was not entirely confident about whether the developmental state could serve as a model for China as a whole. For this reason, Shanghai, the biggest industrial center, was denied the right to employ special policies to innovate and experiment. Obviously he did not want to

Shenzhen Revolution and Central-Local Synergism 187

take a risk of killing the goose laying golden eggs for the central government under the state-planned economy. Later he regretted his decision, seeing it as a mistake. But his doubts did not prevent him from allowing Shenzhen to have a try.

The status of Shenzhen as a SEZ was established in 1980 by the NPCSC. "The Regulations Concerning the SEZs of Guangdong Province" delegated special powers to Shenzhen including the power to draw up its own laws, create administrative agencies, determine preferential duties, and approve investment items. The center decided to give privileges to the SEZs so that they might experiment with some bolder reform policies. The NPC passed authorization laws to allow them to have special powers to initiate some innovative economic laws. On April 5, 1989, the NPC passed another resolution authorizing Shenzhen to make laws for the city. This authorization distinguished it from other Chinese cities.

Shenzhen clearly realized that support and information from the central government were essential for innovation. During the initial period of establishing the SEZ, the Guangdong province and later the Shenzhen municipality tried their best to involve the central level. Vice Premier Gu Mu led an investigative delegation to Guangdong and later he played an important role in constructing the SEZs. When the first draft of "The Regulations for SEZs in Guangdong" was drafted, thirteen different versions were written and revised. The State Commission for Import and Export Management participated in evaluating the final report. After it finished in 1979, the drafting group reported the legislative work to the Office for SEZs of the State Council and got, in principle, its agreement. In 1980, Jiang Zemin, then Deputy Director of the State Commission for Import and Export Management, led an investigative group to visit nine export and free trade zones in Sri Lanka, Malaysia, Singapore, the Philippines, Mexico, and Ireland. Later the Shenzhen leaders did not forget to point out that since the beginning, Jiang, the "core of the third generation leadership," had been instrumental in the establishment of the SEZs (Chen and Cen 1991, 192; Guo 1997, 283-285).

In making its "Temporary Regulations for Importing Technologies in the Shenzhen SEZ" in 1983, Guangdong again sent its first draft to the Research Center for Economic Legislation of the State Council for review. One month later, this Center convened a review conference attended by the responsible leaders from the State Planning Commission, the State Economic Commission, the Ministry of Foreign Economic Relations and

188   *The Dual Developmental State*

Trade, the China General Bureau for Patents, the State Industrial and Commercial Administration, the State Foreign Currency Administration, the China Association for Foreign Trade Promotion, the General Custom House, the Office for Hong Kong and Macao Affairs of the State Council, the SEZ Group of the State Council, and legal experts from Beijing. After the draft group got favorable feedback on the first draft and incorporated the suggestions from the officials and experts, they sent the bill to the PPCSC for review and approval (Chen and Cen 1991, 200).

Shenzhen did not disappoint Deng Xiaoping. The Shenzhen SEZ laid down a legal framework for economic actors and instigated some important breakthroughs in the Chinese economic system. Two famous examples are "The Regulations for Corporations in the SEZs" and "The Shenzhen SEZ Land Administration Act." In Sept. 28, 1986, when the national law regarding corporations was still in the stage of exploration and discussion, the Guangdong PPCSC enacted "The Regulations for Corporations in the SEZs," the first legislation concerning corporations in China. It was two years subsequent to this that "The Law of the PRC concerning Enterprises Owned By the Whole People" and "The Law of the PRC concerning Sino-Foreign Cooperative Enterprises" were enacted at the national level. Four years later the "Law of the PRC concerning Sino-Foreign Joint Ventures" was enacted by the NPC. In Dec. 29, 1987, the Guangdong PPCSC passed "Shenzhen SEZ Land Administration Act," allowing the commercial transaction of land-users' rights. At that moment, the sale of land users' rights was not allowed in the "National Land Administration Law." But after the Guangdong's local law was passed, the central government did not contest it as unconstitutional. Rather, the Constitution was revised four months later to accommodate the new development in Guangdong's legislation (Lin 1993, 172-173).

Shenzhen has completely transformed itself into one of the ten largest cities in China, a city full of opportunity, energy and vitality. In 1980, Shenzhen was only a small rural county with a population of 320 thousand; in 1997, its population reached 3.6 million. During these 18 years, its GDP had an average annual growth rate of 36%, and an average annual growth rate of gross industrial output value of 53% (Its 1996 GDP was 482 times greater than that in 1979; its gross industrial output was 150 times greater than that in 1980) (Shenzhen 1990, 12-13, chap. 4). According to an estimate in 1990, Shenzhen maintained a record of 194 "No. 1's" in constructing facilities and developing institutions. In 1998, this record of "No. 1's" increased to 230 (Liu 1990; *PD*, Sept. 14, 1998, 4). Shenzhen's development was the most rapid in the world. "Shenzhen speed" has come to be a well-known phrase in China.

Shenzhen has also not only overhauled its economic, political and social institutions, but also has successfully established a set of new institutions and rules for its political economy. Beginning in 1979, as Hong Kong capital was allowed to flow in, Sino-Hong Kong joint ventures mushroomed in Shenzhen. To accommodate these joint ventures, changes in land and labor regulations were required. Markets for land and labor were created. Later, a stock exchange, stock issuing companies, and markets for technology and information were formed. Consequently, Shenzhen has all but abandoned the traditional socialist planned economy and created its own market economy. With the promotion of the co-existence of various types of property ownership, Shenzhen has given up the emphasis on state-ownership and has converged with the international economy. Stock-sharing and private ownership have come to predominate. For example, in 1995, the enterprises with investment from foreign countries, Taiwan, and Hong Kong were responsible for 82% of the gross industrial output (it was 35% in Shanghai for the same year) (Shenzhen Visiting Scholars 1997, 2).

The fundamental changes brought about by the new system of capital management created dynamic favoring radical changes in the entire society. Social security and labor protection were introduced; personnel management was restructured as people embraced new ideas. Even the government adjusted its way of governing by de-concentrating power, creating a small, efficient bureaucracy, and emphasizing its service function for business and society. The guiding principle for its work has changed to "small government, big society."

Shenzhen was designed as a special economic zone, not a special political zone.[2] But this did not prevent Shenzhen from breaking new ground in political reform. In the early 1980s, its Shekou Industrial Zone was hailed as "an experimental zone for reforms in the economic system, and also as a laboratory for exploring reforms in the political system" (Hu 1986). By introducing freedom of speech, the selection of officials through competition, votes of confidence on cadres, and by creating a tolerant environment, the so-called Shekou Impact (*Shekou Fengbo*) challenged the Communist control over the mass media, the traditional mode of political education, and many old norms and values. As new economic institutions

190 *The Dual Developmental State*

expanded, they unavoidably intensified the tensions between politics and the economy.

Political institutions have increasingly become the main obstacle to further reform. Shenzhen's steps toward political reform may amount to a breakthrough in the political realm as dramatic as that in China's economy.[3] Although no one single city can lead China out of a one-party system and empower the people with full freedom of expression, Shenzhen may nonetheless have a larger impact upon the way the central government does business, China's state-society relationship, and the accountability of officials to the people. Actually, several Shenzhen officials have expressed their desire to break new ground in the political realm to maintain the leading role of Shenzhen in the national political economy. The challenge from Shanghai has made this more urgent. If the market economy is embedded in a political, legal, social, and cultural environment, further changes in the political realm will be unavoidable, and Shenzhen has a new role to play in the process of China's transition: to experiment with some new political institutions as practiced by most market economies.

The great achievements in Shenzhen can also be viewed from the national perspective. To Deng Xiaoping, Shenzhen was expected to play four important roles for his reforms: First, it was to be "an experimental field" (*shiyantian*). Second, it was to be "an advance party of soldiers" (*xiandoubing*). Third, it was to be a "window" for technology, management, knowledge, and the policy of openness and reform. Fourth, it was to be a "bridge" connecting Hong Kong and mainland China. Playing these four roles, Deng instructed local officials that Shenzhen should boldly learn from foreign countries, especially from Hong Kong, with which it might eventually converge. Shenzhen should take new ideas and policies from capitalist countries and apply them to the environment of China. After a trial and error process, it should provide lessons and experiences for other localities in China. Its own success should have a strong demonstrative effect and finally help China smoothly finish a transition from the centrally-planned economy to a market-oriented economy (Ma and Ling 1998, 147-150; Xiao 1996, 213-219; Tang 1997, 191-204).

Shenzhen has become a window to demonstrate the latest achievements of China's modernization drive. By establishing a new SEZ, the central government expected it to attract western capital, technology, managerial skills and experiences, and ultimately to transform the Chinese economic structure from an out-dated socialist planned economy to a market oriented economy. Over the past 20 years, many new economic policies were first tested in Shenzhen, and then popularized in other areas of China. Despite an ongoing heated debate about whether the Shenzhen experiment has been a success or a failure, its national impact has been enormous. Far beyond what we can evaluate simply by calculating its contribution to the earning of hard currency and the learning of new technology, its real value to the nation lies in its importance for Deng's institutional design for China's transition and its avant-garde role in embracing capitalism.

For example, "Time is money, efficiency is life," one of the ten most famous slogans of the past two decades in China, was first shouted out by Shenzhen builders in 1979 and caused revolutionary changes in the Chinese way of work and life. In 1987, Shenzhen allowed individuals and companies to sell and buy land use rights (Liu 1989, 1990). This caused a constitutional change later. Shenzhen plays the role of an "experimental field" and "bellwether" for China's economic reform. Many crucial components for a market economy were first developed in Shenzhen, such as stock-ownership, stock issuing companies, the stock exchange, enterprise groups, the sale of land use rights, the contract system for cadres and labors, the social security system, insurance for laborers, and the open bidding process for government procurement, among others. No wonder a Shenzhen official told me with pride: "If you want to see the China of the past, look at Beijing; the China of the present is in Shanghai; but Shenzhen is the China of the future." This echoes Lee Kuan Yew's comments that "Shenzhen's today is China's tomorrow" (Wang and Gong 1998).

In 1989, Shenzhen announced that "a complete, organic, uniform, and dynamic market system" had already been formed. More than 90% of the goods, products, and means of production were regulated only by the market price. State-owned enterprises and private-owned businesses were treated equally. Foreign companies were given "treatment as nationals" when it came to water and electricity supply, access to foreign exchange, and bank interest rates. The Shenzhen officials also claimed that they had abandoned a series of old ideological taboos and made four fundamental breakthroughs: "Four old ideas were transformed and abandoned: the idea of planning that sticks to the state monopoly for purchasing and marketing in production and exchange; the traditional idea that socialism has no circulation (of materials for living and production in the form of commodity); the belief that the market is equivalent to capitalism; and the

192 *The Dual Developmental State*

idea that the market and the plan are incompatible. Four brand new ideas were embraced: market first, competition first, circulation first, consumption first" (Liu 1989b, 1-20, 21). If we compare these new ideas to Deng's major ideological innovations during his 1992 tour, we can clearly see the close connection between them. But there were four years between these ideas and Deng's innovations. As a result, when the whole of China was involved in a heated debate on the market vs. the plan, Shenzhen entrepreneurs were perplexed: Why again? "[Our] reality is so far ahead of Beijing's. Beijing is still talking about the best way to accomplish what we've already achieved. It would take an army of occupation to reverse the trends"(*Asia, Inc.*, July 1992).

Perhaps the best example for Shenzhen's central role in Deng's national strategy is that in the "three emancipations of the mind," Shenzhen had played a pivotal role in affecting the tone of the national debate and shaping the direction of the national political economy by supplying ammunition to Deng. In return, Deng became the strongest patron for Shenzhen and, indeed, came to its aid several times when it was under siege.

The establishment of the SEZs, to some degree, was a direct product of the first debate on the criterion of truth. If Deng needed ideas for his reform agenda, some local leaders suggested the experiences from the "Four Little Dragons" would do. Deng decided to put these ideas into practice in the hope of "seeking truth from facts." The experiment immediately caused heated debate about the nature of the SEZ economy. Some conservatives regarded the Shenzhen SEZ as a "new colony," or "a new concession." Some reportedly held the national flag and said, here only this is red. In 1981 and 1982, Chen Yun criticized the problems in the SEZs and pointed out the need for them to learn from and rectify these problems. He made the following observations: "Shenzhen, Zhuhai, Shantou and Xiamen are just experiments. We can have just these four zones and no more....Now every province wants a SEZ and wants to open up (to foreign investment). If that's the case, every foreign capitalist and speculator in our country will appear. Everyone might as well engage in speculation and profiteering. That's why we cannot do this"(*Asia, Inc.*, August, 1992).

In 1983, when the "anti-spiritual pollution campaign" was going on, Hu Yaobang, then Party General Secretary, went to Shenzhen and expressed his strong support for the SEZ. Accompanied by Yang Shangkun and Wang Zhen, Deng Xiaoping went to Shenzhen and the two other SEZs in 1984 to see personally whether the SEZs had succeeded or failed. Deng concluded his trip with a famous statement, "The development and experiences of Shenzhen have testified that our policy for setting up the SEZs was correct." With this encouragement, the other three SEZs were expanded, as fourteen more coastal cities were granted more power to open up to direct foreign investment. In 1985, the center further decided to allow fifty-nine cities and counties in the Yangtze delta, Pearl Harbor delta, and southern Fujian delta more freedom to interact with foreign capital and markets.

But when the Shenzhen model was widely appraised, an article written by a professor at the University of Hong Kong published in a popular Hong Kong magazine in 1984, asked this rhetorical question, "What went wrong with Shenzhen?" (*Shenzhen de wenti zai nali?*), another round of debate was stirred. At this moment Deng gave his assessment: "I am certain on two points: First, the decision for setting up SEZs was correct; Second, SEZs are still an experiment. It takes time for us to judge whether we have taken a right path or not. We wish them a success. If they failed, they were still an useful experience." The newly arrived mayor from Beijing also expressed his reservations by emphasizing that since the SEZs were an "experiment," we should be ready to pay a "tuition fee." After another three years, Deng finally became confident enough to tell foreign visitors, "We now can safely say, not only the decision for setting up SEZs was correct, but they are also very successful." With strong support from the central reformers, Shenzhen survived its first several tumultuous years (He 1988, 127-140; Tang 1997, 199-204; *RMRB*, February 2, 1984, 1).

For Deng, Shenzhen was an institutional investment that provided an experimental field for testing and generating new ideas, and ultimately enriched Deng's theoretical arsenal in policy debates with other leaders, most prominent being Chen Yun. In 1992, Shenzhen provided a stage for Deng to air his bold policies, and a base to mobilize local support for his endangered reforms. Because of the setback in 1989 and the dramatic changes in other socialist countries, the conservative forces suddenly found the courage to mobilize and fight back. The conservatives insisted that the supreme criterion for reforms was to judge whether they are socialist or capitalist. "To take the class struggle as the key link" became a formidable slogan and influenced Deng's teachings on "taking economy as the focus." Many reforms faced the danger of being undone.

194   *The Dual Developmental State*

From 1989 to 1992, when Deng stayed in Shanghai for the Spring Festival, he tried to send out his political message that economic development still should be the paramount task and should not be compromised by ideological factors. But his words were ignored. Four editorials published in the Shanghai official newspaper in 1991 were actually paraphrasing Deng's words but faced strong attack from the conservatives. Deng went to Shenzhen and launched his battle against the conservative forces in Beijing. During his "Southern Inspection Tour" in Shenzhen, he put forward his theory of "the three conducives," gave his support to the market economy, praised the success in Shenzhen and encouraged it to become another Hong Kong or Singapore. He also warned, "Only development will pass the test of reason." Two local newspapers, *The Shenzhen Commercial News* (*Shenzhen Shangbao*) and *The Shenzhen Special Zone Daily* (*Shenzhen Tequbao*) acted as devoted drummers for Deng's policy by carrying eight positive editorials in a series. As two Chinese commentators write, "Through the impact of public opinion from these two leading newspapers in Shenzhen, this spring wave from the south finally rushed northward and reached Beijing, the political central nerve of the nation. After the endorsement of the Politburo meeting, it rapidly overwhelmed the nation and radiated overseas. A new wave of reforms were generated" (Yuan and Han 1992, 65). We may say, Shenzhen salvaged Deng Xiaoping's reforms; in return, Deng's new call for reforms also consolidated Shenzhen's strategic role in China's transition.

Another crucial year for Shenzhen was 1994 when the special authorization of many favorable policies for Shenzhen was to expire after a 15 year run. In addition to this "weaning-off" crisis, Shenzhen's strategic position increasingly was being challenged by other cities as they developed their own special zones and competed for investments by matching each other's concessions. After the development of Pudong, with support from Jiang Zemin and Zhu Rongji, Shanghai became the new favorite son of the center and posed the biggest threat to Shenzhen's bellwether role. Another debate about the future of Shenzhen was conducted in China among officials and scholars. Some people believed that now it was time for Shenzhen to "return to the system" since a market economy had been endorsed as the fundamental structure of the Chinese economy. It did not make sense any more to maintain a privileged role for Shenzhen. And when the new tax-sharing system was carried out, the East-

West gap widened. This disparity made it more unjustifiable for any developed region to enjoy privileges unavailable to the inland region.

Hu Angang, an influential economist, was a vocal advocate for revoking the SEZs' special privileges. But the central government seemed to have no intention of transforming the SEZs back into normal cities. To assure the SEZs, Jiang Zeming visited Shenzhen and reiterated this basic principle toward the SEZs: "On behalf of the Party Central Committee and the State Council, I think it is necessary to repeat here that the basic policy of the center toward the SEZs will not change. The historical position and role of SEZs in national reform, the opening of the economy, and modernization will not change. Developing SEZs will be part of the entire process of constructing a socialist modernization. How long it takes us to realize the modernization of our nation, will decide how long we will stick to the development of SEZs." (Cited from Zhang, et al, 1997, vol. 2, 238).

For the Chinese central leaders, if marketization is a long process, Shenzhen is still needed for generating lessons and experiences pertaining to "institutional innovations." The Shenzhen Municipal Government has taken some important steps in fulfilling this function. One important step was that the Shenzhen government adopted a new guideline, the so-called "three firsts": "Those international practices the nation intends to adopt shall be first introduced in Shenzhen; new policy adjustments for the WTO membership should be first tried here; new mechanisms for establishing a new socialist market economy should be first used here" (Zhang, et al, 1997, vol. 2, 232-253).

This function indeed helped Jiang Zeming in formulating his agenda of restructuring the ownership system by resorting to "stock sharing" reforms. In 1997, before the Party endorsed the stock sharing system, and private ownership, Li Youwei, Party Secretary of Shenzhen, published an article casting doubt on state-ownership and endorsing privatization. He argued that: "Whatever ownership best fits and fosters the development of productive forces is the best" (Li 1997). His viewpoint stirred a nationwide debate on the advantages and disadvantages of state ownership and private ownership, and ushered in resolutions in the Party's National Congress that legitimated private ownership and a stock sharing system that were a milestone for the "third emancipation of the mind" (Yuan and Han 1992; Ma and Ling 1998; Zhang, et al, 1998).

Deng Xiaoping wanted his political legacy to be remembered as "the Second Revolution" for China after Mao Zedong's "First Revolution"

196   *The Dual Developmental State*

more than half a century ago. After the Long March, Mao took Yanan as his "red base" to accumulate and expand Communist influence over the following difficult years, to experiment with new strategies and tactics, then to systematize and popularize them in other places. Eventually he won the final victory. His strategy was summarized as "the Yanan Road" and was later made popular in the West by foreign observers like Edgar Snow, the author of *Red Star over China*. Shenzhen is to Deng Xiaoping what Yanan was to Mao Zedong. Deng's "Shenzhen model" has the same, in fact a greater, historical significance than Mao's "Yanan Road." Once allowed "to jump out of the current system," it is no exaggeration to say that Shenzhen has been an Archimedean point for Deng Xiaoping's strategy.

Shenzhen Model and the Transition Costs

With respect to the Shenzhen model, many scholars have two questions to ask: Why was not Shanghai chosen since it has better human resources, thus potentially making it a better bell-whether for the Chinese national economy? Why was not Wenzhou favored as a model for national emulation, since as some recent studies have argued, in terms of input-output analysis, the "Wenzhou model" was more efficient and less expensive (Fong 1998; Parris, 1993)? Why then didn't Deng Xiaoping use either Shanghai or Wenzhou as his Archimedean point? To shed light upon these questions, it is necessary to consider the central place of the transition costs in Deng's strategic thinking and planning.

According to Douglass North (1990, 94), the choice of one specific path of economic development is always constrained by its past course, or the effect of "path-dependence," meaning that "the consequence of small events and chance circumstances can determine solutions that, once they prevail, lead one to a particular path." This is like Karl Marx's idea that human beings can create history, but only under the constraints of history. With respect to Deng's challenges in the late 1970s, the antiquated but powerful institutions under a Stalinist political economy defined the circumstances of path-dependence. Deng considered three possible options for transcending the constraints, for introducing institutional innovations, and ultimately for replacing the old Communist system with a new one: (1) a radical, coordinated effort to rebuild the ship at sea, (2) a laissez faire, individual approach to let passengers save themselves, and (3) a conservative, coordinated effort to build a new ship with more compartments before the ship sinks.

Most post-Communist countries in the former Soviet Union and East Europe have followed the first option (Elster, et al, 1998). The rationale for this option is very simple: Since the old socialist system is the biggest stumbling block for liberalization and marketization, the first thing that should be done is to demolish this old building and clear it away to give space to the new system. If demolition is planned, it should be carried out in one stroke, because it does not make sense to cut off the tail of a cat piece by piece. This simply prolongs the process of pain and suffering. Guided by this rationale, the captains (old or new) in Eastern Europe and the former Soviet Union let their passengers destroy the old ship and start the process of rebuilding a new one at sea. However, this strategy did not work very well in these countries, primarily for two reasons: The leaders exaggerated their own and their people's ability and resolution to abandon the old ship (remember, institutions are "man-made man") and underestimated the difficulty of instituting a market economy. As a result, when the old system was under siege, the attack itself mobilize the conservative forces.

The radical reformers engaged in a Herculean battle with the defenders of the status quo. What followed were military coups, economic crises, the change of power through new elections, the come-back of the communist old guards, political stagnation, a protracted, painful transition for the people, and the loss of creditability and legitimacy of the reformers. Long before the radical reformers could see the fruition of their strategies, most of them suffered fatal wounds, and many were swept out of office. If Deng Xiaoping had chosen Shanghai or some other large economic actor as the primary target, it would have been a wake-up call not for reformers, but for conservatives, providing them with a banner to rally around and would have led China into the common scenarios found in other post-Communist countries. This is why when Chen Yun expressed his strong opposition against the idea of SEZs, Deng did not attack Shanghai, Chen's favorite base (and the city in which he was raised), to try to win a Pyrrhic victory. Instead, Deng Xiaoping simply walked away and targeted Shenzhen, the weakest link of the socialist central planning system (Jia and Lin 1994, 239-60; Cheung, et al, 1998, 49-88; Yeung and Sung 1996).

The second option sounds like the favorite for the neo-liberals. If everyone knows best what his or her own interests are, why should they

198   *The Dual Developmental State*

need a captain to organize them in a rescue mission? In terms of economic development, it seems proper that a market economy and private ownership should emerge spontaneously, as some orthodox and neo-liberals have argued. Indeed, scholars have found that the role of the government in Wenzhou was less significant than it was in many other provinces that followed a government-guided strategy. The Wenzhou model was a "semi-spontaneous" process (Cheung, et al, 1998, 145-211). Therefore, it would have been advisable for Deng Xiaoping to encourage the Wenzhou path in which the central government paid much less attention than it did in Shenzhen.

But for Deng Xiaoping, a strong nationalist with a national "catch-up" agenda, and an impatient leader who wanted to see the revival of China's old grandeur, this approach had two undesirable qualities: The economic development would have been very slow and its future course more unpredictable. This approach essentially expects the state to be out of the economic business. It goes against the belief in a state role, the conventional wisdom developed among Third World leaders, to which the Chinese leaders took no exception.

In designing new institutions or reshaping old ones, an institutional designer will always consider the general efficiency of the expected institution. According to institutional economists, an institutional designer has to consider both transformation and transaction costs.[4] I have no doubt that Deng understood this: An optimal economy should be a market economy enabling the destruction of the Stanlinist bureaucratic system, because in theory and practice, a market economy has lower production and transaction costs than a centrally planned economy. Certainly, when the Chinese leadership was considering different ideal models and strategies for development, they did take into consideration whether the new system would be more efficient than the current one, and whether the general efficiency of the entire system would be improved. Institutional designers always calculate the different efficiencies of two systems, with the significant difference providing an incentive for change.

This was the case in China. But I would like to propose the following reasons to explain why the allegedly more efficient institution was not adopted, and the "Shenzhen model" was favored for national emulation: (1) The optimal mode of governance in terms of production costs does not necessarily produce a higher net aggregate gain for the whole society than another mode with relatively higher production costs, if the transition costs are incurred in a process of institutional change. I define transition costs as the price paid by the society for moving from one mode of governance to another one. (2) With regard to dynamic institutional change, the transition costs will be added to the transformation costs and transaction costs. Together they determined the path of institutional change. (3) The transition costs arise from the path-dependence effect in institutional change. The path-dependence effect will be magnified the greater the intensity and the larger the scale of change. Deliberately managing the intensity and scale of change will help overcome the constraints from the former path. (4) The intensity of change is largely determined by the degree of divergence between the current system and the expected one. A gradual strategy for institutional change, or the "chipping-away" strategy, often makes the resistance from the old system more manageable. Had the Chinese leadership, especially Deng Xiaoping, not thought about the transition costs, the transition costs could have easily canceled out the gains of the new system. It is quite possible that the differential gains by switching systems are smaller than the transition costs. If this is the case, it does not make any sense to reshape institutions. Unless the net aggregate gains are still positive after the transition costs are deducted from the differential gains, a transition from one system to another cannot be justified and cannot be regarded a success.

Deng decided to bypass inland provinces and industrial centers like Shanghai and Tianjian, for he did not want to stir up a hornet's nest right from the start. He chose Shenzhen and the other three SEZs, for he wanted to tap into the resources of overseas Chinese networks for quick results. Fujian and Guangdong are the home provinces of the largest number of overseas Chinese. Shenzhen is close to Hong Kong, Zhuhai to Macao, and Shantou and Xiamen to Taiwan. In the early 1980s, the "Four Little Dragons" became newly industrialized economies and had a strong "demonstration effect" upon the Chinese coastal areas. In addition, these nations and areas also were restructuring their economies by transferring out of labor-intensive industries and upgrading to value increasing industries. These demonstration and restructuring effects met Deng's "opening-up" policy and the SEZs, a Shenzhen Revolution, and eventually a Southern China Miracle were created. Actually, Hong Kong and Taiwan's capital have been the dominant driving force behind the Chinese economic boom in these areas. Therefore, scholars have argued, "the bamboo network" transcended the political barriers, permeated mainland China, and finally created there a *"guanxi* capitalism" in their own images

200 *The Dual Developmental State*

(Castells 1998, 293; Naughton 1997; Weidenbaum and Huges 1996; Hsin 1998; Wank, 1999).

The Chinese scholars have generalized the experiences of Shenzhen with the phrase: "introducing from the outside and linking with the interior" (*waiyin neilian*). The SEZs used special policies to attract foreign direct investment, technologies, joint ventures, and foreign enterprises. As these all poured in, the SEZs needed more talented people and investment in infrastructure from other Chinese areas. Many interior provinces and central ministries also wanting to take advantage of the special policies granted exclusively to SEZs, brought in a large amount of capital and established offices and factories. As Yao Yiling put it, Shenzhen needed "national support." Indeed, many provinces and ministries invested heavily there to set up their "window enterprises" in order to get access to global markets. According to one study, up to 1984, central ministries had invested 1.6 billion yuans; from 1980 to 1985, the ratio between the foreign investment and domestic capital (in the form of loans, investment from other provinces and ministries, etc.) of the total of 6.4 billion yuans invested for basic construction during the past five years was 1 to 4 (He 1988, 131-132). Therefore, direct foreign investment and the "blood transfusion" from the inland provinces, created a boomtown, with Shenzhen being the crucial link between foreign capital and Chinese enterprises.

This strategic position made it possible for Shenzhen to exert its demonstration and restructuring effect upon the inland once its economy succeeded. According to Li Youwei, Shenzhen Party Secretary, Shenzhen formed a "two-dimensional cooperation" with less developed inland provinces. In 1996, Shenzhen had more than 600 enterprises based on such cooperation. At the same time, Shenzhen enterprises invested 15 billion yuans in 1,390 projects nationwide and transferred 600 labor-intensive factories to other regions, reaching as far as Northeast China. Thus, these beneficial interactions between Shenzhen and the inland provinces were frequent occurrences (Zhang, et al, 1997, vol. 2, 241).

After Deng's Southern Tour in 1992, a new round of developmentalism surged. Thousands of special developmental zones or technological zones were set up by provinces nationwide, (in 1991, 117 developmental zones nationwide; after the "developmental zone fever," in 1992, the number increased to 2,700; and in 1993, there were more than 6,000 developmental zones.) emulating the Shenzhen model, and attracting foreign capital (Montinola, et al, 1995, 77; Ming 1993).

The Shenzhen model was nationalized. This spread of the Shenzhen experience turned the exceptionalism of the SEZs into a national standard. Accordingly, China's "economic identity" also changed from state socialism to a state-guided market economy. or state-led capitalism (Crane 1994). In response to the challenge from Shenzhen, and other developed coastal areas, many Chinese inland provinces adopted two important state-led strategies: "To force the officials to enrich the people" (*biguan fumin*) and "The officials force the people to become rich" (*guanbi minfu*). On the one hand, the high level officials pay attention to the appointment of entrepreneurial leaders and put pressure on them, using their achievement in developing the economy as the most important consideration for promotion (Bo 1996). The officials are forced to make the economy their priority. On the other hand, the leaders also play an active role inspiring, leading, and guiding the people to overcome the traditional anti-business mentality and to actively participate in the market economy in order to get rich.[5] With these policies, China now has a pervasive "fear-of-poverty culture." The developmental states and excessive developmentalism are certainly responsible for the rapid economic development in China.

Here I must point out, unlike Mao's disastrous strategy of massive immediate mobilization (i.e., the Great Leap Forward and the Cultural Revolution), Deng's strategy was much more successful, because he did not put all his eggs into one basket. Instead, he encouraged experiments in different places with different ideas. Shenzhen was one of his places for experimenting with new ideas and generating new experiences for his strategic planning. Meanwhile, more than a hundred cities were chosen as pilots to experiment with comprehensive reforms or reforms in one specific issue area. These reforms included restructuring urban government, instituting a financial system. a housing policy, and starting the reform of resource allocation (Gao 1987, 184; Zhou 1984).

Shenzhen's promising potential and vitality convinced his cynical colleagues and other local leaders who were reluctant to reform. Other places started to emulate Shenzhen, and Shenzhen became a seed for change sowed by Deng. Ultimately, this seed grew into a tree, and then a forest, and finally this forest surrounded and buried the old state socialism.

202 *The Dual Developmental State*

State-based Power Networks

How can Communist countries move away from their old political and economic institutions to more desirable ones? What salient factor or factors shape the path of institutional change? This chapter uses the case of the Shenzhen SEZ to demonstrate the role of the transition costs in institutional design, and the function of networks to reduce both transaction and transition costs. By focusing on the central-local interaction, it has been made apparent how China's institutional designer, Deng Xiaoping, used the Municipality of Shenzhen as an Archimedean point to turn the Chinese political economy up-side down, setting state socialism on the track of a market-oriented economy. This strategy of "building a new ship before the Titanic sinks," is in contrast to the "rebuilding the ship at sea" strategy adopted by East European post-communist countries.

Shedding light on the key question in this chapter: Why was "the Shenzhen model" favored by Deng, despite the fact that this model per se was neither more efficient nor less expensive than some alternatives available in other parts of China? In this chapter I argue "the transition costs" occupied a central place in the strategic thinking of institutional design. In other words, I argue that besides the concerns for the transformation costs and transaction costs, the transition costs, which I define as the price paid for moving away from the old mode of governance to the new one, determined the path of the Chinese transition.

Transition costs can refer to the deterioration of the economic growth rate and standard of living, political disorder (such as a coup d'etat or civil war leading to political paralysis), psychological suffering, and cultural dislocation (loss of identity). They can be either paid by one segment of the population, the ruling class, or the entire society. In this chapter I put a finger on a crucial concept, the transition costs, in order to provide a bridge between the concept of path-dependence and the choice of a path for transition. When we talk about institutional change from one mode of governance to another one, the transition costs must be included. The production costs (both the transformation and transaction costs) are useful for providing a static comparison of two systems, but cannot fully account for the dynamic process of system transitions we have seen in China, Eastern Europe and the post-Soviet states. Once identified, it is easy to understand the importance of transition costs for the institutional designers.

Shenzhen Revolution and Central-Local Synergism 203

Since China has been regarded as a success in the transition from state socialism to a market economy, with Shenzhen two steps ahead of other Chinese regions (since Guangdong is one step ahead), concentrating one's research on Shenzhen is useful if one is to build a theory directed to explaining the importance of transition costs. This case study of Shenzhen, which includes its interactions with the central state, the developmental synergism between micro and macro linkages, and its demonstration effect upon other provinces and cities surely will generate meaningful theoretical conclusions for "transiotology" (Elster, et al, 1998) as well as practical guidance for any transition.

The development and transformation of Shenzhen also has provided an excellent perspective from which to examine the developmental synergism between the center and localities. The Shenzhen case shows that local developmentalism has played an indispensable role in China's national transition. The traditional approaches to the central-local relationship tend to treat it as a zero-sum relationship. They often exaggerate the tensions and incompatibilities between the center and local levels, ignoring the networks developed between the center and localities and ignoring their ability to manage their conflicts. As a result, they issue alarmist warnings about China's inevitable disintegration. But if we can see a symbiotic relationship existing between an authoritarian developmental state in Beijing and the most liberalized city in China, we have no reason to doubt that the Chinese central government can manage its relationship with the localities.

Actually, both sides are aware of how this indispensable relationship serves the interests of each. This is apparent in the efforts to give reassurance (*gei dingxingwan*) to Shenzhen by the center and to find a new patron in the center (*zao kaoshan*, finding the backing) by Shenzhen. The center has reassured Shenzhen of its "special status" on several occasions. Menawhile, Shenzhen has found Jiang Zemin as its new patron by emphasizing Jiang's early involvement in the establishment of the SEZs.

Several other studies have also argued that the relationship between the center and localities in China is characterized by "interdependence" and "mutuality." It is a "non-zero-sum game" (Lieberthal and Oksenberg 1988; Linda Li 1998; Wu and Zheng 1995). To explain this equilibrium between the center and localities, Oksenberg and Lieberthal have emphasized that the two levels each possessed some resources that are essential to the central control and local autonomy, but neither the center

204 *The Dual Developmental State*

possessed enough to command nor the local governments possess enough to take an independent path. Instead, both need the valuable resources that each provides. They have "portrayed central-provincial relations neither in terms of central dominance nor provincial autonomy. Rather, interdependence characterizes the relationship with the balance generally in favor of the center" (Oksenberg and Lieberthal 1988, 346).

Wu Guoguang and Zheng Yongnian (1995) emphasize the separation of administrative decentralization and political decentralization to maintain and institutionalize the "bargaining relationship, or a de facto federalism." This conclusion was supported by other studies.[6] From a rational choice perspective, Linda Li concludes her study on the center-provinces relationships by placing them within a non-zero sum framework: Both the center and provinces have irreducible power over one another. For the center it is coercion; for the provinces, it is their intermediary role in the Chinese structure. Therefore, they form a mutual interdependence and are indispensable to each other. This condition makes for protracted conflicts in which total victory or total failure is not feasible. Ultimately, a politics of compromise as a non-zero-sum game have formed (Linda Li 1998, 34).

From my studies of the developmental state, I like to draw several inferences relevant to the aforementioned conclusions. When we talk about the central-local relationship, it is unlikely that the provinces or localities are one uniform actor vis-à-vis the center, as Linda Li's study has assumed. It is nearly impossible to provide a clear-cut framework accounting for the relationships between the center and 31 provincial, and many local units. Since the two-tier developmental state in China has revealed an uneven "geographically sliding policy," some localities have received more favorable policies and privileges (like the SEZs), some have not; in some provinces, the center has taken more aggressive actions to try to boost local developmentalism through appointing competent and reform-minded leaders (such as Zhao Zhiyang to Sichuan, Wan Li to Anhui, Rui Xinwen, Jiang Zemin, and Zhu Rongji to Shanghai), in other provinces, the center took no action (cases in Zhejiang in the 1980s and Shaanxi) (Cheung, et al, 1998). There has been no universal pattern with regard to the center-localities relationships in China.

From the provincial perspective, the provinces seldom act collectively at the same time to engage in bargaining with the center, therefore, even from a rational choice perspective, the central power should not be evaluated against the resources of 31 provincial units as a collective actor in collective action. Moreover, the provinces have never been able to be at equal footing with the center. It is still the case that there is a strong developmental state vis-à-vis the localities with a power relationship in favor of the center, as Oksenberg and Lieberthal have argued. This is because the parameters structuring this relationship have been defined more by the center than by the localities, not to mention the many other crucial resources that give the center an upper hand in bargaining with the provinces.

The feature of unevenness, or particularism reflected in the center-localities relationship, is a conspicuous character of network governance. A network society is always in favor of particularism instead of universalism. This has made the Chinese state structure appear less institutionalized, and lacking legibility. However, this amorphism provides freedom for the Chinese state to explore new ways to structure or regulate the center-localities relationship. For a huge country, this should not be seen as a problem. Rather it is a strength, a great advantage for the Chinese state in transition. Besides, the existence of networks between the center and local governments, (as demonstrated in Shenzhen case) as well as among the provinces, has made it easier for political actors and institutions to be connected and to communicate with each other. The more efficient and free flow of information certainly reduces miscalculations, helps smooth out differences and work out compromises, and contributes to the maintenance of an equilibrium between the center and localities.

Many scholars in recent studies have pointed out the importance of networks, or *guanxi*, in Chinese local politics (Oi, 1987; Wank 1999; White 1998; Yang 1994; Yan 1996a, 1996b; Wilson 1997; Herrmann-Pillath 1996; Wang Huning 1991; Dongfang 1998). But most studies approach the *guanxi* from a cultural, sociological, anthropological, or historical perspective, treating it as an abnormal phenomenon. They treat *guanxi* as a Chinese cultural and political phenomenon lacking objectivity, or as an art featuring interactions within a limited group, or at micro-level such as a family, work unit, or interpersonal relations, etc. Or at best, networks are treated as linkages between societal forces, or informal actors, and institutionalized, formal authority. Few scholars have treated the networks in Chinese society as a new mode of governance for the macro-management of the political economy. Although I agree that network is affected by its old traditional *guanxi* culture, it also should be understood as a political and economic governance. Lynn White rightly

206 *The Dual Developmental State*

points out that the networks have played an important part in transforming the Chinese hierarchy. He writes,

> Power in small collectivities is as effective, in the long term, as power in the national government, which has more obvious coercive sanctions. Networks are a more useful object of political study than is power conceived as merely centralized or decentralized, supra- or infra-politics. Networks come in many types. Some are vertical, others horizontal. Many networks exchange protection and sustenance for obedience and service, other exchange commodities or reputation. They can be isolated or widely connected. Some are official; others are not. Links between people and groups, as described by networks, are institutions that frame most exercises of power and also serve many other human purposes. It would be difficult to study politics while ignoring these platforms in which they are based. Organized horizontal relationships between networks were hardly new in China before reforms came, and they are not necessarily modern in any country. But nonstate networks, both productive and corrupt, have expanded rapidly during reforms. They might be said to engage in infrapolitics; but if so, the bottom certainly constrains the top. (White 1998, vol. 1, 36-37)

However, in White's study, he uses the local networks and the nonstate networks interchangeably in opposition to the state or hierarchy. Based on my study, the networks have certainly been a part of local institutions. Furthermore, the central state has also resorted to networks to transform its own institutions, and to regulate its relationships with the local states. This is its fundamental characteristic: A network form of governance excludes neither a hierarchy nor market mechanisms. Instead, it incorporates both. Therefore, instead of seeing a dichotomy, or an antagonism between the state and local networks as does White, my study reveals that the networks have become a basic feature of the states both at the central and local levels and framed their interactions. The networks have transcended informal politics and have been incorporated into the formal Chinese body politic. They have become the fundamental principle used to organize the order of the political economy, and are now a conspicuous feature of institutional transformation in transitional China.

Notes

1   It is said, one day Deng brought his grandson to visit Chairman Mao. Mao wanted the grandson to call him "Grandpa" and was refused. Mao took out some candies and said if he called him, he could get candy. Deng's grandson immediately said, "hello, Grandpa Mao." Deng made these comments to Mao: "Look, even such a little boy knows the material incentive." See: Xiao 1996, 202-203.

2   In 1981, the Central Party Committee and the State Council agreed upon the guideline for the SEZs. The first guideline was that the SEZs are special economic zones, not political economic zones. As Fang Sheng, an economist, puts it: With regard to the SEZs, economy is special not politics, they are anti-pollution not anti-foreign. Guo 1997, 285; Xiao 1998, 181.

3   One very significant move towards political and social changes is the "Overseas Training of Shenzhen High-Level Personnel" project. Since 1996, Shenzhen has sent hundreds of government officials to the United States, Japan, EU, Australia, and Hong Kong for short and long term professional training. It is expected to last at least for ten years. The Municipal Government expects, at that time, all important leaders at the city, bureau and department levels will have acquired a comparative approach to look at their own work. More details can be found in: Lu Ruifeng, *Shenzhen Ganbu Zhidu Gaige Lun* [Reforms on Cadre System in Shenzhen] (Shenzhen: Haitian Chubanshe, 1997); The Organization Department, Shenzhen Municipal CPC Committee, *Shenzhen Gaoji Rencai Peiyang Gongcheng Shilu* [Records on the Project for Training Senior Cadres in Shenzhen] (Shenzhen: Haitian Chubanshe,1997); Training and developing Bureau of Senior Civil Servants of Shenzhen People's Government: *Overseas Training of Shenzhen High-Level Personnel* (Shenzhen: Municipal Government, 1998). You can also visit their website at "http://www.szii.gov.cn/overseas_training".

4   Douglass North (1990, 28) states, "The total costs of production consist of the resource inputs of land, labor, and capital involved both in transforming the physical attributes of a good (size, weight, color, location, chemical composition, and so forth) and in transacting-defining, protecting, and enforcing the property rights to goods (the right to use, the right to derive income from the use of, the right to exclude, and the right to exchange)."

5   Xiao 1998, 27-30. In Jean Oi (1992, 1995)'s study, she calls this phenomenon "local state corporatism" in which a local government coordinated economic enterprises in its territory as if it were a diversified business corporation.

6   Montinola, Qian and Weingast believe that China has been a federalist state, its de facto federalism has also been "market-preserving." See: Montinola, et al, 1995. Another Nobel laureate, James Buchanan (1997) also suggests that "competitive federalism" will be the optimal institution for China.

8 The Logic of the Dual Developmental State

The discussion on the dynamic interactions among political arrangements for China's transition constitutes the basic focus of the book. In my study, development strategy, political institutions, and market institutions have been treated both as explicandums (the phenomenon to be explained) and the explicans (the factors accounting for explicandum) as the context of research varies. First, by focusing on political and economic institutions and their legacies, I explained why and how the developmental state strategy was adopted and adapted in China. The targeted goals for the economy and the path-dependent constraints arising from the political context constituted the framework for the changes of the development strategy. Through interactions with the international environment, Chinese leaders experimented with different strategies and finally settled on the East Asian developmental state model. However, there were substantial modifications due to China's vastness and the legacy of state socialism.

Political institutions, specifically the central state, the National People's Congress (NPC), the Provincial People's Congresses (PPCs), and central-local relations are treated within the context of the development strategy and marketization. The goal of building up a market economy explains the dynamics behind political institutionalization. The chosen development strategy, namely the developmental state model, constituted a constraint upon the process of political institutionalization, and defined its character and logic. Consequently, the institutional development has been harnessed to serve, instead of harm, the state capacity of a developmental state.

Finally, the process of market creation in China has been attributed to the choice of a developmental state strategy with assistance from deliberate political arrangements. The successful adoption of the developmental state strategy generated more opportunities for the Chinese economy to evolve toward a market-oriented one. However, this was achieved with assistance from a developmental political system at both the central and local levels that involved the synergism between the two. In particular, the NPC and

PPCs were crucial to the creation of a market economy and its maintenance, and also have been an indispensable part of the Chinese developmental state.

In the following section, I will summarize the main arguments and findings of my study.

The Duality of the Chinese Developmental State

The failure of state socialism and Hua Guofeng's new radical adventure discredited Mao's development strategy and ushered in Deng Xiaoping with his pragmatic reform agenda in the late 1970s. For Deng, economic development (for a while it was reflected in the call for the realization of Four Modernizations) was his major concern. Understandably, even he did not develop a clear vision for China's future, Deng underscored general efficiency as the bottom-line for evaluating different economic strategies as demonstrated and practiced by the United States and countries in Asia and Eastern Europe. Transformation costs, transaction costs, and transition costs all played a part in Deng's considerations. Consequently, a variety of experiments guided by different models were conducted. The achievements in the coastal regions, especially in Shenzhen and other SEZs, convinced Deng that the East Asian developmental state model was preferable and should be emulated. By emulating the successful model of East Asian developmental states, Deng turned China into a developmental state.

However, under the constraints arising from its vastness and Communist legacy, China has had to creatively transform its institutional arrangements and modify the developmental state model in order to be market-facilitating and maintain a strong state capacity. The two most important modifications are seen in the relationships between the government and the legislative system, between the center and localities. If a strong executive is a continuation of the past regime, an active legislative system is an innovation that took hold after the reforms were initiated. While China's industrial policy is an adoption, its regional policy is an adaptation. Decentralization is a further development of the developmental state model, serving as a precondition, not a consequence, of Chinese economic development over the past two decades. If China has turned into a developmental state, it has done so by following a dual developmental state model. The duality of the Chinese developmental state is illustrated by an active role played by the People's Congresses (PCs) in the

210 *The Dual Developmental State*

developmental system, in partnership with the central state, makes it appropriate to speak of a two-tiered structure involving the center and localities.

My empirical studies on Chinese legislative development have revealed that both the NPC and the PPCs have become more institutionalized over the past two decades. They also have been instrumental in fostering a market economy. Extensive empirical data demonstrate that since the start of China's reforms, the NPC and PPCs have built up their own structures, expanded accessory institutions, established rules and norms for their operation and interaction with other institutions, and created institutional linkages with the public and other political actors. They have also improved the qualities of their personnel. Deputies, especially the members and Chairmen of the SC, have become better educated and better connected in the regime. Increasingly, the NPC and PPCs have achieved relative autonomy and identity, distinguishing themselves from other institutions of the state and the Party. They also have laid down an institutional foundation for their emergence as increasingly influential actors in national and sub-national politics, which is reflected in their legislation, supervision over the executive and judicial branch, oversight of the law enforcement, and their contestation with other political actors.

The strategy for legislative development in China was guided by the criterion of developmentalism. To be developmental was the first step for the legislative development of the Communist representative institutions. The activities of the PPCs in the market creation, and in preventing and remedying the "market failures" and "state failures," demonstrated their developmental role in the Chinese economy. The interactions among the NPC, the PPCs and other political actors demonstrates that the NPC and the PPCs did not hesitate to exert their powers to challenge the government, judicial branch, and even the Party, when they thought that their actions could be justified by the larger interests of national development. Relative to the past, Chinese legislative system has achieved remarkable progress. Even in a comparative context, the legislatures both at the central and national levels in China have consolidated some degree of legitimacy and autonomy in the political system, and their contestation with other political actors has sown the seeds of liberalization among the ruling elite, which might bring the Chinese political system to the threshold of democratization. Nonetheless, their emphasis on developmentalism has suppressed the potential impact of the NPC and PPCs upon democratization and explains the phenomenon of "democratic deficit" in their institution building. However, this failing is not a reason for denying the reality of Chinese legislative development.

The Chinese legislative development is a Fabian strategy, with a conservative pace at the beginning leading to a cumulative achievement in the long term. The tragic setbacks in Russian legislative development and democratization led some parliamentary scholars to conclude that a subordinate role of new legislatures to the executive may contribute more to legislative development and long-term democratization (O'Brien 1994; Hahn 1995, 237). However, the choice for the legislatures in their early development had gone beyond that of being either subordinate or unruly. Sophisticated political entrepreneurs within the PCs, even those at the local level, were able to expand their power, and at the same time, convince the executive and the whole ruling elite that they could be of help in making and implementing policy, and even at times indispensable to the maintenance of the whole system by serving the goals of political integration and control. Once the legislatures were organically integrated into the process of governing, their institutionalization could be justified. A more institutionalized legislature certainly would be less exposed to the danger of abolition or executive dictatorship. For most countries in transition and those developing countries, the easiest way to pursue this strategy is to resort to economic developmentalism, as the Chinese experiences have demonstrated.

The tensions between the center and localities, between the government and legislative branch have made the Chinese dual developmental state look awkward. Many people doubt its ability to survive. If the conventional knowledge generated by the developmental state theory is that suppression of legislative and regional power strengthens the state capacity, then, how China has remained a strong state under the circumstances of legislative activism and decentralization becomes very intriguing. However, political actors in China have been able to institutionalize a sustainable relationship between a developmental state at the national level and local developmentalism, between an active legislative system and strong governments by forming a non-zero sum, or a cooperative, game. It can be viewed as a larger Nash equilibrium game at the national level embedded within smaller games at the local level (local developmentalism in thirty-one provinces), as the former is able to set the rules for the latter, and the latter generally play by these rules (Granick 1990, 23).

212 *The Dual Developmental State*

Explanations for the possibility of such an arrangement are multiple. First, the major players (the center and local states, the governments and legislatures) share compatible goals. The optimal goal for the center is to keep ruling. To achieve this goal, it needs economic prosperity, and usually also political and social stability. But the center knows its limitations in these areas, and therefore looks to the local states to play an active role. Local leaders are expected to take the primary responsibility for keeping their region prosperous and stable. Prosperity and stability often become the main criteria the center uses to evaluate the performances of local leaders. For local leaders, whether they are in the government or the PC, their primary aim is to secure their position. Many provincial government leaders also may want to be promoted to the central government. Therefore, they have a strong incentive to boost the local economy and maintain stability. Their performance in these two areas are closely watched by the PPCs which have the constitutional rights to elect and to dismiss the provincial governments. High ratings (e.g., strong election results, and favorable government work reports) from the PPCs do not automatically translate into promotion, but low ratings, and objections in other forms (for example, impeachment, inquiry, and criticisms on the floor, etc.) will indicate that the governmental leaders have no future in the official hierarchy. To some extent, we can say the PPCs have veto power over the promotion of provincial governmental leaders, for the central government does pay attention to how provincial governmental officials are judged by the PPCs.

Second, both the center and local states have realized that their functional resources are interdependent. The center controls the power of appointment and dismissal that determines the political careers of governmental officials. It also has control over key economic resources. For example, it can provide funds to and implement favorable policies for a province. This can be a big boon to the local economy, as the Shenzhen and Pudong cases have shown. Besides, the center controls the military and the ideological and propaganda apparatus and relies on them to make the center's threats creditable. Furthermore, the center has some instruments to adjust the larger game at the national level and discipline the regional governments to abide by the basic rules set by the Center: (1) Administrative control through the Party organization, personnel appointments and sanctions, (2) Monetary and fiscal control over the national economy (Huang 1996); (3) The Party's and Center's embedded ties with the provincial legislatures, mass organizations, and economic

Logic of the Dual Developmental State 213

units; (4) The military as a last resort for quelling challenges from the localities and separatist forces (Lieberthal and Oksenberg 1988, 138-140). Therefore, the center has the capacity to define the parameters of the central-local relationship.

But this does not mean the thirty-one provinces have no resources to counter-balance the center. Two important institutional arrangements have given institutional bases to local developmentism: First, regional property rights. As David Granick (1990) has argued that the existence of property rights individually owned by the regional governments has changed the relationship between the center and regional governments: the center no longer can treat the regional governments as agents as is the case with the central government ministries and state-owned enterprises. Regional governments now enjoy property rights, and are also "principals," just as the center is in relation to the state-owned enterprises. The regional governments have some countervailing power against the center (Huang 1996). Second, the PPCs now have some legislative autonomy. Because the provinces have been allowed to initiate legislation according to their own needs and characteristics, the provinces are able to define the rules of their own games, providing they are not challenging the equilibrium of the whole system.

Finally, the equilibrium of the Chinese system is also maintained by the self-constraints from both the center and the localities, from their mutual understanding and cooperation. The center and provinces have shared the following pool of common knowledge: First, in the near future, the CPC will continue its rule. It is very unlikely that the CPC will be replaced by another political organization very soon. Second, the central authority should be respected and the national interest should take precedence over the local interest. Since it is almost impossible for thirty-one provinces to coordinate a collective action against the center, the center will always have the upper hand when it so chooses. Third, they all are aware of the iron law in the central-local relationship: if the center loses too much control, chaos often ensues; if the center has excessively tight control, it always stifles the localities. Repeated bad experiences and the shared political culture they fostered warn the leaders not to go to extremes. The institutional linkages and personnel overlaps facilitate complete information and efficient communication. They encourage strategic cooperation. The major political players have been responsible and cautious

214 *The Dual Developmental State*

in using their power to challenge other branches of the state. Self-constraint has been followed most of time.

In summary, all the important political institutions have developed networks, and have become interdependent. To borrow two terms from M. Nakano (1997, 65) on Japanese politics, here I can argue that, in terms of the horizontal relationships among major institutions, China has also been characterized by "elite accommodation politics," in which political elites have created institutionalized channels for conflict management. In terms of the relations between the central state and local officials, or between the elite and the common citizens, "client oriented politics" has also formed, in which social actors seek and expect patronage and benefits from those in power as well as the subordinate officials vis-à-vis their superiors. The structural qualities of these relationships impose constraints upon the actors and discipline their behavior.

The Network as a New Mode of Governance

In designing new institutions or reshaping old ones, an institutional designer will always consider the general efficiency of the expected institution. The institutional economists, particularly the transaction costs theorists, have identified both the transformation costs and transaction costs as being responsible for the total costs of economic activities. In my study I have note that the transformation costs and transaction costs are sufficient to explain a static comparison of two systems with respect to their relative advantages or disadvantages, but leaves gaps in the account of the dynamic process of regime transitions. When we talk about the institutional change from one mode of governance to another, the transition costs must be included. In the Chinese transition of their political economy, because of the transition costs, its development strategy and institutional arrangements have been tailored in a peculiar way to avoid incurring high transition costs. This will have an important impact upon the general gains of the entire regime and society in pursuing the transition. Because transformation costs are more technological, neo-liberal economists have shown a greater interest; transaction costs are more institutional and have attracted the attention of neo-institutional economics. In contrast, transition costs are more political and have been ignored in the discussion among economists. As a political scientist, I cannot ignore them.

Logic of the Dual Developmental State 215

In the light of "market" versus "hierarchy" mode of governance, the Chinese political economy has not completely, and unambiguously chosen one of them. China's economy has been characterized by a hybrid mode. It is not a planned state socialism anymore, but it has not fully become a pure type of market economy. Large state-owned enterprises have not been privatized but have been forced to marketize. Chinese politics has done away with the old Stalinism but not embraced pluralist democracy. At best, China can only be treated as a "consultative authoritarian regime" (Harding in Barnett and Clough 1986, 33), or an "authoritarian pluralist system" (Scalapino 1998). In my study, I coin the term "the dual development state" to indicate the diversification in the Chinese political structure and the ensuing frequent bargaining and consultation among important actors and institutions in the political life. These new features of Chinese politics can be attributed to the emergence of the network mode of governance in the Chinese economy and their politics.

The network mode of governance is characterized by embeddedness, connectedness, and reciprocity. Reflected in Chinese political governance, it is characterized by the development of institutional linkages among various institutions and the *"mohe"* strategy they follow to guide and manage their interactions. These two characteristics are related. Because of institutional mutual embeddedness and connectedness, the common interests of different institutions in the system create an imperative to cooperate; and institutional linkages provide channels for actors to exchange information and make it possible to manage conflicts. When we look at the Chinese political system, it is difficult to define a clear-cut boundary between the various institutions. Instead, they are intertwined through institutional linkages and the overlapping of personnel. The CPC is clearly embedded in the NPC and PPCs, the local governments and PPCs are also embedded in the NPC and the Central Party Committee. Many officials wear several hats at different levels (it is not unusual to see one county head as a PPCSC member and a NPC deputy at the same time). This mutual embeddedness makes the Chinese state look amorphous, and for this reason, many scholars have expressed their doubts about its survivability. But actually, this is the strength the Chinese state has counted on for an incremental transition and the maintenance of the dual developmental state, because the network strategy provides flexibility for institutional adaptation without jeopardizing long-term stability.

216 *The Dual Developmental State*

The strength of the Chinese dual developmental state also lies in the fact that it is compatible with its social and cultural environment. It is not news to point out that the Chinese have long been obsessive with networks and connections. In Chinese society, to be a Chinese starts with the socialization into the network society. People are taught to know how to weave networks, cultivate good relationships, care about other people's human feelings, save instead of hurt your own and other's faces, behave in accordance with propriety, respond to other people's greetings, and practice anticipate reciprocity. To care about other person's feeling constitutes the keystone for personal relationships and interactions in Chinese society. This quality is emphasized not only because of its instrumental value, but also for its intrinsic value as a part of human cultivation and development. (Yang 1994; Yan 1996) These values pervade every aspect of Chinese social life, and are reflected in Chinese political behavior. The most important utility of this network society is to nurture mutual trust, obligation and loyalty that help integrate the formal structures, reduce the transaction costs in interpersonal and inter-organizational interactions, and create an environment for organized, orderly change (Pye 1968, chapter 9; Lieberthal and Oksenberg 1988, 155-7). In addition, the porous nature of the state created by complex relations provides venues for any sector of society to gain access to the authoritative distribution of values and defuses opposition forces that can easily turn to destructive. Once these merits of networks had been instilled into the mode of governance for the Chinese political economy, Chinese political life and the economy were revitalized. They helped to reconcile the conflict between the traditional values of order, authority and hierarchy, and the recent commitment to the pursuit of efficiency, adaptiveness, and decentralization. Consequently, in comparison to the past situation under a Soviet-style authoritarianism the tension between the Chinese state and society has been less.

The praise for the merits of the Chinese developmental state certainly applies to the East Asian model. The current crises of the East Asian developmental states do not necessarily mean the crisis for this model. Rather, they reveal the long and painful process of implanting capitalism and democracy, two foreign systems, into Asian soil, and the difficulties of reconstruction and adjustment. In his provocative 1994 article, "The Myth of Asia's Miracle," Paul Krugman correctly warned the Asian NIEs to pay attention to productivity to sustain their development. Since he exclusively focused on the transformation costs, he did not consider the following three

Logic of the Dual Developmental State 217

factors that are also responsible for the improvement of efficiency: First, as Krugman correctly pointed out, it is impossible for the East NIEs to turn 70% of their population into Ph.D.s. But he argues that once the education level of workers reaches its limit, it will become one factor that slows down the inputs. This is unlikely to materialize, since knowledge, unlike the level of education, will never meet its limit. Second, he did not consider that the transaction costs are much lower under the East Asian model than under the Soviet Union. The demise of the Soviet Union to a large degree was due to its rigid bureaucracy and central planning. Third, the network strategy enables the East Asian institutions to be flexible and adaptable in seeking change. Under this mode of governance, the transition costs for adjusting their strategies and institutions are much lower than for a Stalinist system. Therefore, Krugman overstated the "surprising similarities" between the East Asian NIEs and the Soviet Union. The lower transaction costs and transition costs under the East Asian model provide enough reason for us to remain confident about its future.

If we say that five years ago it was naive to claim the coming of an Asian or Chinese century, then now it is too early to declare the demise of the East Asian model and the final triumph of the Anglo-Saxon model. Since these two patterns of political and economic governance have been deeply embedded in their own cultures, their tenacity should never be underestimated. If ideological rivalry and military confrontation have disappeared with the end of Cold War, cultural diversity (instead of Huntington's "clash of civilizations, or the West against the Rest" scenario) may be counted on to provide new momentum for human development and the progress of history. For our common human fate, the differences between the East Asian model and Anglo-Saxon model should not become a reason for mutual fear, and a call for a cultural crusade. These differences should be viewed as a fountain of inspiration for us to explore new ideas and institutions for a better human future.

But I do not mean that East Asian countries have no reason to seek change. Sometimes their very successes under this model create new challenges. For example, the economic achievement under an authoritarian political system eventually creates a middle class and fosters a civil society. The autonomous state will face increasing challenges from the newly created social forces. The developmental state somehow has to adopt the policies of the welfare state. The economic growth rate can drop, and conflicts can arise. The network has been a strength for East Asian development; however,

218 *The Dual Developmental State*

it can also turn into a liability. Since a network society is characterized by contextual, relational, and personalitistic ties, it is amorphous and lacks clear boundaries between the state and society. Particularism, instead of universalism, prevails in East Asian countries. Lack of well-defined rules for the political economy leaves room for corruption and collusion among powerful officials, capitalists, and their cronies at the expense of economic efficiency and the national interest. Therefore, the East Asian model risks becoming a perversion of "crony capitalism" (Safire 1998). In the East Asian financial crises, where crony capitalism was more out of control, the economy was hit harder. No wonder, the crises started in Thailand, then swept over Indonesia, Malaysia, and South Korea. If we compare the early (Four Little Dragons, or "Tiger Economies") and later NIEs (three "cubs": Indonesia, Malaysia, and Thailand), the latter were hit harder because they had a larger problem with crony capitalism (MacIntyre 1994). This bitter lesson will certainly help the East Asian countries when they reflect upon their developmental model.

Selective Targeting and State Capacity

My discussion on the formation of a developmental state, institutionalization of the NPC and the PPCs may shed light upon the debate between "political decay" versus "political instituionalization" with regard to the Chinese body politic. The "political decay" thesis is based on the writings of two famous authors. Samuel Huntington (1968, 86) argues that modernization and mobilization tend to produce differentiation, and heightened tensions and political demands beyond the capacity of the political system to resolve them. Political decay is the result. Many societies suffer a loss of political community and the decay of political institutions during the most intensive phrases of modernization. Alexis de Tocqueville claimed that "the most perilous moment for a bad government is one when it seeks to mend its ways" (Pei 1994, 45). Since China has reformed to "mend her ways," the odds are against China escaping the political decay resulting from the above double jeopardy. Many scholars have pointed out the accelerated institutional decay of the party-state and its major institutions in China (Pei 1994, 65; White 1993; Segal 1994). The 1989 crackdown further made some of them have "a strong sense of pessimism about China's future" and "concern" that "the social forces in China seem to lead inexorably to more

Logic of the Dual Developmental State 219

massacres, more suffering, and more anguish" (Lichtenstein 1991, 1, 19 and 146), or a total collapse of the Chinese Communist rule and a disintegration of China as a nation within a short period of time. "Once Deng dies, great chaos will prevail." One scenario sees disintegration, and warlordism looming large in China (Ruan 1994, 11; Yan in Hamrin and Zhao 1995, 7). Even the thesis of the "death of the state" has been heard. W. J. F. Jenner (1992, 1) argues: "The state, people and culture known in English as China are in a profound general crisis. The very future of China as a unitary state is in question.

The findings in my study contest the argument that the Chinese political system as a whole is in an accelerating decay. Undoubtedly, the Chinese Communist party state has been plagued by permissive political corruption and the atrophy of the party cells at the grassroots. However, it also has managed to adapt to the environment by changing its development strategy, creating alternative institutions, and adding new functions to the existing institutions. My study has presented several cases of creative and positive institutionalization during the reform era: the formation of the developmental state strategy, legislative activism of the NPC, the institutional development of the PPCs and decentralization. In addition, these institutions have also exerted a positive influence on the regime as whole and ameliorated the crises of the system. For example, the developmental state strategy has structured the relationship between the state and economy and made a contribution to economic development. The role of the PPCs includes passing new laws to meet the demands from the market economy, supervising the state agencies to prevent state failures, collecting and passing information to improve the efficiency of decision-making, integrating the state institutions horizontally and vertically, and providing access for the masses and various organizations to participate in the political process. Ultimately, all these will facilitate the political institutionalization of the Chinese system as a whole.

The positive impact of these changes also has been reflected in the strengthening of the state capacity that is a major concern for many scholars. We have seen that the central government has overhauled its tax system to strengthen its extractive capacity, reformed the banking system and developed new macro-policy tools (such as industrial policies) to consolidate its steering capacity. Basically, the NPCs and the PPCs have been encouraged to be more active in using power, and have been involved in market creation to help the central state to maintain its capacity of

220 *The Dual Developmental State*

penetration and legitimization. The coercive capacity has also been strengthened through the use of the military and the police in dealing with political challenges. It is not unimaginable that if someday the CPC collapses, the system of PCs might provide the last democratic resort to maintain the unity of China as a state and a nation. In reality, the system of PCs (3.5 million deputies) constitutes a pervasive system of control and integration with the Party (54 million members), the military (3 million soldiers), and the government bureaucracy (10 million cadres in the state apparatus). Therefore, without counting the system of the PCs as an important bureaucracy, the issue of "governing China" (who and how) cannot be fully understood.

The simultaneity of political institutionalization and partial institutional atrophy does not indicate that the difference between my findings and the "political decay argument" is like the "half empty, half full" metaphor. In fact, some phenomena, such as the dispersion of power resources, the retreat of the party from the life of ordinary people, lax control over some sectors, and decentralization, do not necessarily support the "political decay argument;" they can be interpreted as a husbandry of power. Since power is a scarce commodity, for effective policy and control, the state is advised to be highly selective in choosing areas to intervene, and limits its role mostly to "economic transformation," in crucial sectors of the population and policy. According to Peter Evans and Dietrich Rueschemeyer, "Increased penetration of civil society by the state activates political responses and increases the likelihood that societal interests will attempt to invade and divide the state" (Evans, et al, 1985, 69). The most important key to a successful developmental state is the "embedded autonomy" of the state (Evans 1995). For an effective coordination of economic development, the state should stand apart from societal forces. However, it should not isolate itself totally from the society, severing its connection with it; but should be embedded within the society and some important industrial sectors and economic organizations to gather information and monitor their development. In other words, selectivity is important, as excessive intervention weakens a state's autonomy. If one state wants to follow the developmental model successfully, it has to deal well with the dialectical relationships between autonomy and embeddedness, penetration and selectivity, and centralization and decentralization.

The selective penetration strategy is reflected in the social, political and economic policies of the Chinese government. For example, economic liberalization is parallel to autocratic politics. On the one hand, apolitical ordinary citizens are left alone; for them, freedoms have been increased. But, on the other hand, political activists, especially those in sensitive institutions of big cities, have had to face tighter political control and personal surveillance. As the control of the Party over the grassroots has loosened up, its penetration into the PCs has deepened, its control over the personnel appointment at the provincial and bureau levels has been strengthened, and the security apparatus (the army, the armed police, the public security and state security agencies) has been strengthened and given a bigger role in political life. In the economy, decentralization, marketization, and liberalization have been accompanied by a stress on the macro-economic control, industrial policy, and the centralization of regulation through the banks, etc.

Future of the Chinese Developmental State

The East Asian financial crises dramatically slowed down economic growth in many countries and destroyed the dreams of hundreds of thousands people in this region. But, because it is at least one step behind these countries, China enjoys the advantage of backwardness, and is able to learn from their successes and failures. The East Asian developmental states can provide rich experience and their failures can also teach the Chinese good lessons. It is not unreasonable if we see that the gain is even larger than the loss for the Chinese in this crisis. Certainly, this depends on whether the Chinese government can transform these lessons into sound policies.

For example, Singapore has been doing better than other NIEs and, of course, the three "cubs" (Indonesia, Malaysia, and Thailand), in defending its economy. The call to "Learn form Lee Kuan Yew" encouraged by Deng Xiaoping in China might not be wrong. But what exactly can China learn from Lee Kuan Yew? Lee's lesson can be summarized in three points: to pursue justice, to clean government, and to provide good order. Lee points out the relationship of these three goals: "The existence of a new nation primarily depends on a clean government. A developing nation needs justice more than democracy. If the government is corrupt, it loses the faith of the people and cannot function in accordance with justice. The public policies will lose meaning and will be unable to succeed as expected. The failure of public policies will do harm to social and economic development, and cause

222 The Dual Developmental State

further decay and corruption" (Yang 1991, 4). To examine China in light of these three policy goals, we can see clearly that injustice, corruption and social disorder have posed a serious threat to the integrity of the Chinese developmental state and its ability to govern the market and steer the transition in China.

In the early 1980s, Chinese officials were still clean relative to the officials in the other Third World countries. Today, China has become one of the most corrupt societies judged by international business. This judgment is corroborated by the perception of the Chinese themselves: 54.4% of the Chinese thought the officials were corrupt, 74.9% believed that you have to have the support of the powerful to make money (Wu and Xu 1997, 91). The blatant activities of turning the public properties into private holdings, and the transactions between political power and money are permeating up to the higher levels and developing into a larger group phenomenon. The collusion between the officials and business, the commodification of power, the stealing of state-owned properties, and the transferring of them out of China to overseas under the names of officials or their children are the political cancers in Chinese society. In her very popular and provocative book, *The Pitfalls of Modernization*, He Qinglian sheds light upon this phenomenon:

> The problem in China recently does not arise from the distribution or redistribution of the national income, but from the disposition of resources under the influence of political power even before people participate in the market....In the several rounds of competition for accumulating wealth during the past ten years, the people who have benefited most are those in positions of power who control the resources in the two bureaucracies of governmental departments and state-owned enterprises. These select few formed a group for sharing the booty in the process of social transition. By using the political, social and economic resources under their control, for the purpose of mutual benefits, they have engaged in large-scale rent-seeking activities. (He Qinglian 1998, 16)

The unequal accesses by the Chinese to resources in the process of marketization have shattered the old egalitarian society and turned it into one with several classes: the capitalists, the bureaucratic elites, the white-collar middle class, the wage laborers, the peasants, and the poor. Since the most wealthy capitalists have been transmuted from the bureaucratic elite, this fusion of capital and power has created an unfathomable impact upon

Logic of the Dual Developmental State 223

the Chinese social structure. The wage laborers and peasants have few resources apart from owning their own bodies and free time and can only make a living by selling their time and labor. Since China has an oversupply of human bodies, their large number itself constitutes an obstacle to their upward social mobility. But the most unfortunate people are those who cannot even find an employer to sell themselves to, namely the jobless urban and rural people, the *nouveaux pauvres*. More accurately, the most hurt are the children of workers and peasants who even have been deprived of the right, and denied the opportunity, to be a worker or a peasant. As many as 200 to 300 million have either become a part of the laid-off and jobless, or a part of the "floating population." This is a number equivalent to the total population of the US, France, and Great Britain combined (Li Tongwen 1998, 49, 100). The poor are taking the brunt of the transition and are forced to pay a high human cost for Chinese development. Meanwhile, there are now more than a million millionaire households in China (Li Tongwen 1998, 513). Certainly the development process in China is not a "pastoral song." Many people in China have been both relatively and absolutely deprived. The gap between rich and poor has been created and is widening.

As the Chinese state is troubled by rampant corruption, and mounting complaints from the disadvantaged population, its social order has been placed in jeopardy. To make matters worse, the secret societies and gangs have expanded like a prairie fire and constitute another big threat to the state system. Now that Chinese society is in a state of rapid transition and becoming chaotic and unstable, the large number of victims of social transition provides hotbeds for social unrest. The increasing number of jobless rovers in urban and rural areas provides limitless human resources for secret societies. Once these criminals got themselves organized, the "secret societies" (gangs) were revived in China. For example, in 1994, 46% of the crime was committed by the "floating population" in Beijing (He Qinglian 1998, 255). These crimes are their revenge against the a society that has done an injustice to them. Their influence is fully demonstrated in three colorful businesses: the white one: drug smuggling and using; the black: gang crimes and violence; and the yellow: prostitution (The Chinese like to use these three colors to describe these crimes).

According He Qinglian (1998, 17), "the money politics, collusion between officials and secret societies, the floating population and mobs are

224 The Dual Developmental State

three root reasons for the future social crises in China." Unfortunately, these three time-bombs are interconnected with each other. As the market economy has torn down the traditional social structure, anomie and dislocations have been created. For the poor victims, the best strategy to claim back a part of the wealth they think they deserve may be to organize themselves into criminal gangs, given that legitimate channels are blocked. For many rich people, if the social order is non-existent, the protection from the secret societies becomes necessary. After the gang members accumulated enough money, they can invest in officials to seek state protection or at least benign neglect. The regime can easily become captive to the gangs. If we think about the influence of gangs in the Taiwanese politics, and the Mafia connections within the Russian government, the odds for China (both a Chinese cultural unit and a Communist country) to avoid the rampant rule by gangsters are not very good.

As John Rawls (1971) argues, justice starts with fairness and any just institution should make some people better off without making the least advantaged worse off. If the Chinese development has provided a "socialist free lunch" for the power-holders, and power is the most efficient and effective "gold touch," then an injustice has been done to those without power or access to power. The issue here is not that the equal distribution of poverty under the old egalitarianism is more desirable, or that an equality of condition shall be guaranteed in the process of marketization. The central issue is that even the equality of opportunity has been illusive to achieve as the resources have been distributed unequally and the traditionally disadvantaged people (the over-exploited peasants under the dual economy and the low-paid workers under the excuse of life-term work-units benefits) are forced to sacrifice disproportionately.

Under developmentalism, the Chinese state has been forced to be economy-oriented. Its achievements are great, but its price has been the neglect of social and political issues. Since the economic actors have become more and more mature, governments at every level should be gradually phased out of many economic activities and return to their other fundamental functions, namely, social and political management. The experiences of Western countries reveal that governments often take the responsibility for public goods (social equity, and social order are some of them) as the private citizens are let free to pursue their selfish interests. The government should take primary responsibility for solving the problem of injustice and for generating a moral renewal. If the Chinese

Logic of the Dual Developmental State 225

population has been restructured, the traditional system of political management has become antiquated; the state has to learn how to manage social and political crises arising from the clashes of social strata.

In the current China, social tensions following the process of stratification, and political and social crises are looming large. It is quite possible that future social and political crises will come from the newly formed classes who will challenge the old status quo for more political power and higher social status. These crises will also come from the victimized classes who will try to seek revenge against other better-off classes through their destructive actions. But how can we make sure that the government is a guardian of justice, instead of the source of injustice? In order to guarantee each social stratum an equal access to political power, political pluralism must be gradually introduced. It has become impossible for the CPC to act as a representative of all social groups. Interest group politics and competitive party politics will be inevitable. If the governmental officials share the same human nature as ordinary people, we cannot simply expect them to behave in a more moral way. Based on this general agnosticism and skepticism about human nature, we have to allow democratic political processes that provide channels for social participation and encourage disadvantaged people to use legitimate means to protect themselves. Otherwise, they will retaliate against the whole society through illegal channels. Actually it is happening now.

To maximize the responsibility and minimize the immorality of the government, the Western countries have developed a democratic culture arising from three pillar institutions: The religious associations have been the guardian of moral values by advocating universal fraternity; academia has been the conscience of the society by acting as a social gadfly constantly criticizing social ills; communities have been the fountain for civic values and civilities by sustaining the grassroots self-governments (Alexis de Tocqueville discussed the roles of these three institutions in a democracy in his *Democracy in America*). Unfortunately in China, the three biggest legacies from the Communist rule are the absence of independent academia, the absence of autonomous churches, and the disintegrating communities. The collective image of Chinese intellectuals is that they are spineless double-thinkers who have been corrupted either by power or by money. Despite the fact that religious believers in China have increased from 30 million to 100 million from 1982 to 1992 (Wu and Xu 1997, 360-1), we have not seen influential religious groups or leaders

226 *The Dual Developmental State*

committing to philanthropy and fraternity. Any indication of a religious renaissance is not in sight. In contrast, superstitions, voodooism, *feng-shui*, witchcraft have gotten out of control. Meanwhile, the foundations for communities, namely, work-units (*danwei*) in urban areas and communes in the countryside, have been damaged or dissolved in the process of marketization. All these do not give us enough reason to be overly optimistic about the future of China over the long run.

Under the developmental state model, the Chinese leadership has been almost completely occupied by the priority of efficiency and growth. The CPC has been called "the Party of Production Force" (Zhang et al, 1996, 25) and the Chinese state has been an "economic state." But the tradition of political economics reminds us that the creation of national wealth is as important as its distribution. The Chinese developmental state is now facing an enemy created by its own successful economic development. Now it is time for the state to give sympathy, care, and attention to the Chinese people by addressing the issue of economic inequality and social injustice. If the CPC fails to adjust its policy to address this issue and to strike a balance between development and justice, the CPC may have difficulty in maintaining its reform alliance, and might be torn apart by the irreconcilable interests and policies from its two wings within the CPC. The voices of the old and new Left wing are gradually being heard, for example, in the form of several Ten Thousand Character Documents (*wanyanshu*), and they have an appeal to the vast number of people who have been hurt in the transition.[1] Conceivably, an alliance among the progressive intellectuals, some former party elites, and the disadvantaged people will take shape and pick up the issue of justice. This may well presage a new party. Hopefully, the Chinese developmental state will demonstrate a new organizational adaptativeness and pave the way for a new system. Will this be a Confucian democracy, or a communitarian democracy? Or will everything turn totally awry and end up as a crony capitalism? Only the future will tell.

Note

1   The most important documents representing the old and new Left wing, for example, "Certain Factors Affecting China's National Security," Deng Liqun's speech, Xin Mao's "Reform and Economic Man," can be found at

the website, "www.chinabulletin.com/doc". For the articles and books by Cui Ziyuan, one strong voice overseas for economic democracy and social justice, you can visit his wetsite at "http://web.mit.edu/polisci/www/faculty/z.cui.html". From there, you will also find many related debates and articles on the New Leftism (*xin zuopai*).

Bibliography

* Articles from the *People's Daily* (*Renmin Ribao*, both National and Overseas edition), magazines and other newspapers are not listed.

A Ji. 1997. *Da Lifa* [Great Legislation: China's Legislative progress in the Eyes of a Reporter]. Chengdu: Sichuan Renmin Chubanshe.

Abegglen, James C. 1994. *Sea Change: Pacific Asia as the New World Industrial Center*. New York: The Free Press.

Aberbach, Joel, David Dollar, and Kenneth Sokoloff. 1994. *The Role of the State in Taiwan's Development*. Armonk: M.E. Sharpe.

Aikman, David. 1986. *Pacific Rim: Area of Change, Area of Opportunity*. Boston: Little, Brown.

Almond, Gabriel A. 1991. "Capitalism and Democracy." *PS: Political Science and Politics* (September).

Almond, Gabriel A., and G. Bingham Powell, Jr. 1978. *Comparative Politics: System, Process, and Policy*. Boston: Little, Brown.

Alston, Lee J., Thrainn Eggertsson, and Douglass C. North, eds. 1996. *Empirical Studies in Institutional Change*. New York: Cambridge University Press.

Amsden, Alice H. 1989. *Asia's Next Giant: South Korea and Late Industrialization*. New York: Oxford University Press.

Applebaum, Richard P., and Jeffrey Henderson, eds. 1992. *States and Development in the Asian Pacific Rim*. Newbury Park: Sage Publications.

Avtorkhanov, A. 1966. *The Communist Party Apparatus*. Chicago: Henry Regnery.

Bachman, David M. 1985. *Chen Yun and the Chinese Political System*. Berkeley: University of California Press.

Bachman, David and Li Cheng. 1989. "Localism, Elitism, and Immobilism: Elite Formation and Social Change in Post-Mao China." *World Politics* 41 (October): 64-91.

Balassa, Bella. 1991. *Economic Policies in the Pacific Area Developing Countries*. New York: New York University Press.

Balassa, Bella, and others. 1982. *Development Strategies in Semi-Industrial Economies*. Baltimore: Johns Hopkings University Press.

Barnett, Doak, and Ralf N. Clough, eds. 1986. *Modernizing China: Post-Mao Reform and Development*. Boulder, Colorado: Westview.

Baum, Richard. 1992-93. "The China Syndrome." *Harvard International Review* (Winter).

---. 1993. The Road to Tiananmen: Chinese Politics in the 1980s. In *The Politics of China*, ed. by Roderick MacFarquhar. New York: Cambridge University Press.

---. 1995. *Burying Mao: Chinese Politics in the Age of Deng Xiaoping*. Princeton: Princeton University Press.

---. 1996. "China After Deng: Ten Scenarios in Search of Reality." *China Quarterly* 145 (March): 153-175.

Berger, Peter, and Hsin-Huang Michael Hsiao, eds. 1988. *In Search of an East Asian Developmental Model*. New Brunswick: Transactions Books.

Bibney, Frank. 1982. *Miracle by Design: The Real Reasons Behind Japan's Economic Success*. New York: Times Books.

Bihari, Otto. 1970. *Socialist Representative Institutions*. Budapest: Akademiai Kiado.

Black, Cyril E., et al. 1975. *The Modernization of Japan and Russia: A Study of Comparison*. New York: Free Press.

Blanchard, Olivier Jean, Kenneth A. Froot and Jeffrey D. Sachs, eds. 1994. *The Transition in Eastern Europe, vol. 1 Countries Studies; vol. 2, Restructuring*. Chicago: the University of Chicago Press.

Blecher, Marc J., and Vivienne Shue. 1996. *Tethered Deer: Government and Economy in a Chinese County*. Stanford, CA: Stanford University Press.

Blommestein, Hendrikus J. and Bernard Steunenberg, eds. 1994. *Governments and Markets: Establishing a Democratic Constitutional Order and a Market Economy in Former Socialist Countries*. Boston: Kluwer Academic Publishers.

Bo, Zhiyue. 1996. "Economic Performance and Political Mobility: Chinese provincial leaders." *Journal of Contemporary China*, no. 5 (12), 135-154.

Bonavia, David. 1989. *Deng*. Quarry Bay, Hong Kong: Longman.

Bowles, Paul, and Gordon White. 1993. *The Political Economy of China's Financial Reforms*. Boulder: Westview.

Breslin, Shaun Gerard. 1996. *China in the 1980s: Center-Province Relations in A Reforming Socialist State*. New York: ST. Martin's Press.

Bromley, Daniel W. 1989. *Economic Interest and Institutions: The Conceptual Foundations of Public Policy*. New York: Basil Blackwell.

Brown, Richard Harvey, and William T. Liu, ed. 1992. *Modernization in East Asia: Political, Economic, and Social Perspectives*. Westport, CT: Praeger.

Brus, Wlodzimierz and Kazimierz Laski. 1989. *From Marx to the Market: Socialism in Search of An Economic System*. Oxford: Clarendon Press.

Bryce, James. 1959. *The American Commonwealth*. New York: G. P. Putnam's Sons.

Brzezinski, Zbigniew. 1993. *The Grand Failure: The Birth and Death of Communism in the 20th Century*. Durham: Duke University Press.

Buchanan, James M., Robert D. Tollison, and Gordon Tullock. 1980. *Toward a Theory of the Rent-Seeking Society*. College Station: Texas A & M University Press.

230 *The Dual Developmental State*

Buchanan, James. 1997. "Economic Liberties and Federalism." In *Jingji Minzhu yu Jingji Zhiyou* [Economic Democracy and Economic Liberty], ed. by Liu Junning, et al. Beijing: Sanlian Sudian, 32-40.

Cai Dingjian. 1992. *Zhongguo Renda Zhidu* [The System of People's Congresses in China]. Beijing: Shehui Kexue Wenxian Chubanshe.

Calder, Kent E. 1993. *Strategic Capitalism: Private Business and Public Purpose in Japanese Industrial Finance*. Princeton: Princeton University.

Caporaso, James A., and David P. Levine. 1992. *Theories of Political Economy*. Cambridge: Cambridge University Press.

Castells, Manuel. 1996. *The Rise of Network Society*. In *The Information Age: Economy, Society and Culture*, vol I. Maden, MA: Blackwell Publishers.

---. 1998. *End of Millennium*. In *The Information Age: Economy, Society and Culture*, vol III. Maden, MA: Blackwell Publishers.

Chan, Steve. 1990. *East Asian Dynamism* (2nd Ed). Boulder, Colorado: Westview.

Chan, Steve, Cal Clark, and Danny Lam, eds. *Beyond the Developmental State: East Asia's Political Economy Reconsidered*. New York: St. Martin's.

Chavance, Bernard. 1994. *The Transformation of Communist System*. Boulder, Colo.: Westview.

Chen, Derong. 1995. *Chinese Firms between Hierarchy and Market: The Contract Management Responsibility System in China*. New York: St. Martin's.

Chen Hongyi. 1993. "1993 nian, Zhongguo wuji zhengquan huanjie" [The Year of 1993: Five Levels of State Authority Change Term]. *Liaowang* [Outlook] (July 4-5).

Chen Pengsheng, ed. 1993. *Shanghai Fazhi Fazhan Zhanlue Yanjiu* [A Study of the Development Strategy of Shanghai Legal System]. Shanghai: Fudan Daxue Chubanshe.

Chen, Sheying. 1996. *Social Policy of the Economic State and Community Care in Chinese State*. Aldershot, UK: Avebury.

Chen Yun. 1983. *Strategy for China's Development*. ed. by Nicholas Lardy and Kenneth Lieberthal. Armonk, NY: M.E. Sharpe.

Chen Zhaozhong and Cen Xinghe. 1991. *Gaige Kaifang de Guiji: Guangdongsheng Shinian Difang Lifa* [The Course of Reforms and Opening-Up: Ten Years of Local Legislation in Guangdong]. Guangzhou: Guangdong Renmin Chubanshe.

Cheng Chaoze. 1998. *Shiji Zhizheng: Yige Jingji Daguo de Jueqi* [Competition of the Century: The Rise of An Economic Big Power]. Beijing: Xinhua Chubanshe.

Cheng Chuyuan. 1993. *Deng Xiaoping Luxian yu Guangdong Fazhan Jinyan* [Deng Xiaoping's Reform Policy and the Experiences of Development in Guangdong]. Taipai, Taiwan: The Executive Yuan.

Cheng, Joseph Y. S. "How to Strengthen the National People's Congress and Implement Constitutionalism." *Chinese Law and Government* 16 (1983): 88-122.

Cheung, Peter T.Y., Jae Ho Chung, and Zhimin Lin, eds. 1998. *Provincial Strategies of Economic Reform in Post-Mao China: Leadership, Politics, and Implementation*. Armonk, NY: M.E. Sharpe.

Ch'i, Hsi-Sheng. 1991. *Politics of Disillusionment: The Chinese Communist Party under Deng Xiaoping, 1978-1989*. Armonk, NY: M.E. Sharpe.

Chung, Jae Ho. 1995. "Studies of central-provincial relations in the People's Republic of China: a mid-term appraisal." *China Quarterly* No. 142 (June): 487-508.

Clifford, Mark, L . 1994. *Troubled Tiger: Businessmen, Bureaucrats, and Generals in South Korea*. Armonk: M.E. Sharpe.

Close, David, ed. 1995. *Legislatures and the New Democracies in Latin America*. Boulder, Colorado: Lynne Rienner.

Coase, Ronald H. 1937. "The nature of the firm." In Williamson 1993.

---. 1960. "The problem of social cost." In Coase 1988.

---. 1988. *The Firm, The Market, and the Law*. Chicago: University of Chicago Press.

Colclough, Christopher and James Manor, eds. 1993. *States or Markets? Neoliberalism and the Development Policy Debate*. Oxford: Clarendon.

Copeland, Gary W. and Samuel C. Patterson, eds. 1994. *Parliaments in the Modern World: Changing Institutions*. Ann Arbor: University of Michigan Press.

Crane, George. 1990. *The Political Economy of China's Special Economic Zones*. Armonk, NY: M.E. Sharpe.

---. 1994. "'Special Things in Special Way': National Economic Identity and China's Special Economic Zones." *The Australian Journal of Chinese Affairs*, no. 32, July, 71-92.

Crawford, Beverly. 1995. *Markets, States, and Democracy; the Political Economy of Post-Communist Transformation*. Boulder, Colorado: Westview.

Crombie, I.M. 1964. *Plato: The Midwife's Apprentice*. London: Routledge & Kegan Paul.

Cumings, Bruce. 1987. "The Origins and Development of the Northeast Asian Political Economy: Industrial Sector, Product Cycles, and Political Consequences." In Deyo (1987).

Dahl, Robert. 1971. *Polyarchy: Participation and Opposition*. New Haven, CT: Yale University Press.

---. 1985. *A Preface to Economic Democracy*. Berkeley: University of California Press.

---. 1989. *Democracy and Its Critics*. New Haven, CT: Yale University.

Deng Maomao (Deng Rong). 1995. *My Father, Deng Xiaoping*. New York: Basic Books.

Deng Xiaoping. 1983. *The Selected Works of Deng Xiaoping: 1975-1982*. Beijing: Foreign Language Press.

232　*The Dual Developmental State*

---. 1987. *Jianshe Zhongguo Teshe de Shehui Zhuyi* [Building Socialism with Chinese Characteristics]. Beijing: Renmin Chubanshe.

---. 1993. *The Selected Works of Deng Xiaoping*, vol. 3. Beijing: Renmin Chubanshe.

Deyo, Frederic C., ed. 1987. *The Political Economy of the New Asian Industrialism*. Ithaca: Cornell University Press.

Diamond, Larry, Juan Linz, and Seymour Lipset, eds. 1989. *Democracies in Developing Countries*, 3 vols. Boulder, Colorado: Lynne Rienner.

Difangxin Fagui Xuanbian [A Compilation of Local Laws]. 1991. Beijing: Zhongguo Jingji Chubanshe1991.

Ding, Arthur S. 1994. "The reform of the people's congresses in mainland China." *Issues and Studies* 30, no. 4 (April): 14-35.

Di Palma, Giuseppe. 1990. *To Craft Democracies: An Essay on Democratic Transitions*. Berkeley: University of California Press.

Dittmer, Lowell. 1994. *China under Reform*. Boulder, Colorado: Westview.

Dong Yuyu and Shi Binhai. 1998. *Zhengzhi Zhongguo* [Political China]. Beijing: Jinri Zhongguo Chuibanshe.

Dongfang Zhi, ed. 1998. *Guangxixue Quanshu* [Encyclopedia of the Art of Guanxi]. Beijing: Beijing Tushuguan Chubanshe.

Dore, Ronald. 1987. *Taking Japan Seriously: A Confucian Perspective on Leading Economic Issues*. London: Athlone Press.

Dorn, James A. and Wang Xi, eds. 1990. *Economic Reform in China: Problems and Prospects*. Chicago: University of Chicago Press.

Drobak, John N. and John V. C. Nye. 1997. *The Frontiers of the New Institutional Economics*. San Diego, CA: Academic Press.

Durkheim, Emile. 1964. *The Division of Labor*. New York: Free Press.

Dutt, Amitava Krishna, Kwan S. Kim and Ajit Singh, eds. 1994. *The State, Markets and Development: Beyond the Neoclassical Dichotomy*. Brookfield, Vermont: Edward Elgar.

Eaton, Joseph W., ed. 1972. *Institution Building and Development*. Beverly Hills, CA: Sage Publications.

The *Economist*. 1997-98. "China and the Chaebol." 20 December 1997-2 January: 97-98.

---. 1997. "China Adopts the chaebol." June 7, U.S. Edition.

Editorial. 1993. "*Zhonggong baijie renda chuxian de fanduipiao wenti*" [The issue of opposing votes in the Communist 8th NPC], *Zhonggong Yanjiu*, vol. 27, no. 4 (April), 7.

Eggertsson, Thrainn. 1990. *Economic Behavior and Institutions*. New York: Cambridge University Press.

Elegant, Robert. 1990. *Pacific Destiny: Inside Asia Today*. New York: Crown Publisher.

Bibliography 233

Elster, Jon, Claus Offe, and Ulrich K. Preuss. 1998. *Institutional Design in Post-communist Societies: Rebuilding the Ship at Sea.* New York: Cambridge University Press.

Evans, Peter. 1995. *Embedded Autonomy: States and Industrial Transformation.* Princeton: Princeton University Press.

Evans, Peter, Dietrich Rueschemeyer, and Theda Skocpol, eds. 1985. *Bring the State Back In.* New York: Cambridge University Press.

Evans, Richard. 1994. *Deng Xiaoping and the Making of Modern China.* New York: Viking.

Fallows, James. 1994. *Looking at the Sun: The Rise of the New East Asian Economic and Political System.* New York: Pantheon Books.

Fewsmith, Joseph. 1994. *Dilemma of Reform in China: Political Conflict and Economic Debate.* Armonk: M.E. Sharpe.

Fong, Barry Shiaw-Chian. 1998. "Reflections on Guanxi in the Studies of Local Political Economy." APSA Paper, Boston, MA.

A *Foreign Affairs* Reader. 1998. *The Rise of China.* New York: Council of Foreign Affairs.

Foster, Keith. 1990-1991. "The Wenzhou Model for Economic Development: Impressions," *China Information,* vol. V, no. 3 (Winter): 53-64.

Franz, Uli. 1988. *Deng Xiaoping.* Boston: HBJ.

Friedman, Edward. 1995. *National Identity and Democratic Prospects in Socialist China.* Armonk, NY: M.E. Sharpe.

Friedrich, Carl J., and Zbigniew K. Brzezinski. 1956. *Totalitarian Dictatorship and Autocracy.* New York: Praeger.

Fukuyama, Francis. 1989. "The End of History?" *The National Interest* (Summer): 3-18.

Gao Shanquan. 1987. *Jiunianlai de Zhongguo Jingji Tizhi Gaige* [China's Reforms of Economic Institutions after Nine Years]. Beijing: Renmin Chubanshe.

Gao Xin. 1997. *Jiang Zemin de Muliao* [Jiang Zemin's Conselors]. Ontario, Canada: Ming Ching Chubanshe.

Gasper, Donald. 1982. "The Chinese National People's Congress." In Daniel Nelson and Stephen White, ed., *Communist Legislatures in Comparative Perspective.* London: Macmillan.

Gerlach, Michael L. 1992. *Alliance Capitalism; The Social Organization of Japanese Business.* Berkeley: University of California Press.

Gerschenkron, Alexander. 1962. *Economic Backwardness in Historical Perspective.* Cambridge: Belknap Press of Harvard University.

Gilley, Bruce. 1998. *Tiger on the Brink: Jiang Zemin and China's New Elite.* Berkeley: University of California Press.

Goldstein, Steven M. 1991. *Minidragons: Fragile Economic Miracles in the Pacific.* Boulder, Colorado: Westview.

234 *The Dual Developmental State*

---. 1995. "China in transition: the political foundations of incremental reform." *China Quarterly* 144 (December): 1105-1131.

Goodin, Robert E., ed. 1996. *The Theory of Institutional Design.* New York: Cambridge University Press.

Goodman, David S. G. 1986. *The China Challenge: Adjustment and Reform.* London: Routledge.

---. 1989. *China's Regional Development.* Routledge, NY: Royal Institute of International Affairs.

---. 1994. *China's Quiet Revolution.* New York: St. Martin's.

Goodman, David S. G. and Gerald Segal, ed. 1991. *China in the Nineties: Crisis Management and Beyond.* Oxford: Clarendon Press.

---. eds. 1994. *China Deconstructs: Politics, Trade and Regionalism.* London: Routledge.

---. 1997. *China Without Deng. China News Digest* Internet Special Issues (February 24-March 1).

Granick, David. 1990. *Chinese State Enterprises: A Regional Property Rights Analysis.* Chicago: University of Chicago Press.

Granovetter, Mark. 1994. "Business Group." In Smelser and Swedberg (1994).

Gray, Jack and Gordon White, eds. 1982. *China's New Development Strategy.* London: Academic Press.

Griffin, Keith. 1989. *Alternative Strategies for Economic Development.* London: Macmillan.

Gui Shiyong, ed. 1987. *Lun Zhongguo Hongguan Jingji Guanli* [On the Macro-Economic Management in China]. Beijing: Zhongguo Jingji Chubanshe.

Guo Dehong. 1997. *Dang he Guojia Zhongda Jueche de Licheng* [Processes of Important Party and Government Decisions]. Beijing: Hongqi Chubanshe, vol. 5.

Guojia Jingji Tizhi Gaige Weiyuanhui [The State Commission of Economic Institution Reform], ed. 1988. *Zhongguo Jingji Tizhi Gaige Guihuaji* [Bluprints for the Economic Institution Reforms in China]. Beijing: Zhonggong Zhongyang Dangxiao Chubanshe.

Gustafsson, Bo, ed. 1991. *Power and Economic Institutions: Reinterpretations in Economic History.* Vermont: Edward Elgar Publishing Co.

Habermas, J. 1973. *Legitimation Crisis.* Boston: Beacon Press.

Haggard, Stephan. 1990. *Pathways from the Periphery: the Politics of Growth in the Newly Industrializing Countries.* Ithaca: Cornell University Press.

---. ed. 1995. *The International Political Economy and Developing Countries*, vol. 1, and vol. 2. Brookfield, Vermont: Edward Elgar Publishing Company.

Haggard, Stephan, and Robert R. Kaufman, eds. 1992. *The Politics of Economic Adjustment.* Princeton: Princeton University Press.

---. 1995. *The Political Economy of Democratic Transitions.* Princeton: Princeton University Press.

Bibliography 235

Hahn, Jeffrey W., ed. 1995. *Democratization in Russia: The Development of Legislative Institutions*. Armonk, New York: M.E. Sharpe.

Halpern, Nina. 1985. "Learning from abroad: Chinese view of the East European economic experience, January 1977-June 1981." *Modern China* 1 (January): 77-109.

Hamilton, Edith, and Huntington Cairns, eds. 1961. *Plato: The Collected Dialogues*. Princeton, NJ: Princeton University Press.

Hamilton, Garry, ed. 1991. *Business Networks and Economic Development in East and Southeast Asia*. Hong Kong: Center for Asian Studies, University of Hong Kong.

Hamrin, Carol Lee and Suisheng Zhao, eds. 1995. *Decision-Making in Deng's China: Perspectives from Insiders*. Armonk, NY: M.E. Sharpe.

Harding, Harry. 1987. *China's Second Revolution: Reform after Mao*. Washington D.C.: Brookings Institution.

Harwit, Eric. 1994. *China's Automobile Industry: Policies, Problems, and Prospects*. Armonk, NY: M.E. Sharpe.

Hayek, Friedrich. 1945. "The use of knowledge in society." *American Economic Review* 35 (September): 519-30.

He Bochuan. 1988. *China on the Edge* [Shanao shangde Zhongguo]. Guizhou Renmin Chubanshe.

He Qinglian, 1998. *Xiandaihua de Xianjing: Dangdai Zhongguo de Jingji Shehui Wenti* [The Pitfalls of Modernization: Economic and Social Problems in Contemporary China]. Beijing: Jinri Zhongguo Chubanshe.

Herrmann-Pillath, Carsten. 1996. *Wangluo Wenhua yu Huaren Shehui Jingji Xingwei Fengxi* [Networks, Culture, and the Socioeconomic Behavioral Patterns of the Chinese]. Taiyuan: Shanxi Jingji Chubanshe.

He Yiqun. 1993. *Qianlong Zai Yuan: Jiaofeng hou de Zhongguo* [Hidden Dragon at Bay: China after the Cross of Swords]. Hongqi Chubanshe.

Hobbes, Thomas. 1968. *Leviathan*. London, UK: Penguin.

Hodgson, Geofry M. 1988. *Economics and Institutions: A Manifesto for a Modern Institutional Economics*. Philadelphia: University of Pennsylvania Press.

Horner, Charles. 1994. "Losing China again." *Commentary* (April)

Hornik, Richard. 1994. "Bursting China's bubble." *Foreign Affairs* 73, no. 3 (May-June): 28-42.

Howell, Jude. 1993. *China Opens Its Doors: The Politics of Economic Transition*. Boulder: Lynne Rienner.

Hsiao Yun. 1993. "*Dui zhonggong renda jinnian biaojue xinwei zi fenxi*" [Analysis of the recent voting behavior in the Communist People's Congress], *Zhonggong Yanjiu*, vol.27, no. 5 (May).

Hsing, You-tien. 1998. *Making Capitalism in China: The Taiwan Connection*. New York: Oxford University Press.

236 The Dual Developmental State

Hu Jiwei. 1986. "Cong Shegou de yici Piping Baodao kan Zhenzhiti Gaige" ["From a Report on Shekou to Reforms on Political System"]. *Nanfang Ribao* [Southern Daily], August 19.

Hu Shikai. 1993. "Representation without Democratization: the 'Signature Incident' and China's National People's Congress." *Journal of Contemporary China* 2(1), Winter-Spring, 3-34.

Hu Xitao. 1997. *Zhongguo Hangkong Shiye de Jianshe yu Fazhan* [The Construction and Development of the Airplane Industry in China]. Beijing: n.p.

Huang, Yasheng. 1996. *Inflation and Investment Control in China*. New York: Cambridge University Press.

Hunan Nianjian 1989 [The Yearbook of Hunan]. 1990. Changsha: Hunan Nianjian Chubanshe.

Huntington, Samuel. 1968. *Political Order in Changing Societies*. New Haven, CT: Yale University.

---. 1970. "Social and Institutional Dynamics of One-Party System." In *Authoritarian Politics in Modern Society: The Dynamics of Established One-Party System*, edited by Samuel Huntington and Clement Moore. New York: Basic Books.

---. 1991. *The Third Wave: Democratization in the Late Twentieth Century*. Norman: University of Oklahoma.

---. 1993a. "The coming clash of civilization—or, the West against the rest." *The New York Times* (June 6).

---. 1993b. "The clash of civilizations?" *Foreign Affairs* (Summer 1993): 22-49.

In Depth. 1993. Special Issue: Establishing Democratic Rule. no. 1 (Winter).

Islam, Shafiqul, and Michael Mandelbaum, eds. 1993. *Making Markets: Economic Transformation in Eastern Europe and the Post-Soviet States*. New York: Council of Foreign Relations Press.

Ito, Takatoshi, and Anne O. Krueger, eds. 1995. *Growth Theories in Light of the East Asian Experience*. Chicago: The University of Chicago Press.

Jenner, J. F. 1992. *The Tyranny of History: The Roots of China's Crisis*. Allen Lane: The Penguin Press.

Jia, Hao, and Lin Zhimin. 1994. *Changing Central-Local Relations in China: Reform and State Capacity*. Boulder, Colorado: Westview Press.

Jilingsheng Renda Changweihui Yanjiushi. 1989. *Difang Renda Xingshi Jianduquan Jicui* [Cases of Using Supervisory Power by the Local People's Congresses]. Changchun: Jiling Renmin Chubanshe.

Johnson, Chalmers. 1982. *MITI and the Japanese Miracle: The Growth of Industrial Policy: 1925-1975*. Stanford: Stanford University.

---. 1987. "Political Institutions and Economic Performance: The Government-Business Relationship in Japan, South Korea, and Taiwan." In Deyo (1987).

---. 1995. *Japan: Who Governs? The Rise of the Developmental State*. New York: W. W. Norton.

The Joint Economic Committee, Congress of the United States, ed. 1992. *China's Economic Dilemmas in the 1990s*. Armonk, NY: M.E. Sharpe.

Keith, Ronald C. 1994. *China's Struggle for the Rule of Law*. New York: St. Martin's.

Keyfitz, Nathan. 1988. "The Asian road to democracy." *Society* 26, no. 1 (November/December): 71-76.

Kim, Eun Mee, ed. 1998. *The Four Asian Tigers: Economic Development and the Global Political Economy*. San Diego, CA: Academic Press.

Kim, Ilpyong and Jane Shapiro Zacek, eds. 1993. *Establishing Democratic Rule: The Reemergence of Local Governments in Post-Authoritarian Systems*. Washington, D. C.: Paragon Press.

Kleinberg, Robert. 1990. *China's "Opening" to the Outside World: the Experiment with Foreign Capitalism*. Boulder, Colorado: Westview.

Knight, Jack. 1992. *Institutions and Social Conflict*. New York: Cambridge University Press.

Knight, Jack and Itai Sened, eds. 1995. *Explaining Social Institutions*. Ann Arbor: University of Michigan Press.

Knoke, David. 1990. *Political Networks: The Structural Perspective*. New York: Cambridge University Press.

Kornai, Janos. 1990a. *The Road to a Free Economy: Shifting from a Socialist System: the Example of Hungary*. New York: W.W. Norton.

---. 1990b. *Vision and Reality, Market and State: Contradictions and Dilemmas Revisited*. New York: Routledge.

---. 1995. *Highway and Byways: Studies on Reform and Post-Communist Transition*. Cambridge: The MIT Press.

Kornberg, Allan, and Lloyd D. Musolf, eds. 1970. *Legislatures in Developmental Perspective*. Durham, NC: Duke University Press.

Kristof, Nicolas D. 1992. "Chinese Communism's Secret Aim: Capitalism." *The New York Times*, October 19, pp. A1, A.6.

Kristof, Nicholas, and Sheryl WuDunn. 1994. *China Wakes*. New York: Times Books.

Krugman, Paul. 1994. "The Myth of Asia's Miracle." *Foreign Affairs* vol. 73, no. 6: 62-78.

Lam, Willy Wo-Lap. 1995. *China after Deng Xiaoping: The Power Struggle in Beijing since Tiananmen*. New York: John Wiley & Sons.

Lavigne, Marie. 1995. *The Economics of Transition: From Socialist Economy to Market Economy*. New York: St. Martin's.

Lawrence, Susan V. 1994. "Democracy, Chinese Style." *The Australian Journal of Chinese Affairs* 32 (July): 61-68.

Lee, Hong Yung. 1991. *From Revolutionary Cadres to Party Technocrats in Socialist China*. Berkeley: University of California Press.

Levy, Jr., Marion J. 1966. *Modernization and the Structure of Societies: A Setting for International Affairs*. Princeton: Princeton University Press.

238   *The Dual Developmental State*

Li Buyun and Wang Yongqing. 1998. *Zhongguo Lifa de Jiben Lilun he Zhidu* [Fundamental Principles and Systems of Legislation in China]. Beijing: Zhongguo Fazhi Chubanshe.

Li, Cheng, and Lynn White. 1988. "The thirteenth Central Committee of the Chinese Communist Party: from mobilizers to managers." *Asian Survey* 28 (April): 371-99.

Li, Linda Chelan. 1998. *Centre and Provinces: China 1978-1993-Power as Non-Zero-Sum*. Oxford, UK: Clarendon Press.

Li Ronggeng. 1998. *Bada Tixi* [Eight Great Systems]. Shenzhen: Haitian Chubanshe.

Li, Tongwen, ed. 1998. *Zhongguo Minsheng Baogao: Zhongguo Shehui Gejieceng de Xianzhuang yu Weilai* [A Report on the Lives of Chinese People: The Current Situation and the Future of Social Strata in China]. Beijing: Jincheng Chubanshe.

Li, Wei, and Lucian W. Pye. 1992. "The Ubiquitous Role of the Mishu in Chinese Politics." *The China Quarterly*, no. 132 (December): 913-36.

Li Youwei. 1997. "Several Reflections upon the Ownership." *Zhongguo yu Shijia* [China and the World], no. 8, at: http://www.chinabulletin.com.

Liang, Xiaosheng. 1997. *Zhongguo Shehui Gejieceng Fengxi* [An Analysis of Social Strata in China]. Beijing: Jingji Ribao Chubanshe.

Lichtenstein, Peter. 1991. *China at the Brink: The Political Economy of Reform and Retrenchment in the Post-Mao Era*. New York: Praeger.

Lieberthal, Kenneth. 1995. *Governing China: From Revolution through Reform*. New York: W.W. Norton.

Lieberthal, Kenneth G. and David Lampton, eds. 1992. *Bureaucracy, Politics, and Decision Making in Post-Mao China*. Berkeley: University of California Press.

Lieberthal, Kenneth and Michel Oksenberg. 1988. *Policy Making in China: Leaders, Structures and Processes*. Princeton; Princeton University Press.

Lijphart, Arend. 1969. "Consociational Democracy." *World Politics* XXI, no. 2.

---. 1984. *Democracies: Patterns of Majoritarian and Consensus Government in Twenty-one Countries*. New Haven, CT: Yale University Press.

---. 1996. "The puzzle of Indian democracy: a consociational interpretation." *American Political Science Review* 90, no. 2 (June): 258-268.

Lin Sen. 1993. China's Decentralization and Provincial Legislation, 1980-1989. Ph.D. Diss., Political Science, University of Calgary.

---. 1992-93. "A new pattern of decentralization in China: the increase of provincial powers in economic legislation." *China Information* VII, no. 34 (Winter): 27-38.

Lin, Zhiling and Thomas W. Robinson, eds. 1994. *The Chinese and Their Future: Beijing, Taipei, and Hong Kong*. Washington D.C.: The AEI Press.

Lindblom, Charles E. 1977. *Politics and Markets: the World Political Economic Systems*. New York: Basic Books.

Ling Zhijun and Ma Lichen. 1999. *Huhan: Dangjin Zhongguo de Wuzhong Shengyin* [Shout: Five Voices in the Current China]. Guangzhou: Guangzhou Chubanshe.

Lingle, Christopher. 1996 *Singapore's Authoritarian Capitalism: Asian Values, Free Market Illusions, and Political Dependency*. Fairfax, VA: Edicions Sirocco.

---. 1998. *The Rise and Decline of the Asian Century: False Start on the Path to the Global Millennium*. Hong Kong: Asia 2000.

Little, Reg, and Warren Reed. 1989. *The Confucian Renaissance*. Sydney: The Federation Press.

Liu Pin-yen. 1990. *China's Crisis, China's Hope*. Cambridge: Harvard University Press.

Liu Binyan. 1993. "The Long March from Mao: China's De-Communization." *Current History* (September): 241-244.

Liu Zheng, Chen Xiangqin, et al. 1992. *Renmin Daibiao Dahui Zhidu Jianghua* [Lectures on the System of People's Congresses]. Beijing: Zhongguo Minzhu Fazhi Chubanshe.

Liu Zhifeng. 1998. *Diqici Geming* [The Seventh Revolution]. Beijing: Jingji Chubanshe.

Liu Zhigeng. 1989a. *Kaituo yu Chenggong* [Development and Success]. Shenzhen: Haitian Chubanshe.

---. 1989b. *Shenzhen Shichang Tixi Toushi* [Examination on the Market System in Shenzhen]. Shenzhen: Haitian Chubanshe.

---. 1990. *Shenzhen de Quanguo Zhizui* [Shenzhen's "No. One" Records in the Nation]. Shenzhen: Haitian Chubanshe.

Lyons, Thomas P. and Victoe Nee, eds. 1994. *The Economic Transformation of South China: Reform and Development in the Post-Mao Era*. Ithaca: Cornell East Asia Program.

Ma Hong. 1983. *New Strategy for China's Economy*. Beijing: New World Press.

Ma Licheng and Ling Zhijun. 1997. *Jiaofeng: Dangdai zhongguo sanci sixiang shilu* [Cross of Sword: Narrative History of Three Emancipations of the Mind]. Beijing: Jingji Chubanshe.

MacFarquhar, Roderick, ed. 1993. *The Politics of China, 1949-1989*. New York: Cambridge University Press.

MacIntyre, Andrew, ed. 1994. *Business and Government in Industrializing Asia*. Ithaca: Cornell University Press.

Manion, Melanie. 1993. *Retirement of Revolutionaries in China: Public Policies, Social Norms, Private Interest*. Princeton: Princeton University Press.

---. 1996. "The electoral connection in the Chinese countryside." *American Political Science Review* 90, no. 4 (December): 736-748.

240 *The Dual Developmental State*

March, James G. and Herbert Simon. 1958. *Organizations.* New York: John Wiley & Sons.

McCord, William. 1991. *The Dawn of the Pacific Century: Implications for Three Worlds of Development.* New Brunswick, NJ: Transaction Publishers.

McCormick, Barrett L. and Jonathan Unger, eds. 1996. *China After Socialism: In the Footsteps of Eastern Europe or East Asia?* Armonk, NY: M.E. Sharpe.

McKinnon, Ronald I. 1992. "Spontaneous order on the road back from socialism: an Asian perspective." *The American Economic Review* 82, no. 2 (May).

Migdal, Joel S. 1988. *Strong Societies and Weak States: State-Society Relations and State Capabilities in the Third World.* Princeton: Princeton University Press.

Ming Hua. 1993. "*Tingzhi Shenpi Suoyou de Kaifaqu*" [Stop Allowing New Developmental Zones]. *Jiushi Niandai* [*The Nineties*], August, 46.

Ming Qi. 1989. *Zhongguo Zhengzhi Wenhua* [The Chinese Political Culture]. Kunming: Yunnan Renmin Chubanshe.

Moe, Terry M. 1989. "The Politics of bureaucratic structure." In *Can the Government Govern?* edited by John E. Chubb and Paul E. Peterson (Washington D.C.: The Brookings Institution).

---. 1990. "Political institutions: the neglected side of the story." *Journal of Law, Economics, and Organization* 6 (Special Issue 1990).

---. 1995. "The politics of structural choice: toward a theory of public bureaucracy." In Williamson (1995).

Montinola, Gabriella, Yingyi Qian and Barry Weingast. 1995. "Federalism, Chinese Style: the political basis for economic success in China." *World Politics* 48 (October): 50-87.

Moody, Peter R. 1977. *Opposition and Dissent in Contemporary China.* Stanford, Calofornia: Hoover Institute Press.

---. 1988. *Political Opposition in Post-Confucian Society.* New York: Praeger Press.

Mosca, Gaetano. 1939. *The Ruling Class: Elementi Di Scienza Politica.* New York: McGraw-Hill Book Company.

Mueller, Dennis C. 1989. *Public Choice II.* New York: Cambridge University Press.

Muramatsu Michio. 1997. *Local Power in the Japanese State.* Berkeley, CA: University of California Press.

Myers, Ramon H., ed. 1991. *Two Societies in Opposition: The Republic of China and the People's Republic of China after Forty Years.* Stanford, California: Hoover Institution Press.

Nakano, M. 1997. *The Policy-Making Process in Contemporary Japan.* Basingstoke: Macmillan.

Nathan, Andrew J. 1985. *Chinese Democracy.* New York: Alfred A. Knopf.

---. 1990. *China's Crisis: Dilemma of Reform and Prospects for Democracy.* New York: Columbia University Press.

Naughton, Barry. 1995. *Growing Out of the Plan.* Princeton: Princeton University Press.

Bibliography 241

---. 1997. *The China Circle: Economics and Technology in the PRC, Taiwan, and Hong Kong*. Washington, D.C.: Brookings Institution Press.

Nee, Victor. 1992. "Organizational dynamics of market transition: hybrid forms, property rights, and mixed economy in China." *Administrative Science Quarterly* 37:1-27.

Nee, Victor and David Stark, eds. 1989. *Remaking the Economic Institutions of Socialism: China and Eastern Europe*. Stanford: Stanford University Press.

Nee, Victor and Sijin Su. 1990. "Institutional Change and Economic Growth in China: The View form the Villagers." *Journal of Asian Studies* 1:3-25.

Nelson, Daniel, ed. 1980. *Local Politics in Communist Countries*. Lexington: The University Press of Kentucky.

Nelson, Daniel, and Stephen White, eds. 1982. *Communist Legislatures in Comparative Perspective*. London: Macmillan.

Nohria, Nitin and Robert G. Eccles, eds. 1992. *Networks and Organizations: Structure, Form, and Action*. Boston, MA: Harvard Business School.

Nolan, Peter. 1995. *China's Rise, Russia's Fall: Politics, Economics and Planning in the Transition from Stalinism*. New York: St. Martin's.

Nolan, Peter and Dong Furen, eds. 1990a. *The Chinese Economy and Its Future*. Cambridge: Policy Press.

Nolan, Peter, and Dong Fureng, eds. 1990b. *Market Forces in China: Competition and Small Business-The Wenzhou Debate*. London: Zed Books.

North, Douglass C. 1981. *Structure and Change in Economic History*. New York: W.W. Norton.

---. 1990a. *Institutions, Institutional Change and Economic Performance*. Cambridge: Cambridge University Press.

---. 1990b. "A Transaction Cost Theory of Politics." *Journal of Theoretical Politics* 2(4): 355-367.

---. 1992. "Institutions, ideology, and economic performance." *Cato Journal* 11, no. 3 (Winter): 477-488.

---. 1995. "Five Propositions about Institutional Change." In *Explaining Social Institutions*, edited by Jack Knight and Itai Sened (Ann Arbor: The University of Michigan Press), pp. 15-26.

Norton, Philip, and Nizam Ahmed, ed. 1999. *Parliaments in Asia*. London: Frank Cass.

Novak, Michael. 1991. *The Spirit of Democratic Capitalism*. Lanham, Maryland: Madison Books.

O'Brien, Kevin J. 1990a. *Reform Without Liberalization: China's National People's Congress and the Politics of Institutional Change*. New York: Cambridge University Press.

---. 1990b. "Is China's National People's Congress a conservative legislature?" *Asian Survey* 30: 782-794.

242 *The Dual Developmental State*

---. 1994a. "Agents and remonstrators: role accumulation by Chinese people's congress deputies." *China Quarterly* no. 138 (June): 357-380.

---. 1994b. "Chinese people's congresses and legislative embeddedness: understanding early organizational development." *Comparative Political Studies* 27, no.1 (April): 80-109.

O'Brien, Kevin J. and Lianjiang Li. 1993-94. "Chinese political reform and the question of deputy quality." *China Information* VIII, no. 3 (Winter): 20-31.

O'Donnell, Guillermo, Philippe Schmitter, and Laurence Whitehead, eds. 1986. *Transitions from Authoritarian Rule*, 4 vols. Baltimore: Johns Hopkins University Press.

Ogden, Suzanne. 1993. "The Changing Content of China's Democratic Socialist Institutions." *In Depth* 3, no. 1 (Winter): 237-256.

---. 1995. *China's Unresolved Issues: Politics, Development, and Culture*, 3rd ed. Englewood Cliffs, NJ: Prentice Hall.

Oi, Jean C. 1987. *State and Peasant in Contemporary China: The Political Economy of Village Government*. Berkeley: University of California Press.

---. 1992. "Fiscal Reform and the Economic Foundations of Local State Corporatism," *World Politics*, no. 45 (October).

---. 1995. "The Role of the Local State in China's Transitional Economy." *China Quarterly* vol. 144 (December).

Okimoto, Daniel. 1989. *Between MITI and the Market: Japanese Industrial Policy for High Technology*. Stanford: Stanford University.

Olsen, Jr., Mancur. 1971. *The Logic of Collective Action*. New York: Schocken Books.

Olson, David, and Michael Mezey, eds. 1991. *Legislatures in the Policy Process: The Dilemmas of Economic Policy*. New York: Cambridge University Press.

Olson, David, and Philip Norton, ed. 1996. *The New Parliaments of Central and Eastern Europe*. London: Frank Cass.

Orru, Marco, Nicole Woolsey Biggart, and Gary G. Hamilton. 1991. "Organizational Isomorphism in East Asia." In Powell and Dimaggio (1991).

Oshima, Harry T. 1993. *Strategic Processes in Monsoon Asia's Economic Development*. Baltimore: The Johns Hopkins University Press.

Ostrom, Elinor. 1990. *Governing the Commons: The Evolution of Institutions for Collective Action*. Cambridge: Harvard University Press.

Ouchi, William G. 1984. *The M-Form Society*. Reading, MA: Addison Wesley.

Overholt, William. 1993. *The Rise of China*. New York: W.W. Norton.

Park, Jung-Dong. 1997. *The Special Economic Zones of China and Their Impact on its Economic Development*. Westport, CT: Praeger.

Parris, Kristen. 1993. "Local Initiative and National Reform: The Wenzhou Model of Development." *China Quarterly*, no. 134 (June):243-263.

Pei, Minxin. 1994. *From Reform to Revolution: The Demise of Communism in China and the Soviet Union*. Cambridge: Harvard University Press.

Bibliography 243

Perkins, Dwight H. 1986. *China: Asia's Next Economic Giant?* Seattle: University of Washington Press.

Perry, Elizabeth and Christine Wong. 1985. *The Political Economy of Reform in Post-Mao China*. Cambridge: Harvard University Press.

Pfeffer, Jeffrey. 1981. *Power in Organizations*. London: Pitman Books.

---. 1982. *Organizations and Organization Theory*. London: Pitman Books.

Phelps, Edmund S. 1985. *Political Economy: An Introductory Text*. New York; W.W. Norton.

Pitelis, Christos, ed. 1993. *Transaction Costs, Markets and Hierarchies*. Cambridge, MA: Basil Blackwell.

Polanyi, Karl. 1957. "The Economy as Instituted Process." In Karl polanyi, Conrad Arensberg and Harry W. Pearson (eds), *Trade and Market in the Early Empires*, Glenco, IL.: The Free Press.

---. 1975 [1944 original edition]. *The Great Transformation*. New York: Octagon Books.

Polsby, Nelson W. 1968. "The institutionalization of the U.S. House of Representatives." *American Political Science Review* (March): 144-168.

Porter, Pittman B., ed. 1994. *Domestic Law Reforms in Post-Mao China*. Armonk, NY: M.E. Sharpe.

Powell, Walter W. and Paul DiMaggio, eds. 1991. *The New Institutionalism in Organizational Analysis*. Chicago: The University of Chicago Press.

Powell, Water and Laurel Smith-Doerr. 1994. "Networks and Economic Life." In Smelser and Swedberg (1994).

Prybyla, Jan S. 1990. *Reform in China and Other Socialist Economies*. Washington, D.C.: The AEI Press.

Przeworski, Adam. 1991. *Democracy and the Market: Political and Economic Reforms in Eastern Europe and Latin America*. New York: Cambridge University Press.

Pu Xinzhu, ed. 1990. *Dangdai Zhongguo Zhengzhi Zhidu* [Contemporary Chinese Political System]. Shanghai: Shanghai Renmin Chubanshe.

Putterman, Louis and Dietrich Rueschemeyer. 1992. *State and Market in Development: Synergy or Rivalry?* Boulder, Colorado: Lynne Rienner.

Putterman, Louis and Randall S. Kroszner, eds. 1996. *The Economic Nature of the Firm: A Reader*. New York: Cambridge University Press.

Pye, Lucian W. 1968. *The Spirit of Chinese Politics: A Psychocultural Study of the Authority Crisis in Political Development*. Cambridge: M.I.T. Press.

---. 1985. *Asian Power and Politics: The Cultural Dimensions of Authority*. Cambridge: The Belknap Press of Harvard University Press.

---. 1988. *The Mandarin and the Cadre*. Ann Arbor: University of Michigan Press.

244 *The Dual Developmental State*

Qi Mo, ed, 1991. *Xinquanwei Zhuyi: Dui Zhongguo Dalu Weilai Minyun de Lunzheng* [Neo-Authoritarianism: Debates over the Future of Mainland China]. Taipai: Tangshan Chubanshe.

Qian, Yingyi and Chenggang Xu. 1993. "Why China's economic reform differ: The M-form hierarchy and entry/expansion of the non-state sector." *Economics of Transition* (June).

Qiao Shi. 1994. "Zai Shoudu gejie jinian renmin daibiao dahui chengli sishi zhounian dahui shang de jianghua" ["Speech to the Commemoration Meeting by All Circles in Beijing for the Forty Years Anniversary of the Establishment of People's Congress"]. *People's Daily* (Overseas Edition) (September 16): 3.

Quan Gu. 1993. "*Duizhonggong tiaozheng zhengquan xitong nindao renshi zi pinxi*" [Analysis on the Personnel Changes within the Chinese Communist Political System]. *Zhonggong Yanjiu*, vol. 27, vol. 4 (April 1993).

Quanguo Renda Changweihui Bangongting Yanjiushi [The Research Office of the General Bureau of the NPC Standing Committee]. 1990. *Zhonghua Renmin Gongheguo Renmin Dasibiao Dahui Wenxian Ziliao Huibian (1949-1990)* [A Compilation of Documents and Files of the People's Congresses of the People's Republic of China]. Beijing: Minzhu Fazhi Chubanshe.

---. 1992. *Difang Renda Shi Zenyang Xingshi Zhiquan de* [How the Local People's Congresses Use Their Power]. Beijing: Zhongguo Minzhu yu Fazhi Chubanshe.

---. 1996. *Difang Renda Xinshi Zhiquan Shili Xuanbian* [Selected Cases on the Use of Authority by the Local People's Congresses]. Beijing: Zhongguo Minzhu Fazhi Chubanshe.

Quanguo Renda Changweihui Banguongting Yanjiushi, Guangdongsheng Renmin Daibiao Dahui Zhidu Yanjiuhui [The Research Office of the General Office of the NPC Standing Committee and the Guangdong Association of the System of People's Congresses]. 1994. *Shehui Zhuyi Shichang Jingji yu Renda Gongzuo* [Socialist Market Economy and the Work of People's Congresses]. Guangzhou: Guangdong Renmin Chubanshe.

Rawls, John. 1971. *A Theory of Justice*. Cambridge, MA: Belknap Press of Harvard University Press.

Redding, S. Gordon. 1990. *The Spirit of Chinese Capitalism*. New York: de Gruyter.

---. 1996. "Societal Transformation and the Contribution of Authority Relations and Cooperation Norms in Overseas Chinese Business." In Tu Wei-ming, ed.

Remington, Thomas F., ed. 1994. *Parliaments in Transition: New Legislative Politics in the Former USSR and Eastern Europe*. Boulder, Colorado: Westview.

Robert, Stephen. 1994. "In China, Let Free Markets Aid Liberty." *The New York Times*, April 24.

Robinson, Thomas W., ed. 1991. *Democracy and Development in East Asia: Taiwan, South Korea, and the Philippines*. Washington D.C.: The AEL Press.

Rosemont, Jr., Henry. 1991. *A Chinese Mirror*. La Salle, Il.: Open Court.

Bibliography 245

Rosen, Stanley, ed. 1990-91. The debate on the new authoritarianism. *Chinese Sociology and Anthropology* 23, no. 2 (Winter); 24.

Rosenbaum, Arthur Lewis. 1992. *State and Society in China: The Consequences of Reform.* Boulder, Colorado: Westview.

Rozman, Gilbert, ed. 1981. *The Modernization of China.* New York: Free Press.

---. 1991. *The East Asian Region: Confusion Heritage and Its Modern Adaptation.* Princeton: Princeton University Press.

---, ed. 1992. *Dismantling Communism: Common Causes and Regional Variations.* Baltimore: Johns Hopkins University Press.

Ruan, Ming. 1994. *Deng Xiaoping: Chronicles of An Empire.* Boulder, Colorado: Westview.

Ru Xin, Lu Xueyi, and Chan Tianlun. 1998. *1998: Zhongguo Shehui Xingshi Fengxi yu Yuce* [China's Social Conditions in 1998: Analyses and Prospects]. Beijing: Shehui Kexue Wenxi Chubanshe.

Safire, William. 1995. "Singapoverty." *The New York Times,* sec. OPED, February 21.

---. 1998. "Crony Capitalism." *The New York Times* magazine, February 1, Sunday.

Sakakibara, Eisuke. 1993. *Beyond Capitalism: The Japanese Model of Market Economics.* Washington D.C.: University of America Press.

Samuels, Warren J., ed. 1989. *Fundamentals of the Economic Role of Government.* New York: Greenwood Press.

Sanzhong Quanhui yilai de Zhongyao Wenxian Xuanbian [A Selection of Important Documents since the Third Plenum]. 1982. Beijing: Renmin Chubanshe.

Scalapino, Robert A. 1989. *The Politics of Development: Perspective on Twentieth Century Asia.* Cambridge: Harvard University Press.

---. 1998. "Will China Democratize? Current Trends and Future Prospects." *Journal of Democracy* (January): 35-40.

Scalapino, Robert A, Sato Seizaburo, and Jusuf Wanandi, eds. 1985. *Asian Economic Development: Present and Future.* Berkeley: University of California Press.

Schell, Orville. 1989. *Discos and Democracy: China in the Throes of Reform.* New York: Anchor Books.

---. 1994. *Mandate of Heaven: A New generation of Entrepreneurs, Dissidents, Bohemians, and Technocrats Lays Claim to China's Future.* New York: Simon & Schuster.

Schlossstein, Stephen. 1991. *Asia's New Little Dragons: The Dynamic Emergence of Indonesia, Thailand, and Malaysia.* Chicago: Contemporary Books.

Schotter, Andrew. 1981. *The Economic Theory of Social Institutions.* New York: Cambridge University Press.

Schram, Stuart R., ed. 1985. *The Scope of State Power in China.* Hong Kong: The Chinese University Press.

246 The Dual Developmental State

Scott, James C. 1998. *Seeing Like a State: How Certain Scheme to Improve Human Condition Have Failed.* New Haven, CT: Yale University Press.

Seidman, Ann, and Robert B. Seidman, 'Beyond Contested Elections: The Process of Bill Creation and the Fulfillment of Democracy's Promises to the Third World,' *Harvard Journal on Legislation*, Winter, 1997.

Seidman, Ann, Robert B. Seidman, and Janice Payne. 1997. *Legislative Drafting for Market Reform: Some Lessons from China.* New York: St. Martins's.

Segal, Gerald, ed. 1990. *Chinese Politics and Foreign Policy Reform.* London: Kegan Paul International.

---. 1994. "China's changing shape." *Foreign Affairs* 73, no. 3 (May/June).

Shambaugh, David L. 1985. *The Making of a Premier: Zhao Ziyang's Provincial Career.* Boulder, Colorado: Westview.

---, ed. 1993. *American Studies of Contemporary China.* Armonk, NY: M.E. Sharpe.

Shenzhen Visiting Scholars. 1997. *The 1997 Shenzhen Report.* Shenzhen: Hefei Chaoyang Print Limited.

Shibusawa, Mashihide. 1992. *Pacific Asia in 1990s.* New York and London: Routledge.

Shi'erda yilai de Zhongyao Wenjian Xuanbian [Selected Important Documents since the CPC Twelfth National Congress]. 1988. Beijing: Renmin Chubanshe.

Shiraishi, Takashi, and Shigeto Tsuru. 1989. *Economic Institutions in a Dynamic Society: Search for a New Frontier.* New York: St. Martin's.

Shirk, Susan. 1993. *The Political Logic of Economic Reform in China.* Berkeley: The University of California.

---. 1994. "Playing to the province-Deng Xiaoping's political strategy of economic reform." In Lin and Robinson (1994): 23-57.

Shue, Vivienne. 1988. *The Reach of the State: Sketches of the Chinese Body Politic.* Stanford: Stanford University Press.

Sichuansheng Renda Changweihui Yanjiushi [Research Office of the Sichuan PPC Standing Committee]. 1991. *Difang Rendai Gongzuo Wenjian Xuanbian* [A Selected Compilation of Documents of the Work of Local People's Congresses]. Chengdu, Sichuan: Sichuansheng Renda Changweihui.

Siebert, Horst, ed. 1993. *Overcoming the Transformation Crisis: Lessons for the Successor States of the Soviet Union.* Tubingen: J.C.B. Mohr (Paul Siebeck).

Simon, Herbert. 1961. *Administrative Behavior.* New York: Macmillan.

Simone, Vera and Anne Thompson Feraru. 1995. *The Asian Pacific: Political and Economic Development in a Global Context.* New York: Longman.

Singh, Inderjit. 1992. *China: Industrial Policies for an Economy in Transition.* World Bank Discussion Papers, no. 143.

Sjostrand, Sven-Erik, ed. 1993. *Institutional Change: Theory and Empirical Findings.* Armonk, NY: M.E. Sharpe.

Skopol, Theda. 1979. *The State and Social Revolution: A Comparative Analysis of France, Russia and China.* Cambridge: Cambridge University.

Bibliography 247

Smelser, Neil J. and Richard Swedberg, eds. 1994. *Handbook of Economic Sociology*. Princeton, NJ: Princeton University Press.

Smith, Joel, and Lloyd Musolf, eds. 1979. *Legislatures in Development: Dynamics of Change in New and Old States*. Durham, NC: Duke University.

Solinger, Dorothy J. 1982. "The Fifth National People's Congress and the process of policy-making: reform, readjustment and opposition." *Asian Survey* 22: 1238-1275.

Solnick, Steven L. 1996. "The breakdown of hierarchies in the Soviet Union and China." *World Politics* 48 (January): 209-38.

Stavis, Benedict. 1983. "The dilemma of state power: the solution becomes the problem." In *State and Society in Contemporary China*, edited by Victor Nee and David Mozino, Ithaca: Cornell University Press.

---, ed. 1987. Reform of China's Political System. *Chinese Law and Government.* 20:1 (Spring special issue).

---. 1988. *China's Political Reforms: An Interim Report*. New York: Praeger.

---. 1990. "Contradictions in Communist reform: China before June 4, 1989." *Political Science Quarterly* 105:1 (Spring): 31-52.

---. 1993. "Decay, conflict resolution, and institutions at Tiananmen Square." *Conflict Resolution Quarterly* 13:1 (Winter): 48-67.

Steinmo, Sven, Kathleen Thelen, and Frank Longsterth, eds. 1992. *Structuring Politics: Historical Institutionalism in Comparative Analysis*. New York: Cambridge University Press.

Streeten, Paul P. 1992. "Against Minimalism." In Putterman and Rueschemeyer.

Su Shaozhi. 1988. *Democratization and Reform*. Nortingham, England: Spokesman.

---. 1993. *Marxism and Reform in China*. Nottingham, UK: Spokesman.

Sun Qiming and Zhang Qianyuan, eds. 1996. *Zhongguo Shichang Jingji yu Difang Lifa* [China's Market Economy and Local Legislation]. Beijing: Zhongguo Minzhu Fazhi Chubanshe.

Tai, Hung-chao, ed. 1991. *Confucianism and Economic Development: An Oriental Alternative?* Washington D.C.: The Washington Institute Press.

Tan, Qingshan, Peter Kien-hong Yu, and Wen-chun Chen. 1996. "Local Politics in Taiwan: Democratic consolidation." *Asian Survey*, vol. 36, no. 5 (May): 483-494.

Tang Xiaokui, et al. 1992. *Difang Lifa Bijiao Yanjiu* [A Comparative Study of Local Legislation]. Beijing: Zhongguo Minzhu Chubanshe.

Tang Yingwu 1997. *1976 Nian Yilai de Zhongguo* [China since 1976]. Beijing: Jingji Chubanshe.

Tanner, Murray Scot. 1991. The Politics of Law-Making in Post-Mao China. Ph.D. Diss., University of Michigan.

---. 1994a. "The erosion of Communist Party control over law-making in China." *China Quarterly* no. 138 (June): 281-403.

248 *The Dual Developmental State*

---. 1994b. "Organizations and politics in China's post-Mao lawmaking system." In Porter 1994.

---. 1995. "How a bill becomes a law in China: stage and processes in lawmaking." *China Quarterly* no. 141 (March): 39-64.

Thurow, Lester. 1992. *Head to Head: The Coming Economic Battle Among Japan, Europe, and America.* New York: William Morrow.

Tien Hung-Mao. 1989. *The Great Transition: Political and Social Changes in the Republic of China.* Stanford; Hoover Institution.

Tu Weiming, ed. 1996. *Confucian Traditions in East Asian Modernity.* Cambridge: Harvard University Press.

Tullock, Gordon. 1989. *The Economics of Special Privilege and Rent Seeking.* Boston: Kluwer Academic Publishers.

Tyler, Patrick E. 1996. "Rebel's new cause: a book for Yankee bashing." *The New York Times*, September 4, A4.

Unger, Jonathan, and Anita Chan. 1995. "China, Corporatism, and the East Asian Model." *The Australian Journal of Chinese Affairs* Issue (January) 33.

van Ness, Peter. 1989. *Market Reforms in Socialist Societies: Comparing China and Hungary.* Boulder, Colorado: Westview.

van Wolferen, Karel. 1989. *The Enigma of Japanese Power.* New York: Vintage Books.

Vogel, Ezra F. 1989. *One Step Ahead in China: Guangdong Under Reform.* Cambridge: Harvard University Press.

---. 1991. *The Four Little Dragons: The Spread of Industrialization in East Asia.* Cambridge: Harvard University.

Wade, Robert. 1990. *Governing the Market: Economic Theory and the Role of Government In East Asian Industrialization.* Princeton: Princeton University.

---. "East Asia's economic success: conflicting paradigms, partial insights, shaky evidence." *World Politics* (January, 1992).

Wang Chu and Gong Wen. 1998. "Yige Yaoyan de Zhuobiao: Shenzhen Tequ Gaige Kaifang Shibanian Huimu" ["A Shining Symbol: Review of the Eighteen Year Reforms and Opening-up in Shenzhen"]. *Renmin Luntan* [People's Forum], no. 79, October.

Wang Houde, You Lin, et al. 1998. "Peng Zhen tongzhi shi quanguo renmin daibiao dahui zhidu jianshe de kaituoze he daitouren" [Comrade Peng Zhen is the developer and leader for the construction of the NPC system]. Beijing: unpublished manuscript, March.

Wang, Hui. 1994. *The Gradual Revolution: China's Economic Reform Movement.* New Brunswick: Transaction Publishers.

Wang Huning. 1991. *Dangdai Zhongguo Cunluo Jiazhu Wenhua* [The Culture of Village Clans in Contemporary China]. Shanghai: Shanghai Renmin Chubanshe.

Wang Shaoguang and Hu Angang. 1993. *Zhongguo Guojia Nengli Baogao* [A Study of China State Capacity]. Shenyang: Liaoning Renmin Chubanshe.

Bibliography 249

Wank, David L. 1998. *Commodifying Communism: Business, Trust, and Politics in a Chinese City.* New York, NY: Cambridge University Press.

Wasserman, Stanley, and Katherine Faust. 1994. *Social Network Analysis: Methods and Applications.* New York: Cambridge University Press.

Weidenbaum, Murray, and Samuel Huges. 1996. *The Bamboo Network: How Expatriate Chinese Entrepreneurs are Creating a New Economic Superpower in Asia.* New York: The Free Press.

Weiner, Myron and Samuel Huntington, eds. 1987. *Understanding Political Development.* New York: Harper Collins Publishers.

Weingast, Barry R., and William J. Marshall. 1988. "The industrial organization of Congress; or, why legislatures, like firms, are not organized as markets." *Journal of Political Economy* 96, no. 11: 132-163.

Wekkin, Garry D., et al., eds. 1993. Building Democracy in One-Party Systems: Theoretical Problems and Cross-Nation Experiences. Westport: Praeger.

Westney, D. Eleanor. 1987. *Imitation and Innovation: The Transfer of Western Organizational Patterns to Meiji Japan.* Cambridge: Harvard University Press.

White, Gordon. 1984. "Developmental states and socialist industrialization in the Third World." *Journal of Development Studies* 21, no. 1: 97-120.

---. 1988. "State and market in China's labor reforms." In *Markets within Planning Socialist Economic Management in the Third World* edited by E. V. K. Fitzgerald and M. Wuyts (London: Frank Cass).

---, ed. 1991. *The Chinese State in the Era of Economic Reform: The Road to Crisis.* Armonk, NY: M.E. Sharpe.

---. 1993. *Riding the Tiger: The Politics of Economic Reform in Post-Mao China.* Stanford: Stanford University.

White, Gordon, and Robert Wade, eds. 1988. *Developmental States in East Asia.* New York: St. Martin's.

White, III., Lynn. 1998. *Unstately Power,* vol. 1, *Local Causes of China's Economic Reforms*; vol. 2, *Local Causes of China's Intellectual, Legal and Governmental Reforms.* Armonk, NY: M.E. Sharpe.

White, Lynn T., III, and Cheng Li. 1990. "Elite transformation and modern change in mainland China and Taiwan: empirical data and the theory of technocracy." *China Quarterly* 121 (March): 1-35.

White, Tyrene. 1992. "Reforming the countryside." *Current History* (September).

Whitefield, Stephen, ed. 1993. *The New Institutional Architecture of Eastern Europe.* St. Martin's.

Whiting, Allen S. 1989. *China Eyes Japan.* Berkeley: University of California Press.

Williamson, Oliver E. 1975. *Markets and Hierarchies: Analysis and Antitrust Implications.* New York: The Free Press.

---. 1985. *The Economic Institutions of Capitalism.* New York: The Free Press.

---. 1996. *The Mechanisms of Governance.* New York: Oxford University Press.

250 *The Dual Developmental State*

---. ed. 1995. *Organization Theory: From Chester Barnard to the Present and Beyond.* New York: Oxford University Press.

Williamson, Oliver and Sidney Winter, eds. 1991. *The Nature of the Firm: Origins, Evolution, and Development.* New York: Oxford University Press.

Wilson, Scott. 1997. "The Cash Nexus and Social Networks: Mutual Aid and Gifts in Contemporary Shanghai Villages," *The China Journal,* No. 37 (January): 91-112.

Wittfogel, Karl A. 1957. *Oriental Despotism: A Comparative Study of Total Power.* New Haven: Yale University Press.

Wolf, Jr., Charles. 1988. *Markets or Governments: Choosing between Imperfect Alternatives.* Cambridge: The MIT Press.

Wong, Christine. 1987. "Between plan and market: the role of the local sector in post-Mao China." *Journal of Comparative Economics* 11: 385-98.

---. 1991. "Central-local relations in an era of fiscal decline: the paradox of fiscal decentralization in China." *China Quarterly* 128 (December): 697-715.

Wong, Kwan-yiu and David K.Y. Chu. 1985. *Modernization in China: the case of the Shenzhen Special Economic Zone.* Hong Kong: Oxford University Press.

Woo-Cumings, Meredith. 1994. The 'New Authoritarianism' in East Asia. *Current History* (December).

---, ed. 1999. *The Developmental State.* Ithaca, NY: Cornell University Press.

A World Bank Policy Research Report. 1993. *The East Asian Miracle: Economic Growth and Public Policy.* New York: Oxford University Press.

Woronoff, Jon. 1992. *Asia's 'Miracle' Economies,* 2nd Ed. Armonk, NY: M.E. Sharpe.

Wu Daying and Liu Han, ed. 1991. *Zhengzhi Tizhi Gaige yu Fazhi Jianshe* [Reforms of Political Structure and Legal Construction]. Beijing: Shehui Kexue Wenxian Chubanshe.

Wu Guoguang. 1997. *Zhao Ziyang yu Zhengzhi Gaige* [Zhao Ziyang and Political Reform]. Hong Kong: The Pacific Century Institute.

Wu Guoguang and Zheng Yongnian. 1995. *Lun Zhongyang-Difang Guanxi* [On Central-Local Relations: A Pivotal Issue in China's Institutional Transition]. Hong Kong: Oxford University Press.

Wu Hanmin. 1990. *Renda Huiyi* [Diaries and Notes on My Experiences in the National People's Congress]. Hong Kong: Mingpao Chubanshe.

Wu, Junping and Xu Ying. 1997. *Woshishui?Dangdai Zhongguoren de Shehui Dingwei* [Who Am I? The Contemporary Chinese Social Location] (Huhehot: Neimenggu Renmin Chubanshe.

Wu, Yu-Shan. 1994. *Comparative Economic Transformations: Mainland China, Hungary, the Soviet Union, and Taiwan.* Stanford: Stanford University Press.

Xiao Chong, ed. 1997. *Zhongnanhai Xinzhinang* [The New Braintrust for Zhongnanhai]. Hong Kong: Xiafeier Chubanshe.

Xiao Shimei. 1996. *Deng Xiaoping Moulue* [Deng Xiaoping's Stratagems]. Beijing: Hongqi Chubanshe.

Xie Rong. 1989. "Quanguo renda changwei Huangshunxin xiangshen tan lifa" [Mr. Huang Shunxin, NPCSC member, talks about legislation], *Falu Zhixun* (Shanghai), no. 4, 6-8.

Xin Xiangyang. 1998. *Hongqian Juece* [Decisions behind the Red Wall]. Beijing: Zhongguo Jingji Chubanshe.

Xinzhen Torgquan: Zhongguo Xinyijie Zhenfu Kuashiji Dazhen Ganglin [The Complete Annotation for New Policies: The New Government's Program for the Next Century, four volumes]. Beijing: Jingji Chubanshe, 1998.

Xu Xianghua. 1991. "Woguo Difang Lifa Yanjiu Shinian Pingsu" [A Review of Local Legislation and Their Studies for the Past ten Years]. In Guo Daohui, ed., *Shinian Fazhi Luncong* [Papers on the Legal System During the Past Ten Years], Beijing: Falu Chubanshe.

Yabuki, Susumu. 1995. *China's New Political Economy: The Giant Awakes*. Boulder, Colorado: Westview.

Yan Jiaqi. 1992. *Toward a Democratic China: The Intellectual Autobiography of Yan Jiaqi*. Honolulu: University of Hawaii Press.

---. 1992. *Yan Jiaqi and China's Struggle for Democracy*. Armonk: M. E. Sharpe.

---. 1994-95. "Xinxianzheng Yundong" [New Movement of Constitutionalism]. *Chengming* (September 1994): 85-89, (January 1995): 84-92.

Yan, Yunxiang. 1996. *The Flow of Gifts*. Stanford, CA: Stanford University Press.

---. 1996. "The Culture of Guanxi in a North China Village," *The China Journal*, No. 35 (Janurary): 1-25.

Yang, Benjamin. 1998. *Deng: A Political Biography*. Armonk, NY: M.E. Sharpe.

Yang Jianchen. 1993. *Xian Li Guangyao Xuexi* [Learn from Lee Kuan Yew]. Taipai: Wenshizhe Chubanshe.

Yang, Mayfair Mei-hui. 1994. *Gifts, Favors and Banquets: The Art of Social Relationsaips in China*. Ithaca, NY: Cornell University Press.

Yang Ruilong. 1998. "A Three-stage theory on the transformation mode of institutional change in China." *Jingji Yanjiu*: 3-10.

Yang, Dali. 1990. "Patterns of China's regional development strategy." *China Quarterly* 122 (June): 230-57.

Yeung, Yue-man and Xu-wei Hu, eds. 1992. *China's Coastal Cities: Catalysts for Modernization*. Honolulu: University of Hawaii Press.

Yeung, Y.M., and Sung Yun-wing, eds. 1996. *Shanghai: Transformation and modernization under China's Open Policy*. Hong Kong: The Chinese University Press.

Yeung, Y.M. and David K.Y. Chu, eds. 1998. *Guangdong: Survey of a Province undergoing Rapid Change*, 2nd Edition. Hong Kong: The Chinese University Press.

Yu Daihai. 1995. 'The NPC needs martyr's spirit,' *Beijing Spring* vol. 24 (May), 3.

252 *The Dual Developmental State*

Yuan Ruiliang. 1994. *Renmin Daibiao Dahui Zhidu Xincheng Fazhan Shi* [History of the Formation and Development of the System of the People's Congresses]. Beijing: Renmin Chubanshe.

Yuan Shang and Han Zhu. 1992. *Deng Xiaoping Nanxun hou de Zhongguo* [China after Deng Xiaoping's Southern Tour]. Beijing: Gaige Chubanshe.

Zang, Xiaowei. 1991. "Provincial elite in post-Mao China." *Asian Survey* 16 (June): 512-525.

Zeigler, L. Harmon. 1988. *Pluralism, Corporatism, and Confucianism: Political Association and Conflict Regulation in the United States, Europe, and Taiwan.* Philadelphia: Temple University Press.

Zhang Bingyin. 1992a. *Renda Falu Jiandu Anli Xuanbian* [Selected Cases on Judicial Supervision of People's Congresses]. Beijing: Falu Chubanshe.

---. 1992b. *Renda Gongzuo de Lilun yu Shijian* [Theory and Practice of the Work of People's Congresses]. Beijing: Falu Chubanshe.

Zhang Mingshu. 1993. *Zhonghua Renmin Gongheguo Zhengzhi Zhidu Gaiyao* [Profile about Political Order of the PRC]. Yinchuan: Ningxia Renmin Chubanshe.

----. 1994. *Zhongguo Zhengzhiren* [The Political Man in China]. Beijing: Zhongguo Shehui Kexue Chubanshe.

Zhang Shijun, ed. 1988. *Difang Renda Gongzuo Yanjiu* [A Study of the Work of Local People's Congresses]. Changsha: Hunan Renmin Chubanshe.

Zhang Sutang. 1994. "*Zhongguo yihui lifa neiqing*"[Inside the Legislations in China's Congress]. *Outlook* Weekly, 10 January, no.2: 26-29.

Zhang Wenming, et al, eds. 1996, 1997, 1998. *Zhongguo Jingji Dalunzhan* [Grand Debates on Chinese Economy] (Beijing: Jingji Guanli Chubanshe, 1996, vol. 1; 1997, vol. 2; 1998, vol. 3.

Zhang Weixuan, et al, ed. 1989. *Gongheguo Fengyun Sishinian* [Turbulent Forty Years of the Republic]. Beijing: Zhongguo Zhengfa Daxue Chubanshe.

Zhang Youyu, ed. 1993. *Renda Licheng* [The Milestones of the People's Congresses]. Shijiazhuang: Hebei Renmin Chubanshe.

Zhao, Suisheng. 1992. "From coercion to negotiation: changing central-local economic relationship in the People' Republic of China." *Issues and Studies* 28, no. 10 (October): 1-22.

Zhao Zhiyang. 1987. "Advance along the road of socialism with Chinese characteristics: report delivered at the 13th National Congress of the Communist Party of China on October 25, 1987." *Beijing Review* (November 9-15): 23-49.

Zheng, Shiping. 1997. *Party vs. State in Post-1949 China: The Institutional Dilemma.* New York: Cambridge University Press.

Zheng, Yongnian. 1995. Institutional Change, Local Developmentalism and Economic Growth: The Making of a Semi-Federal System in Reform China. Ph.D. Diss., Princeton University.

Zhongguo Falu Nianjian: 1994 [Law Yearbook of China, 1994]. Beijing: Zhongguo Falu Nianjianshe.

Bibliography 253

Zhongguo Falu Sishinian [Forty Years of Chinese Law]. 1989. Beijing: Beijing Daxue Chubanshe.

Zhonghua Renmin Gonghehuo Difangxin Fagui Huibian [A Collection of Local Laws of the People's Republic of China (1992-1994)]. 1995. Beijing. Zhongguo Falu Nianjianshe.

Zhou, Kate. 1996. *How the Farmers Changed China*. Boulder, Colorado: Westview.

Zhou Lizuo, ed. 1991. *Difang Renda Gongzuo yu Minzhu Fazhi* [The Work of local people's Congresses, Democracy and Legal System]. Guangzhou: Guangdong Gaodeng Jiaoyu Chubanshe.

Zhou Taihe, ed. 1984. *Dangdai Zhongguo de Jingji Tizhi Gaige* [The Structural Economic Reforms in Contemporary China]. Beijing: Zhongguo Shehui Kexue Chubanshe.

Zhou Xirong. 1995. On Socialist Democracy—Making a Clear Distinction between Socialist Democracy and the Parliamentary Democracy of the West. *Renmin Ribao* (April 16), FBIS-CHI-96-114.

Zhu Guanglei. 1997. *Dangdai Zhongguo Zhengfu Guocheng* [Contemporary Governmental Processes in China]. Tianjin: Tianjin Renmin Chubanshe.

Zini Jr., A. A., ed. 1992. *The Market and the State in Economic Development in the 1990s*. Amsterdam: North-Holland.

Ziya, Onis. 1991. "The Logic of the Developmental State." *Comparative Politics* (October).

Author Index

A
Almond, Gabriel, 33, 144
Alston, Lee J., 180

B
Baum, Richard, 24, 55
Black, Cyril, 52
Bromley, Daniel, 31
Bryce, James, 42

C
Castells, Manuel, 4, 27, 38
Chavance, Bernard, 21
Chen, Yizhi, 84
Clark, Christopher, 19
Coase, Ronald H., 9, 63, 64, 65,

D
Dahl, Robert, 12n
Deng, Xiaoping, 24, 46, 50, 58, 81,
   107-108
Deng, Rong (Maomao)
Diamond, Larry, 99n
Ding, Arthur, 105
Durkheim, Emile, 176

E
Eggertsson, Thrainn, 6, 10
Esman, Milton J., 145
Evans, Peter, 4, 76, 220

F
Fukuyama, Francis, 16

G
Gerschenkron, Alexander, 34
Goodman, David, 23
Granick, David, 213

H
Habermas, Jurgen, 40
Hahn, Jeffrey, 132
Hayek, Friedrich, 17, 32
He Qinglian, 12n, 222, 223
Hobbes, Thomas, 81
Hodgeson, Geofry, 31
Horner, Charles, 18
Hu Angang, 195
Hu, Shikai, 124
Huang, Yasheng, 26
Huntington, Samuel, 55, 56, 61,
   217, 218

I
Islam, Shafiqul, 60

J
Jenner, W. J. F., 219
Johnson, Chalmers, 18, 27, 29, 90

K
Kornai, Janos, 26, 49, 66n,
Krugman, Paul, 216

L
Li, Linda Chelan, 204
Li Youwei, 200
Lieberthal, Kenneth, 99n, 203, 205
Lijphart, Arend, 175
Lin, Sen, 135n
Lindblom, Charles, 33,

M
Mandelbaum, Michael, 60
Manion, Melanie, 20, 26
McCormick, Barrett, 23

Moe, Terry, 12n
Montinola, Gabriella, 25, 207n
Morishima, Michio, 52
Muramatsu, Michio, 178
Musolf, Lloyd, 100

N
Naisbitt, John, 37
Nakano, M., 214
Naughton, Barry, 40
North, Douglass, 31, 32, 44, 196, 207n
Nove, Alec, 35

O
O'Brien, Kevin J., 114, 123, 145
Ogden, Suzanne, 19, 26, 123, 135n
Oi, Jean, 207n
Oksenberg, Michel, 99n, 203, 205

P
Polanyi, Karl, 34, 60, 100

Q
Qiao, Shi, 110

R
Rawls, John, 224
Riggs, Fred, 100
Robert, Stephen, 19
Rueschemeyer, Dietrich, 75, 220

S
Scott, James, 183
Segal, Gerald, 23
Seidman, Ann and Robert B., 131

Shirk, Susan, 180
Simon, Herbert, 31
Skocpol, Theda, 35
Smith, Adam, 16
Smith-Doerr, Laurel, 8
Solinger, Dorothy, 113
Solnick, Steven, 61
Stavis, Benedict, 51, 56

T
Tanner, Murray Scot, 114
Thurow, Lester, 36, 37

V
Verba, Sidney, 144
Vogel, Ezra, 50

W
Wade, Robert, 29
White, Gordon, 27
White, III, Lynn, 205-206
White, Tyrene, 20, 26
Williamson, Oliver, 4, 7, 63
Wittfogel, Karl, 160
Wolf, Jr., Charles, 8,
Wu Guoguang, 204

Y
Yan, Jiaqi, 117, 119
Yang, Benjamin, 72
Yoshida, Shiegeru, 50

Z
Zhao Ziyang, 109
Zheng Yongnian, 204

Subject Index

A

adaptation, 2, 43, 209, 215

administrative guidance, 2, 29, 62

adoption, 2, 11, 40, 41, 43, 68, 124, 156, 208, 209

Anglo-American pattern, 16, 18, 24, 26, 41, 44, 100

Anglo-Saxon model, 26, 36, 37, 217

anti-Americanism, 24, anti-foreign, 207n, anti-liberal policy, 22, 47, anti-Western, 51

Asian Century, 71, 217,

Asian values, 71,

Asia's Miracle, 30, 33, 216

authoritarian capitalism, 27

authoritarian development, 24, 178, 203, method, 9-10, 22,184, Samuel Huntington and, 55, system, 2, 12, 13n, 20-21, 25, 29, 58, 67, 75, 99n, 102, 128, 217

authoritarian pluralist system, 215

authoritarianism, 28, 29, 56, 71, 107, 145, 176, 216, consultative, 215, fragmented, 107, 176, neo, 24, 29, 54-55, 56-57, 178, paternalistic-, 29, soft-, 24, 29, 124

B

"BAIRs," 27

bank, 89, central, 86, People's Bank of China, 86, 89, State Bank of Development, 89

Bao, Tong, 84

bicameralism, 24, 54, 68, 117, 124

"bird-in-a-cage" economics, see: Chen Yun

Bismarck, Otto von, 59, 101

Bismarkian-Meiji strategy, 26, 41, 101

bounded rationality, 7, 31, 45

bourgeois liberalization, 24, 58, 68, 186,

bureaucracy, 2, 4, 7, 9, 12n, 17, 28, 29, 46, 63, 77, 93-94, 125, 142, 144, 172, 189, 217, 220

Bureaucratism, 43, 45, 47, 61, 65, 75, 124, 166, 173, 175, Deng's attacks on, 46, 75

C

Capitalism, 21, 26, 27, 33, 34, 58, 62, 69, 71, 100, 178, 186, 191, 216, American-style, 12n, 36-38, communitarian, 36, crony, 5, 218, 226, *guanxi*, 199, in China, 19, 51, 60, 63, 69-70, 73, individual, 36, state-led, 201

CDS (capitalist developmental state), 27, *also see*: developmental state

central-local relationship, 40, 92, 136, 178, 202, 203, 204, 208, 213, as non-zero sum game, 203, 204, 211, as zero-sum game, 180, 203, client oriented politics, 214, cooperative, 180, decentralization, 23, 30, 40, 63, 84, 96, 98, 108, 109,111, 173, 179, 180, 204, 209, 211, 219, 220, 221, determining factors, 203-204, 212-213, dyadic dynamics, 181, interactive pattern, 180-181, interdependent relationship, 3, 178, 181, 203-204, 212, iron law in, 213, symbiotic relationship, 203, two-tiered structure, 3

Central Party School, 68, 84

chaebol, 91

Chen, Ziming, 84

Chen, Yun, 48, 51, 59, 66n, 73, 79, 93, 192, 193, 197, "bird-in-a-cage" economics, 49-50, 51

chief architect, Deng Xiaoping as, see: Deng Xiaoping

chief engineer, Jiang Zemin as, 59, 66n

China, China threat, 14, as a bubble, break-up, 22-23, disintegration, 219

Chinese century, 71, 217

choice-set, 31, 44,

256

civil service, 32, 83, National College of Administration, 83, rejuvenation and professionalism, 83

clash of civilizations, 16, 217

commodity economy, 49-50, 73, 95, 108, 109

Communist Party of China (CPC), 2, 10, 25, 50, 55, 58, 69-73, 82, 102-104, 106-107, 112, 128, 140, 144, 147, 152, 153, 213, 220, 226, Advisory Committee, 84, 116, as a "party of production force," 226, catch-all party, 72, husbandry of power, relationship with the PCs, 102, 105, 112, 114, 118, 128, 131, 134, 169, 173, 215, developing market economy, 49, 59, 108-109, National Party Congress, 72

comparative transaction costs theory, 6-8, 11, 45, 63, 64, 65

Confucian democracy, see: democracy

connectedness, 4, 5, 8, 215

consociational politics, 175

constitution, 9, 12, 29, 48, 68, 72, 103-104, 106, 109, 113, 116, 117, 122, 126, 127, 132, 170, 188

connections, see: *guanxi*

contestation, 125, 131, 133, 168-171, 210

convergence, 15, 18, 19, China with the West, 15-21, 43, with East Asia, 23-25, 50-51, with Eastern Europe, 21-23, 44, 48-49

corporatism, 10, 207n

corruption, 23, 47, 94, 95-96, 105, 110, 127, 163, 218, 219, 222, 223

Council for Economic Planning and Development (Taiwan), 28, 86,

CPC see: Communist Party of China

crimes, 94, 166, 168, 169, 223

crony capitalism, see: capitalism

Cultural Revolution, 42, 45, 47-48, 54, 61, 73, 74, 86, 104, 106, 107, 112, 116, 179, 184, 201, lessons, 45, syndrome, 42

D

decentralization, see: central-local relation

de-communization, 35

democracy, 12n, 18- 23, 28, 29, 32, 40, 84, 95, 99n, 135n, 175, 216, 221, 225, 226,

227n, Chinese-style, 19,-20, 109, 129, 152, communitarian, 226, Confucian, 15, 226, consociational, 175, socialist democracy, 84, 143, western liberal, 15, 16, 17, 18, 19, 22, 24, 27, 44, 47-48, 57, and capitalism,27, 33, 37, Deng's ideas, 45, 47-48, 54, pluralist, 10, 12n, 175, 215, semi-anticipatory, 128

Democracy Movement, 20, 48,

democratic centralism, 126, 135n

democratic deficit, 41, 211

democratization, 18-20, 22, 26, 48, 100, 121, 123, 125, 133, 135n, 145, 174, 177n, 211, and the developmental state, 28, 30, 38, 210

Deng, Xiaoping, as chief architect, 54, 59, 183, 184, 186, as developmental dictator, 61, as general designer, 183-184, as midwife of the Chinese reform, 186, chaos, 65, costs, 65, capitalist-roader, 69, and Japan, 50, legacy, 61, on people's congresses, 107, 108, 124, on reforms, 54, 68, 124, and Shenzhen and SEZs, 50-51, 193, Southern trip, 58, 194, 200, theory of cats, 69, 183, theory of groping stone, 62, 69, theory of three conducives, 69, 58, 81, 154, total efficiency, 65

Deng Xiaoping Thought, 71, also see Deng Xiaoping

development strategy, 27, 41-42, 44, 51, 53, 64-65, 90, 183, 208-209, 214, 219

developmental authoritarianism, 41

developmental dictatorship, 28, 41, 59, 61, 98

developmental state, 1, 93, 98, 201, 208, 209, as a hybrid, 4, as a paradigm, 1-2, built-in tensions in China, 93-98, China's adoption, 208, crisis of, 221, 226, conceptual East Asian, 1, 3, 4, , 5, 11, 25, 27-28, 36-37, 38, 41-42, 44, 59, 71, 72, 102, 136, 208, 209, 216, 221, flaws, 36-38, definition, 27, four part model, 28-29, 41, 48, institutional arrangement, 2, 27-30, 209, institutional deviations in China,2, 3, 209, limitations and strengths, 181, 205, model, 178, network and, 37,

258 The Dual Developmental State

similarities between China and NIE, 1, 53, two-tier, 204, 210

Development Zones, fever of, 156, 200

developmentalism, 3, 12, 36, 87, 92, 97, 136, 181, 210, 224, local, 97, 154, 179-180, 200-201, 203-204, 210-211

dilemma of legislature, 125

dual developmental state, 6, 38, 209, characteristics, 211, definition, 3, 215, strengths and merits, 216

ducal economy, 96-97

E

East Asian exceptionalism, 36

East Asian model, 1, 5, 15-16, 23-24, 28, 38, 41, 42, 45, 51, 57, 62, 67, 85, 124, 208, 209, 216, 217, 218, lessons for China, 85-86, 91

East Wind, 43

Economic Planning Board (South Korea), 28

economic "general staff," 28, China, 86 Japan, Taiwan, South Korea, 87

economic state, 10, 226

economy of dukedom, 96

elite, 4, 10, 21, 28, 29, 45, 55, 59, 106, 118, 143, 149, 173-176, 210, 211, 214, 222, 226

emancipation of the mind, 69-70, 192, 195

embedded autonomy, 4, 91, 220

embeddedness, 5, 8, 153, 215, 220

"end of history," 16

externality, 153, 157-159, 160,

extra-budgetary fund, 88

F

Fang, Lizhi, 18

Federalism, Chinese Style, 25, competitive, 207n, de facto, 204, market-preserving, 25, 207n

financial crisis, East Asia, 1, 30, 38, 216, 221

"flying geese" pattern of development, 1

floating population, 223

Four Fundamental Principles, 69,

"Four Little Dragons," 1, 2, 5, 24, 38, 52, 55, 59, 97, 186, 192, 199, 218

Four Modernizations, 82, 209

function, see: state function

G

general design, 68

general efficiency, 54, 75, 166, 173, 198, 209, 214

"golden partnership," 121, 142

Gorbachev, Mikhail, 57

Gradualism, gradual transition, 24-25, chipping-away, 199, Fabian strategy, 211

Great Leap Forward, 44, 86, 112, 178, 184, 201

Great Leap Outward, 43

Guanxi (connections), 87, 126, 206, capitalism, 199, in the government, 87, 99n, 126, 134, 205, studies on, 205

H

"Hard government, soft economy," 55

hierarchy, 4, 7, 8, 12n, 37, 63, 64, 116, 117, 124, 134, 206, 212, 215, 216

hierarchical control, 145, hierarchical structure, 12n, 139

Hong Kong, 1, 27, 30, 43, 48, 50, 51, 52, 59, 62, 113, 123, 169, 177n, 178, 182, 189, 190,193, 194, 199, 207n

horizontal political competition, 178

horizontal relationship, 136, elite accommodation politics and, 214

household responsibility system, 62, 181, 185

Hu, Jiwei, Signature Campaign, 121

Hu, Yaobang, 52, 80, 81

Hua, Guofeng, 42-43, 49-50, 72, 105, 181-182, 209

Huang, Changxin, 120

Hungarian model, 42, 48, 50, 57

Hybrid, 4, 7, 8, 11, 14, 15, 61, 125, 130, 134, 215, network as a hybrid, 134

I

ideology, 69-75, hollowing-out, 74, orthodox, 73

industrial policy, 28, 90-91, 92, 156, 209, 221, automobile, 90, airplane, 92 industry group, 87, as national team, 91

institution, 2-4, 6, 10-11, 12n, 15, 18-20, 25, 27, 29-32, 34, 37-38, 40, 45, 56, 60, 65, 74, 77, 78, 81, 82, 84, 86, 89, 90, 93, 98, 99n, 100, 103, 107, 109, 111-112, 115-116, 118, 121-123, 126, 128, 131, 136, 140, 144, 145, 149, 152, 153, 161, 168, 173, 175, 176, 188-190, 195-199, 202, 205-206, 207n, 208, 210, 214-215, 217, 219, 225

institution-building, 2, 12, 34, 62, 122, 126, 128, 211, 213

institutional adaptation, 216

institutional arrangements, 1-3, 5-6, 11-12, 23, 26, 34, 36, 41, 44, 61, 65, 67, 136, 153, 183, 209, 213, 214

institutional atrophy, 220

institutional change, 34, 45, 117, 131, 136, 198-199, 202, 214

institutional decay, 21, 218,

institutional design, 35, 62, 126, 130, 134, 136, 183, 191, 197-198, 202, 214

institutional development, 102, 116, 136, 145, 170, 208, 219

institutional economics, 11, 15, 30, 124,

institutional linkages, 5-6, 12, 144-149, 174, 210, 213, 215

institutional investment, 193

institutional maintenance, 122, 174

institutional maturity, 112, 118, 132, 139, 172

institutional transaction, 31

institutionalism, 13n, 15, 30-31, 34

institutionalists, 9, 30-31, 33

institutionalization, 6, 12, 64, 98, 102, 105-107, 112-113, 116-117, 122, 124-125, 133-134, 136, 138, 140, 144, 159, 172, 173, 174, 208, 211, 218-219, 220, re-, 105

intellectuals, 225-226

intermediate stasis, 97, 179

invisible hand, 33, 34

Issues of "CPC" (corruption, pollution and crime), 94

J

Japan, 1-2, 5, 10, 11, 27-30, 50-53, 79, 85, 87, 101, 178, 207n, Japan, Inc., 10, Deng

Xiaoping and Hua Guofeng and, 50, image in China, 50, 52-53

Japanese model, 26, 36-37, 50, 52, 101

Jiang, Zemin, 57, 68, 72, 75, 77, 79, 84-85, 115, 130, 169, 187, 194-195, 203-204, as chief engineer, 59, 66n

Jiang-Li axis, 115

Judicial branch, 122, 129, 147, 153, 169, 174

June 4th crackdown, 57, *also see:* Tiananmen crackdown

justice, 221, 224, 225

K

keiretsu, 5

L

late-comer, 35

Lee, Kuan Yew, 28, 191, 221

Leftism, 58, old and new Left wing, 226-227

legitimacy, 10, 27, 29, 37, 40, 42, 49, 50, 58, 72, 96, 111, 127, 132, 144, 148, 152, 163, 166, 173, 197, 210, legitimacy crisis, 95, 106, 111, 132, Habermas and, 40

legislation, 100, 109, 110, 123, 127-128, 149-150, 155, 159, 160, 166, 188, 210, 213, as a shuttle process, 153, economic legislation, 127, 154-157, 188, plan, 149, process, 129, 149-153, three-readings, 151

legislative activism, 5, 12, 23, 105, 133, 211, 219

legislative development, 2, 12, 101-107, 116, 118, 124-125, 132-34, 144, 149, 153, 210-211, dynamics of, 105-107, Fabian strategy, 144, 211, in Russia and East Europe, 23, 125, 131-133, 136, 144, 211, strategy, 211

legislature, 2-4, 6, 9, 29-30, 39, 98, 100-103, 107-108, 110-112, 116, 118, 125, 131-134, 139, 144, 174, 177n, 210- 212, conservative, 101, economic development, 100, 110-111, negligible role, 29-30, Western, 139, 144

Leninist, party, 25, political structure, 22, regime, 23, relationship, 20, state, 23, system, 21, 23

260 *The Dual Developmental State*

liberalization, 18, 19, 22, 51, 60, 81, 93, 114, 127, 132, 133, 145, 197, 210, 221
Li, Nanqing, 80
Li, Peng, 78-81, 114, 115, 120- 122, 128, 130
Li, Ruihuan, 113
Li, Youwei, 195, 200
Liu, Ji, 57, 66n
liberal democracy, 15-18, 20, 24, 44
liberalism, 16, 24, 28, 31, 33, 56
List, Friedrich, 16
local autonomy, 2, 59, 203,
local developmental state, 6
localism, 22-23, 56, 179-180

M
martial law, 56
macro-economic, control, 78, 85-86, 90, 96, 154-155, 205, policy, 31, 97, 219, 221
Mao, Zedong, 42, 45, 61, 69, 72, 76, 84, 104, 106, 170, 181, 184, 195, 201, 207n, 209, judgement on Deng, 69, Yanan Road and, 182-183, 196
market, 17, as institution, 31-32, as mechanism of provider, 32, as mechanism of denial and exclusion, 32, as a spontaneous order, 17, 46, 67, 179, institutionalist definition, 31-32, 98, creation, 3, 6, 17, 34, 47, 60, 98, 107, 125, 136, 153-154, 179, 208, 210, 219, making-, 34, 60, 98, mode, 4, 7-8, 125, 130, 134, 136, 174, 215, the self-regulating, 17, and state relationship, 10, 33-35, 46, 49, 51, 55, 61, 67, 70, 73,78, 92, 95-96, 191-192, 222, as "fingers" and state as "thumbs," 33
market economy, 13n, 16-19, 21-22, 30, 40-44, 47, 51, 55, 60, 70, 72-73, 74, 77-78, 87, 93-94, 96-97, 106, 109-110, 154-155, 161, 179, 198, 203, socialist, 55,59, 74, 109, 110, 111, 122, 162, 166, 175-176, 179, 189-191, 194-195, 208-210, 215, 219, 224, state-guided, 201
market facilitating, 6, 27, 65, 98, 172, 209,
market failure, 7, 32-33, 45-47, 63, 153-154, 210
Market-Leninism, 21, 69-70

market mechanism, 10, 28, 34, 43, 46-47, 62-63, 157, 161, 206
market socialism, 42, 44, 48-50, 52-53, 62, 65
marketization, 6, 10, 17, 21-22, 25, 35, 60, 64, 73, 77, 88, 93-94, 97-98, 102, 106-107, 111, 125, 136, 153, 156-157, 162, 173, 176, 180, 195, 197, 208, 221-222, 226, three wheels of, 60
Meiji Restoration, 101
Meritocracy, 29, 81
MITI, 28, 86
mode of governance, 4, 7-8, 11, 14, 37, 64, 125, 130, 134, 198-199, 202, 205, 214-215, 217, *see also*: market, hierarchy, hybrid, and network
mohe (co-petition), 124, 129-130, 134, 135n, 215
"Muddle Kingdom", China, 14

N
Nash equilibrium game, 211
nationalism, 23, 24, 28, 71
Network, 4-5, 8-9, 14-15, 37, 147, 154, 174, 102, 129, 133, 202, 205-206, 214, 216, as a governance, 8, 37, 205-206, 214-215, bamboo, 199, Chinese traditional culture and, 205, definition, 8, formal, 126, informal, 116-117, 126, information, 174, in East Asia, 4-5, 37, 199, 217, state-based network, 202
network approach, 4, 11, 37-38, 126,
network strategy, 5-6, 8-9, 12, 38, 62, 102, 130, 134, 136, 145, 174, 215, 217
network society, 4, 37-38, 205, 216-218
networking, 4, 37, model, 37
neo-authoritarianism, 25, 55, 178, debate on, 55-56, 57
NIEs (Newly Industrialized Economies), 1-2, 11, 24-25, 26, 43, 57, 178, 216-218, 221
NPC (National People's Congress), as rubber stamp, 113, 135n, and martial law, 114, "bee-hive structure," 119Chairmen Group, 121-122, delegation meeting, 119, democracy and NPC, 119, 135n, early years, 103, expansion of power, 127-128,

210, faction, 115, negative votes, 120-121, Standing Committee, 121-123, studies on NPC, 113-115, parliamentarization, 117, plenary session, 118-121, Qiao Shi and, 115, Wan Li and, 114

O

official profiteering, 95, 163
opportunism, 7, 45, 98
organization costs, 7-8
orthodox paradox, 47

P

Park, Chun Hee, 28, 55, 61
Parkinson's law, 77
parliament, 23, 100-101, 125-126, 134, 136, 146, in Eastern Europe and Soviet Union, 22, 131-132, role in economy, 100-101, 134, parliamentarization of Chinese PCs, 117, Soviet-style, 136, Western-type, 136
parliamentary arrangement in China, 23
parliamentary democracy, 22-23, 132,
parliamentary election, 23-24, 54, 123
parliamentary legislation, 100
parliamentarism, 18, 105
particularism, 126, 205, 218
partocracy and legislature, 101
party-state, 101, 131, 219
path-dependence, 44, 199, China and, 44, 202, definition, 44, 196, transition costs and, 202
peasants' burden, 164-165
Peng, Chong, 113, 121, 122
Peng, Zhen, 106, 113-114, 117, 121, 130, 138, 145
people's congresses, anti-corruption, 96, evolution, 102-103, 112, 117, people's deputies, 147-148, *also see*: NPC and PPC
personnel reform, 82, 84, downsizing, 77, 83, civil service, 82-83, National College of Administration, 83
pillar industry, 90-92, automobile, 90-92, airplane, 92
political decay, 218, 220
political firms, 9-10,

political reform, Deng's ideas, 54, disparity between economic reform and, 40, 109, 208, general design, 68, principles, 75, taboos, 68, three waves, 68
politics of smoothness, 175
PPCs (Provincial People's Congresses), 136-176, 177n, Chairmen Group, 137-138, corruption and, 167, impeachment, investigation, 168-169, institutions, 139, institutional linkages, 145-149, institutionalization, 172, 210, judicial supervision, 166-167, legislation, 143, 149-153, legislative contestation, 168-172, market economy and, 153-167, Party and, 147, personnel change, 140-144, reinstitutionalization, 136-140, relationship between the Party and, 169, 170, relationship with the NPC, 145, 146, size, 137, role in the developmental state, 210, staff, 138, Standing Committee, 137
pragmatism, 41, 51, 65, 72
pricism, 17
privatization, 60, 195
production costs, 31, 65, 198, 202
property rights, 10, 31-32, 34, 60, 153, 161-162, 166, 179, 207n, 213, regional and provincial, 179, 213
public good, 34, 97, 111, 153-154, 159-160, 224

Q

Qiao, Shi, 110, 115, 120, 121, 130, 131, 169

R

reciprocity, 5-6, 9, 215-216
regime transition, *see* transition
religions, 225
rent-seeking, 17, 93-96, 161-163, 98, 222, society, 93, behavior in China, 94, 161, 163, 222, and marketization, 94, 222,
retirement, 81-82, veteran cadres, Deng Xiaoping, 80-81, impact upon the PCs, 116
revolution, 81, 161, 170, democratic, 74, 128, from above, 178, from bottom, 179, mundane, 20, of de-communizing, 69, silent, 124

262 *The Dual Developmental State*

revolutionary committee, 104
River Elegy, 20
rubber-stamp, 102, 109, 112, 131
rule by law, 74
rule of law, 73, 74, 115
rule of man, 74,
Russian legislature, *see* legislative
   development

S
Second Revolution, 43, 46, 70, 195
secret societies, 223-224,
selective, emulation, 52, 64, penetration,
   220, targeting, 51, 76, 156, 218, 220,
   selectivity, 28, 76, 128, 220
semi-legislative power, 105
separation of the party from the government,
   80
SEZ (Special Economic Zone), 5, 45, 50-53,
   58-59, 62, 93, 181, 207n, Deng and, 182,
   190, 192-194, debate on, 193, 194-195,
   establishment, 182
Shenzhen, as SEZ, 52, 182-183, 187, as
   Archimedean point, 196, demonstration
   and restructuring effect, 200, its roles in
   Deng's strategy, 190-191, 192, 194, Jiang
   Zemin and, 187, 195, 203, model, 53, 193,
   196, 198, 201, political reform and, 189-
   190, 207n, Revolution, 199, relations with
   Hong Kong and Taiwan, 189, 199,
   transformation, 188-189, 191-192, 203,
Singapore, 60, 187, as a model for China,
   221-222, Deng's praise, 59, 194
sinomania, 19
small government, big society, 76, 189
Smith, Adam, 16-17, 34, 36
socialist legacies, 2, 44, 48, 134, 225
soft budget constraints, 87
Solidarity Movement in Poland, 48
Song Defu, 83
South Korea, 25, 27-30, 50, 53, 87, 91, 218,
   Inc., 10
South Wind, 43, 52
Southern Inspection Tour, 58, 70, 74, 184,
   194, also see: Deng Xiaoping
"spiritual pollution," 81, anti-spiritual
   pollution, 68, 192,

spontaneous order, 17, 46, 67, 100, 180
stability, 48, 54, 56-58, 61-62, 75, 81, 83,
   86, 125, 138, 175-176, 178, 212, 216
Stalinist model (or system, strategy), 2, 9-
   10, 23, 33, 42, 43-45, 49, 61, 63, 65, 72,
   93, 97, 107, 125, 175, 196
state, definition, 35, as an artificial man, 81,
   central state, 35, local states, 3-5, 36, 164-
   165, 207, 212
state capacity, 2, 5-6, 12, 38, 40, 48, 54, 75,
   88, 101, 124, 133, 136, 145, 152, 173-
   174, 178-179, 208-209, 211, 218-220,
   definition, 2, Deng's concern, 124-125
State Council, 53, 76, 79, 82-84, 89-90, 93,
   103-105, 150, 187-188, 195, 207n
State Development Planing Commission,
   86-87
state-economy relationship, 67, synergism,
   33, "driver and engine", 67, *also see*:
   market
state failure, 7, 33, 46-47, 63, 154, 161, 165,
   210, 219
state function, 76-78, 99n
state minimalism, 17
state socialism, 60, 62, 178, 186, 201, 203
state ownership, 10, 22, 45, 94, 161, 195
strategic thinking, 62, 196, 202
strategy, 2, 8-9, 12-13, 15, 19, 21-22, 26,
   37-38, 40-44, 47, 49-59, 61-64, 90- 93,
   97, 102, 106, 124, 126, 128, 130-134,
   136, 145, 147, 173-174, 179-180, 182-
   183, 186, 192, 196-199, 201-202, 208-
   215, 217, 219, 221, diversification, 53,
   201, geographical sliding policy, 90, 204,
   hard government and soft economy, 55,
   middle ground, 63, muddling-through, 54,
   62, of capitalism, 26, product-sliding
   policy, 90, regional inclining, 92, under
   Mao, under Deng, 54, 180, 186, also see:
   development strategy, developmental
   state
strong state, 9-10, 28, 30, 38, 75, 211
student movement, 53, 56
Sunan model, 179
super-firm, 9
synergism, 3, 13, 33, 178, 203

Subject Index 263

T

Taiwan, 13, 25, 27-28, 30, 48, 50, 52-53, 71, 87, 120, 149, 177n, 189, 200, Inc., 10

technocracy, 78, 80

think tank, 83-85, difference from *mishu* politics, 85

Third Plenum of the 11th party Congress, 43, 107-108, 182

The Thirteenth Party Congress, 68, 81, 84

Tian, Jiyun, 115, 120-122, 130

Tiananmen Square, demonstration, 121, crackdown, 56, 186

Tigers' economy, see: Four Little Dragons

transaction costs, 6-9, 11, 13n, 31, 42, 44-45, 62-65, 97-98, 154, 163, 173-174, 176, 198-199, 202, 209, 214, 216-217, definition, 6-7, 31, 154, 207n, Deng Xiaoping and, 65, minimizer, 161, 214

transformation costs, 198-199, 202, 207n, 209, 214, 216

transiotology, 203

transition, 2, 5, 12, 14, 38, 54-55, 62, 93, 95, 98, 102, 125, 135, 161-162, 176, 178-179, 186, 190-191, 197, 203, 208, 211, 214, 215, 222-223, problem, 12, regime, 6, 16, 19, 21-22, 24-26, triple, 14

transition costs, 42, 44, 49, 62, 64-65, 196, 198-199, 202-203, 209, 214, 217

transitional society, 35

triple transition, 14

U

Universalism, 126, 205, 218

V

vertical structure, 9

"visible hand," 33

W

Wan, Li, 93, and NPC, 114, 117, 120-121, 128, 131, in Anhui, 182, 185, 204

Wang, Daohan, 85

Wang, Huning, 75, 85

Wang, Juntao, 84

weak state, 12n,

Wei Jingsheng, 48

Wenzhou model, 179, 196, 198

West Wind, 43, 48

Western model, 16-23, 43-44, Deng on, 24, 47-48

westernization, 18-19, 24

westernization impulse, 18, 21

Whatever doctrine, 72, Whateverists, 113

wholesale Westernization, 18,

work-units (*danwei*), 226

X

Xi, Zhongxun, 113, 182

Y

Yao, Yiling, 79, 81, 93,

Yang, Shangkun, 113, 182,192

Yeltsin, Boris, 22, 70, 131-132,

Z

Zhao, Ziyang, 49, 52, 55, 57-58, 75, 79, 80-81, 83-84, and Yugoslavia, 49, Sichuan Experience, 49, 182

Zhou, Gucheng, 119-120

Zhu, Rongji, 78-79, 82-83, 116, 194, 204